Prologue

Le Corbusier, Unité d'Habitation (1945), Marseille, 1997

Ludwig Mies van der Rohe, Commonwealth Promenade Apartment Buildings (1953–56), Chicago, 1957/58

Yona Friedman, Ville Spatiale, project, 1958/59

René Burri, Office Building by Oscar Niemeyer (1957–60), National Congress, Brasília, 1960

Hans Scharoun, Entry to the international urban-developmental competition "Capital City Berlin," 1957/58

Alexander Naumov, Sketch for the urban-developmental “Competition for ideas for a socialist re-design of the center of the capital of the GDR – Berlin,” 1959

RADICALLY MODERN
Urban Planning and Architecture in 1960s Berlin

Edited by
Thomas Köhler and Ursula Müller
for Berlinische Galerie

With texts by Adrian von Buttlar, Bruno Flierl, Hartmut Frank, Anna Maria Heckmann, Irma Leinauer, Stanislaus von Moos, Ursula Müller, Frank Seehausen, Dirk Weilemann

Catalogue production was supported by Wüstenrot Stiftung.

The exhibition was made possible by

KULTURSTIFTUNG DES BUNDES

BERLINISCHE GALERIE MUSEUM OF MODERN ART

Wasmuth

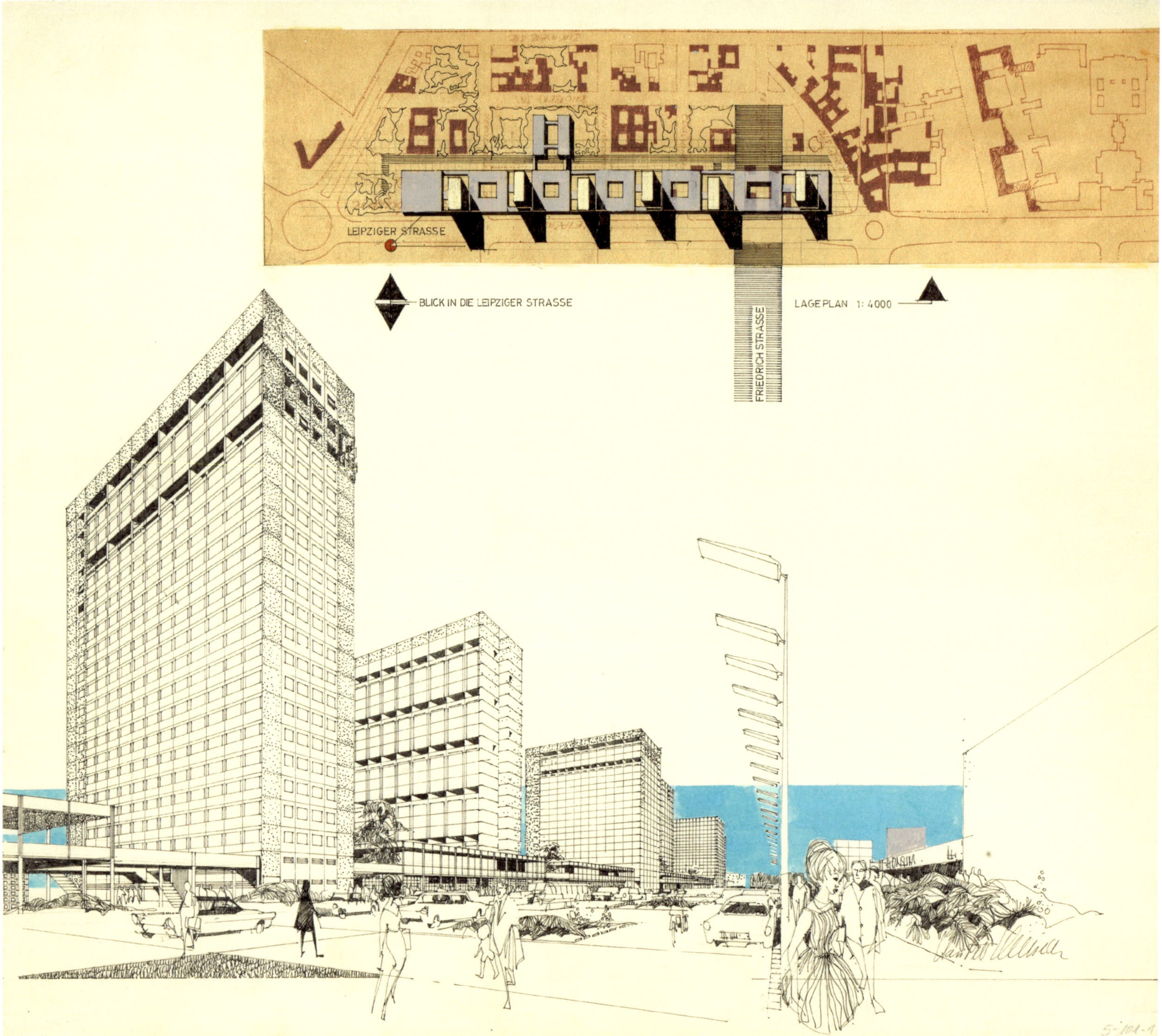

Hans-Peter Schmiedel, Design for a residential and commercial complex, Leipziger Straße, circa 1967

Content

Greeting

"Two rooms, kitchen, bathroom: central heat, telephone, garbage chute: all apartments for ordinary workers. Indubitably impressive. To top it all off, the collective roof garden!" Arno Schmidt has his Berlin alter ego extol the wonderful new socialist boulevard Stalin-Allee with such hymns of praise in his 1954 novel *Heart of Stone*. A year later, American architect Hugh Stubbins visited the war-ravaged landscape of Tiergarten near the zone border, where shortly thereafter West Berlin's Kongresshalle was to be built, today's Haus der Kulturen der Welt, the so-called "miracle building" on the Spree. Stubbins writes, "It was actually a propaganda building directed at the Soviets, just a kilometer away."

A retrospective look at Berlin's post-war architectural history during the short twentieth century is inseparably tied to the image of the "divided city." Berlin was the geopolitical nucleus where the decades of confrontation in the Cold War left an indelible mark on almost all realms of social reality. Architectural policy perhaps represented the clearest expression of the city's partition: on both sides of the Berlin Wall, the most brutal form of the division, one of the main goals of public architecture was to erect monuments in stone to attest to the primacy of the respective system. In the years after 1989, this posturing continued with an approach to the heritage of socialist modernism that was often ruthlessly dismissive.

While thinking in opposites has long shaped the way we think about Berlin's architectural history, this exhibition opens a new chapter that will be pioneering for our future approach to the city's architectural heritage. With the title "Radically Modern," this project refers to lines of development in urban planning and architectural history in both parts of Berlin that today, despite all its heterogeneity, can be understood as two forms of modernism not all too far removed from one another. The buildings of the late 1950s and 1960s are discussed here not as stone antipodes, but as dual monuments. Many of the architects were biographically and aesthetically closely associated with the ideas of the Bauhaus, they took their orientation from principles of industrialization and a view of modernism where the faith in progress was not tempered by any concerns about the limits of growth. From Karl-Marx-Allee to Märkisches Viertel, from Haus des Lehrers to Europa-Center, Kino International or the so-called Ahornblatt (the so-called "Maple Leaf" Pavilion, torn down in 2000) to the Philharmonie, this exhibition can be used to plan a route through the city, crossing the city to locations that show Berlin's architectural history.

Kulturstiftung des Bundes would like to thank Berlinische Galerie, especially its director Dr. Thomas Köhler and Ursula Müller, the director of the architecture collection and her team, for creating an exhibition that promises a "radically modern" view of the joint heritage of post-war modernism in Berlin, which in the end is "indubitably impressive."

For Kulturstiftung des Bundes

Hortensia Völckers	Alexander Farenholtz
Board Member	Board Member
Artistic Director	Administrative Director

Preface

Although post-war modern architecture has been subject to re-evaluation in recent years, this era of architectural history is still struggling for recognition. It continues to be defamed as inhumane and ugly, is subjected to dramatic and destructive alterations, or simply torn down to make room for usually mediocre buildings. In fulfilling its archival task, Berlinische Galerie already focused on the architects of the post-war modern period and their creations early on. While the focus was initially on West Berlin, collecting activities expanded with reunification. The architectural heritage of Berlin was preserved and maintained at the museum and an outreach to the city's architects and urban planners was started.

The exhibition *Radically Modern. Urban Planning and Architecture in 1960s Berlin* goes back to an idea of collection director Ursula Müller and Thomas Steigenberger, a former member of the team at Berlinische Galerie. After systematically studying the holdings at the museum, six years later the idea took shape in six chapters focusing on different themes, presenting the architecture of Berlin using still existing or already demolished buildings. Urban utopias and unrealized projects from both East and West Berlin are explored along with the question of how architects approached the existing historical buildings and the destruction of the Second World War. Large-scale developments and the building projects that are supposed to fulfill a state function are explored alongside the urban planning concepts of a city built for automobile traffic. In addition, works by contemporary artists that deal with the architecture of the 1960s are integrated into the exhibition. They represent a special approach to the subject of architecture by an art museum that goes beyond a mere interest in architectural history.

Ever since Swedish architect Hans Asplund introduced the term "brutalism" to discuss post-war architecture, the façades without ornamentation might lead us to think of a cynical form of architectural discourse. But in fact, the term derives pragmatically and descriptively from the building material used, *béton brut*, raw concrete. The following quotation shows how the term brutalism was given a negative connotation in the 1960s and how the architecture was misunderstood in its reception: "Their buildings recall medieval castles, dungeons and barracks. But the creators of these buildings of concrete and bricks see themselves as advocates of a new freedom, pioneers of a modernism secure for the future. The programmatic label of this new architectural movement: 'brutalism'." *Der Spiegel* used these words in a November 1967 article entitled "Rauh und rissig" (Raw and Cracked)[1] on post-war architecture, which for the first time allowed raw concrete to be used to create façades. The unevenness of prefabricated concrete, the imprints of the formwork and other materials reduced architecture to a purely geometric structure. The structure was no longer hidden by using ornament or "more valuable" construction materials such as granite or marble.

The unadorned, concrete outer skin is dually functional in the street view of Deutsche Oper (1957–1961). Architect Fritz Bornemann used only roughly structured exposed aggregate concrete and moved all the windows to the sides of the building. On the one hand, this serves the purpose of sound insulation between the six-lane Bismarckstraße and the spectators in the opera house. At the same time, it counters the inherently impressive symbolism of an opera building. In contrast, the glass stairwells on the sides of the building attest to a democratic openness, just like the broad, scarcely arched auditorium, where each seat has a good view of the stage. With his 1963 Freie Volksbühne Berlin, Bornemann used raw concrete in the foyer, again to protect the theater from outdoor noise, and in the façade played with an alteration between large glazed surfaces and segments of concrete. In so doing, he created a dialogue with the landscape around the building.

Werner Düttmann, architect and West Berlin's building commissioner, created two outstanding post-war buildings, Akademie der Künste on Hanseatenweg (1958 –1960) and the more radical Kreuzberg church St. Agnes (1965 –1967) Düttmann called his ensemble for the Akademie der Künste a "clear, undramatic box."[2] In a 2006 speech, academy president Klaus Staeck found that "Düttmann and Rossow (the landscape architect) designed this building like a worldly

Werner Düttmann, Akademie der Künste on Hanseatenweg, 1960s

cloister, with corridors, gardens and apartments, as a place of retreat. A kind of intellectual and architectural anti-event concept."

The tripartite academy engages in a dialogue with its environs, the Tiergarten and its own gardens, retreating to the private sphere behind washed concrete walls with spacious glazing for the public, while St. Agnes, completed seven years later, radicalized the sculptural and architectural concept. The ensemble of concrete buildings, almost entirely without windows, is dominated by a square bell tower that seems to be free standing. The inside of the church is a cube, and only receives light from two window slits and glazed bands on the roof. As in *Der Spiegel* article quoted above, this clearly evokes a fortress-like quality, alluding to the free-standing bell towers of medieval Italy. The church, now deconsecrated, has recently been taken over by a gallery, and it is now being remodeled by the architect and theorist Arno Brandlhuber. The transformation of the building can be considered paradigmatic for the changing perception of 1960s architecture.

The exhibition, which included comprehensive research in the collection of Berlinische Galerie, also included the holdings of many other institutions and individuals which could only be realized with substantial funding from Kulturstiftung des Bundes. Our grateful thanks go to those responsible, Hortensia Völckers, artistic director, and Alexander Farenholtz, administrative director.

Wüstenrot Stiftung has made it possible for us to create a more substantial catalogue and to hold a joint conference on post-war modernism, together with the architecture department at Berlin's Technische Universität and Leibniz-Institut für Regionalentwicklung und Strukturplanung Erkner. Kerstin Wittmann-Englert has been a partner of Berlinische Galerie for several years now. She and her department together with Erkner's IRS took on the conception and organization of the conference entitled *Verflechtungen: Planen und Bauen im Berlin der 1960er-Jahre*, which will be held during the exhibition at Berlinische Galerie.

Thanks go to our partners and lenders for their support: Leibniz-Institut für Regionalentwicklung und Strukturplanung in Erkner, Akademie der Künste, Bauhaus-Archiv, Kunstbibliothek Berlin, Neue Nationalgalerie Berlin. I'd especially like to emphasize the support of the families Hopf and Oberste-Wilms. They made it possible for us to take treasures from the archives of the Hermes Hausverwaltung AG and Heinz Mosch Bauunternehmnung and present them to the public. Thanks also to the curator of the exhibition Ursula Müller for her research acumen, her commitment, and for the wonderful implementation of the exhibition idea.

She was superbly assisted by Anna Maria Heckmann, Gunnar Klack, and Dirk Weilemann, who brought in their energy as research trainees at Berlinische Galerie. To support the project, we had an academic advisory board: Andreas Butter (Leibniz-Institut für Regionalentwicklung und Strukturplanung Erkner), Bruno Flierl, architect and writer; Hartmut Frank (HafenCity Universität Hamburg), Stanislaus von Moos (Universität Zürich), and Kerstin Wittmann-Englert (Technische Universität Berlin). My thanks to them for their commitment and their assistance.

I also would like to thank the authors of this volume for their very informative and inspiring contributions, especially Adrian von Buttlar, who could contribute his experience from his committed work as professor at Berlin's Technische Universität and as one of the leading "heads" in the Arbeitsgemeinschaft Gefährdete Nachkriegsmoderne (Working Group: Endangered Post-War Modernism) at the TU's Institut für Kunstwissenschaft und Historische Urbanistik. Thanks also go to David Saik for his design of an aesthetic, functional, logical spatial arrangement for the exhibition. The complex technical and conservational implementation was carried out by our wonderfully professional (and always good-humored) technical and restoration departments, in particular Roland Pohl and Wolfgang Heigl as well as Andreas Piel and Maria Bortfeldt. Ulrike Andres, with the support of Silke Neumann and her team, insured that the project struck a public chord. With this exhibition, Berlinische Galerie hopes to provide an aesthetic and scholarly contribution to the debate on the architecture of post-war modernism.

Thomas Köhler

Werner Düttmann, St. Agnes Church, 2012

NOTES

1 _ Author unknown, "Rauh und rissig," *Der Spiegel* (1967) 47, pp. 188–193.

2 _ Quoted in Thomas Lackmann, "Die schlafende Schöne," *Der Tagesspiegel*, May 8, 2010.

Aerial photograph of Leipziger Platz with adjacent urban area to the east, circa 1955

Introduction

The construction era of the 1960s may have been brief, but our living environment still bears the stamp of its legacy. It was a decade of profound social and cultural transformation, of visions and a deep sense of optimism about the future, a time when Berlin and Germany as a whole experienced a regular building boom, reflecting the profound impatientence to rebuild cities severely scarred by the war. Designs proliferated, and by this time they aimed at more than simply eliminating distress. Offering radically new spaces for life, they drew on rationalized construction techniques and contemporary approaches to development to describe urban planning perspectives and outstanding one-off achievements. Some of them rank among the highlights of recent architectural history and have deeply engraved the collective visual memory.

As a front-line city in the Cold War, Berlin acquired particular significance in the 1960s. Following the foundation of the Federal Republic of Germany and the German Democratic Republic with East Berlin as its new capital, the governments of both countries made it their business, among other objectives, to offset the disadvantages of living in a divided city and prevent a population exodus. By committing to construction and ensuring cogent standards, they sought to uphold the appeal of whichever part of the city lay within their influence. Initially, these ideas and projects related to the city in its entirety, and were expressed in a single *Kollektivplan*, the general tenor of which was intellectually binding for all.[1] When the Wall went up on 13 August 1961, planners in the two halves of the city faced the demanding challenge of continuing what had already begun and completing this modern metropolis despite its enforced division. The historical centre of Berlin had been allocated in 1949 to its eastern sector which now found itself on an urban periphery. West Berlin was now an enclave with neither an economic motor nor financial patrons of its own, and so its chances of survival hinged on the utterly uncertain balance of international forces. Not without justification, the West German government feared its political, economic and cultural isolation.[2] With the continuing rivalry between the two political systems, the development of both halves of the city became a "task beyond any predicted and measurable indicators"[3], and one all Europe was monitoring. The pathways of urban renewal that East and West Berlin separately pursued after the Wall was built have now been forgotten. Views of the architectural legacy are coloured by emotions, misunderstandings and an antipathy that probably originated in the early 1960s – openly in West Berlin, cautiously expressed in East Berlin – with the stirrings of a bourgeois critique directed at the "inhospitality"[4] of its focal points. Half a century later, it appears to have acquired a new relevance. An awareness of "defective material technology, aggressive air-borne pollutants, decades of neglect and social miscalculation"[5] is posing an acute challenge to the preservation and rehabilitation of these architectures, rekindling debate about their perception and value.[6]

The exhibition *Radically Modern. Urban Planning and Architecture in 1960s Berlin* plays its part in this discourse, which was triggered in the late 1990s by a proliferation of events, publications and presentations dealing with post-war modern architecture. In the hope of provoking a critical re-evaluation of this construction era, it draws on models, photographs, drawings and films – some of them on display for the first time – to illustrate the creative aspirations, visions and discussions that accompanied urban renewal throughout Berlin in the 1960s. The urban experience of the presented architectures and places is made possible by guided tours, also by means of a smarthphone-app for iphone and android.

While the selection of projects is inevitably subjective, it does factor in the availability of material and the quality of exhibits. The exhibition essentially takes its cue from the collection held by the Berlinische Galerie, which includes not only original items relating to, for example, the Märkisches Viertel, the Freie Universität and the TV Tower, but also the photographic archives maintained by the former Construction Department in East Berlin, with abundant documentation of the buildings and projects of that period. Additional records were identified in archives belonging to other institutions and private individuals.

Will McBride, 2 young men in Bernauer Straße, the newly constructed Wall in the background, 1961

The focus is on the implementation, in both halves of the city, of modern planning objectives which – for all the heterogeneity and the efforts made during the Cold War to draw distinctions – can be interpreted today as emphasizing common ground between the two cultures of construction. Deeply unsettled by the events of the Second World War, and visually confronted by urban destruction, planners and architects rigorously refused – apart from a few exceptions – to rebuild the traditional city. Instead, they saw the situation as an opportunity to allow a new shape to emerge from the old Berlin and in so doing to put a face on technical progress and rapidly advancing motorization. The form and materiality of their concepts borrowed from both the objective modernism of the Weimar Republic – examples being Bruno Taut's Hufeisensiedlung or Hans Hertlein's Siemensstadt – and contemporary trends in other countries. With that kind of orientation, they sought to overcome twelve years of gigantomaniacal planning under the Nazi dictatorship and to catch up on missed international developments.

The exhibition has been divided thematically into six chapters, well aware that strict demarcations are not always feasible. The first describes the response to historical architectures. Buildings such as Egon Eiermann's Kaiser Wilhelm Memorial Church and Roland Korn's building for the State Council of the GDR share a modern stringency that contrasts vividly with the ruinous fabric of the yesteryear they integrate. Described at the time of construction as built expressions of a "new openness to the world"[7], today they are regarded as vestiges of the quest for an architecture that could reformulate national identity.

The following chapter, devoted to Urban "Spaces/Urban Dreams", shows material from the many struggles with form and content that went into designing and implementing new centres for East and West Berlin, such as Breitscheidplatz and Alexanderplatz, the Kulturforum and Marx-Engels-Platz (now Schlossplatz). The buildings in these places testify to the internationality of creative references: the Europa-Center by architects Hentrich und Petschnigg, for example, to the Rockefeller Center in New York, while Hermann Henselmann's Haus des Lehrers with its conference hall reveals a fascination with Oscar Niemeyer's government buildings in the new capital Brasília.

The chapters "Techno-Geometries" and "Architecture and Art" address the diversity of aesthetic responses to social conditions and demands at the time. The choice of images illustrates the artistic options available to a construction industry primarily driven by technical and economic requirements. Some are spatial visualizations of car-oriented urban planning, or of building experiments and dreams of urban futures which took root in Berlin from the mid-1960s, echoing worldwide visions of life in a "city of spaces", in "clusters" of individual mobile cells, and in cities above and below the ground. These ideas, which never progressed beyond paper, range from "earth architectures" via megastructures to radical thought experiments devoted to the ideal city layout. Architects drew on these in an attempt to eradicate serious wrongs or to provoke socio-political change. Other images depict masterpieces of post-war modernism that were in fact implemented, such as buildings by Mies van der Rohe, Hans Scharoun and Hermann Henselmann.

The next chapter, "Serial Diversity", describes a planning euphoria that gave way in the course of the decade to more sober ways of thinking. Built translations of streamlined construction methods were often bogged down in formal considerations or as yet unresolved issues of prefabrication that led to serialization and repetition. Livelier, although in most cases unrealized designs for various types of housing – for example, by architects Klaus Müller-Rehm and Manfred Zumpe – bear witness to efforts undertaken during those years to counter the risk of monotony imposed by structural typologies. These segue into depictions of the well-known large-scale estates in West Berlin, such as the

Märkisches Viertel and Gropiusstadt. By the mid-1960s at the latest, an intellectual minority was expressing growing discomfort about the "tedium, anonymity and monotony"[8] of the new construction methods they embodied and the "functionalism of the build- ing industry"[9] in West Berlin. Only a few years later, this criticism was one cause of the multifaceted resistance put up by the civil movement in West Germany to the socio-political realities of the 1950s and 1960s.
The six chapters are introduced by a prologue, which argues that planning on both sides of the Wall drew inspiration from the international context, supporting its case with some significant examples.
The concluding epilogue offers a selection of present-day art and photography reflecting some original perspectives on the built legacy of the 1960s. As a counterweight to the historical documentation making up the exhibition, they offer the visitor additional food for thought.
The project benefited from the critical support of an academic advisory board. My cordial thanks to Andreas Butter, Bruno Flierl, Hartmut Frank, Stanislaus von Moos and Kerstin Wittmann-Englert for their constructive and amiable collaboration. I am much indebted to Stanislaus von Moos for his suggestions and enlightenment, not only with regard to the chapter headings. My special thanks go to Adrian von Buttlar for his short-term support.
Warm thanks are due to our research trainees Gunnar Klack, Dirk Weilemann and especially Anna Maria Heckmann for their energetic engagement with this project.
I am extremely grateful to the artists and photographers for their committed involvement.
To those who have loaned exhibits, thank you for placing your trust in the Berlinische Galerie.
And I owe a particular debt of gratitude to the Kulturstiftung des Bundes, without whose generous financial support this project could not have been implemented.
Catalogue production was supported by the Wüstenrot Stiftung.

Ursula Müller

NOTES

1 _ Ulrich Conrads, 2nd version of the introduction for *Casabella*, manuscript, April 4, 1964, p. 1 (UCA BTU Cottbus).

2 _ Dieter E. Zimmer, "Die Literatur-Mafia von Berlin. Eine rabiate Polemik und einige nüchternere Beobachtungen," *DIE ZEIT* (1966), p. 47.

3 _ Ulrich Conrads, "Poelzig Schüler," manuscript, *Neue deutsche Architektur II,* Introduction (UCA, BTU Cottbus, 1961), p. 6.

4 _ Alexander Mitscherlich, *Die Unwirtlichkeit unserer Städte. Anstiftung zum Unfrieden* (Frankfurt am Main, 1965).

5 _ Wolfgang Pehnt, Foreword. In: Adrian von Buttlar/Christoph Heuter, eds., *Architektur der 60er Jahre. Wiederentdeckung einer Epoche* (Berlin, 2007), p. 12.

6 _ *Wie, warum und von wem wird die Architektur dieser Zeit wahrgenommen, wertgeschätzt und weiterverwendet?* Conference proceedings of the Architecture Faculties at Bauhaus-Universität Weimar and TU Dortmund on 12 and 13 March 2015.

7 _ "Neues Bauen in unserer Zeit," January 2, 1962, RIAS II (copy of unrevised manuscript, p. 2), UCA, BTU Cottbus.

8 _ „Bundesbaugesetz," manuscript, circa 1961, *Kleinere Beiträge 1960er* (UCA, BTU Cottbus), p. 4.

9 _ Heinrich Klotz, *Moderne und Postmoderne. Architektur der Gegenwart 1960–1980* (Braunschweig/Wiesbaden, 1987), pp. 24 and 34–35.

PICTURE CREDIT

Will McBride, 2 young men in Bernauer Straße, the newly constructed Wall in the background, 1961, 37.3 x 54.7 cm, silver gelatin paper, Berlinische Galerie BG-FS 028/95,13

Risen from Ruins

BERLINER BANK
U-Bhf Kurfürstendamm

Egon Eiermann, New Kaiser Wilhelm Memorial Church, Interior view into the church, 1963

left: Egon Eiermann, New Kaiser Wilhelm Memorial Church (1956–63), 1963

Paul Baumgarten, Redevelopment of the Reichstag building, sketch for the new dome, handwritten note: "Dome must be rebuilt, although in a different form. It now has 'content' and the large open staircase fulfils a purpose," 1964

Paul Baumgarten, Redevelopment of the Reichstag building (1961–73), assembly hall, circa 1969

Paul Baumgarten, Redevelopment of the Reichstag building, foyer to the plenary chamber with the sculpture *Cosmos* by Bernhard Heiliger, photography circa 1969

right: Doug Hall, Privy Council Building, main entrance hall, ground floor, from the series *Remnants of the GDR*, August 1992

Roland Korn, Hans-Erich Bogatzky and Klaus Pätzmann, Privy Council Building (1962–64), 1965

Roland Korn, Hans-Erich Bogatzky and Klaus Pätzmann, Privy Council Building, insertion of the portal IV from the palace, 1963

Stanislaus von Moos

The Monumentality of the Matchbox

1 _ Bert Sass, Ruins of Kaiser Wilhelm Memorial Church, 1949

2 _ Breitscheidplatz with Europa-Center and Kaiser Wilhelm Memorial Church, postcard, 1975

Power and Ambivalence

For decades, the ruin of Berlin's Gedächtnis-Kirche (Kaiser Wilhelm Memorial Church) alongside its crystalline substitute by Egon Eiermann has played its ambivalent role as tourist logo and mysterious symbol of the city's perseverance in the Cold War (fig. 1). And yet, nobody knows for sure what the combination of old and new exactly represents: the phoenix-like rise of the new from the débris of the old, mourning and soul-searching regarding German responsibility in the war, or a nostalgia for former national glory, romanticized in terms of ruin aesthetics? Considering the endless complications involved in the project's realization, the complex should perhaps rather be seen as emblematic for the difficulties of reaching a compromise when it comes to public representation in democracy.[1] Seen in this way, it is precisely the diffuse nature of its messages, combined with the plastic power of the sign as such (for Alexander Calder, the church ruin was "perhaps the greatest abstract sculpture in the world"[2]) that make the Memorial Church the built paragon of the "New Monumentality."[3]

Eiermann's new church obviously contributes to the potent mystery of the entire complex. Yet even more important as a marker is the slab-shaped office building and hotel of the Europa-Center which towers next to it (fig. 2). Like thesis and antithesis, the ruin and the slab characterize the physiognomy of the place while also, in fact, marking out two extremes within the range of possibilities in architectural signification at hand in the early post-war years. The one form seems to refer dialectically to the other: both are ambivalent in their own way. Towering over and framing the church ruin at the same time, the office building forms a paradoxical alter ego to the Gedächtniskirche, even recreating its toppled tower cross in the form of a colossal Mercedes star.[4]

The decision to build the Europa-Center fell "a few days after the Wall was built." The project, realized in the extremely short time between 1961 and 1963, thus was charged with politics from its very inception.[5] 80 meters high, making it the highest office building in Berlin (two meters higher than the somewhat older Springer tower to which I will return below), the Center unmistakably laid claim to centrality within the city – contrasting sharply in that respect with the earlier buildings on Breitscheidplatz.[6] In fact, on the opening day, *Tagesspiegel* reported on the "magnificient urbanistic conclusion" that the building provided for Kurfürstendamm. The superlatives targeted far beyond the Berlin context: not merely an "exclamation point of free enterprise", the building was even seen as "the most important commercial project of the post-war period on our continent" – in fact, the "first response to New York's famous Rockefeller-Center."[7]

3 _ Skidmore, Owings & Merrill, Model of Lever House, New York, 1949 (with alternative position of the vertical "slab")

Slabs: Economy and Monumentality

The history that interests here begins on the one hand with the dictate of economics – in other words, the ambition of creating a maximum of rentable office space with a minimum of material and structural expense – and on the other with the diffuse need for buildings and places capable of providing a sense of collective identity. Although the term seemed compromised by fascist and Stalinist architecture (or precisely for that reason), architects outside of Germany were more and more intrigued by "monumentality" in the years after 1940. For the Swiss critic Peter Meyer, for example, it was clear that the need for symbolic representation in architecture could not be satisfied on the basis of functionalism. When buildings of a ceremonial nature are needed, he argued, there is simply no alternative to taking recourse to some version of the classical in architecture – regardless of the political system at hand.[8] As becomes clear in their manifesto *Nine Points on Monumenality*, for Sigfried Giedion, Josep Lluís Sert, and Fernand Léger, too, the symbolic deficits of functionalism were an established fact. Yet, unlike Meyer, Giedion combined his campaign with a pathetic attack on the monopoly of classicism in architecture intended to represent state. In Giedion's view, technology and abstract art were the only way of achieving monumentality today – classicism was out. In that respect, the critique was directed at Washington and Oslo no less than at Munich and Moscow.[9] In the U.S., the "Nine Points" were lent a certain urgency by the flagrant decay of the inner cities: commercial revitalization by way of pedestrian streets and plazas seemed the only way to 'give the city centers back to the residents'. In post-war Europe, where so many city centers were left in ruins, things were seen in a similar light – at least in the West. As business moved in and many of the former residents had no choice but to settle in the outskirts, capitalist enterprise often found itself side by side with eerie remnants of war and Holocaust. London had shown interesting ways of going about such unexpected typological encounters. At Breitscheidplatz, Berlin was ready to take up the challenge.

And the slab-shaped office building? – Initially the "blind passenger" in many efforts to constitute meaning by way of architecture, the slab in the 1940s and 1950s increasingly became the projection surface for a particularly American passion to demonstrate technological prowess, if not omnipotence. In order to make this possible, the vocabulary of architecture needed to be reduced to the spectrum of architectural possibilities suitable for such demonstrations: steel skeleton, glass façade, aluminum curtain wall. Within this code, the building form of the slab began to develop its own potential of institutional ceremoniality: its own form of "new monumentality" (fig. 3).

Rockefeller Center: Myth and Recycling

The origin of the slab as a type is rather banal. All that is required is a bank of elevator shafts along a corridor, and then to hang offices onto it. The depth of the offices is a direct function of the desired amount of daylight. The height of the building results from the capacity of the construction chosen and the operating distance of the elevators. Although this simple logic of "form follows function" leaves decisive questions unanswered, it always played a key role as a lubricant in exchanges between architects and clients. The narrow and stepped shape of the 66 stories high RCA Building (Radio Corporation of America), which forms the centerpiece of Rockefeller Center, was a pure question of mathematics, explains Raymond Hood, its main designer. The building's shell reflects the numeric relationship of surface area to the size of the elevator shafts. From the bottom to the top, the rule was that for an office the maximum distance from the inner wall to the window should be 27 feet (around 9 meters). Since the number of elevator shafts decreases toward the top, the stepped profile of the building was a natural result, Hood explains (fig. 4).[10] That there were many other aspects also involved in calculating the height of the building (expected rent yields, the relation to neighboring buildings, the legal and tax policy framework for skyscrapers in Manhattan) remains unsaid.[11]

4 _ RCA Building (Radio Corporation of America), Rockefeller Center, New York City, postcard, circa 1949

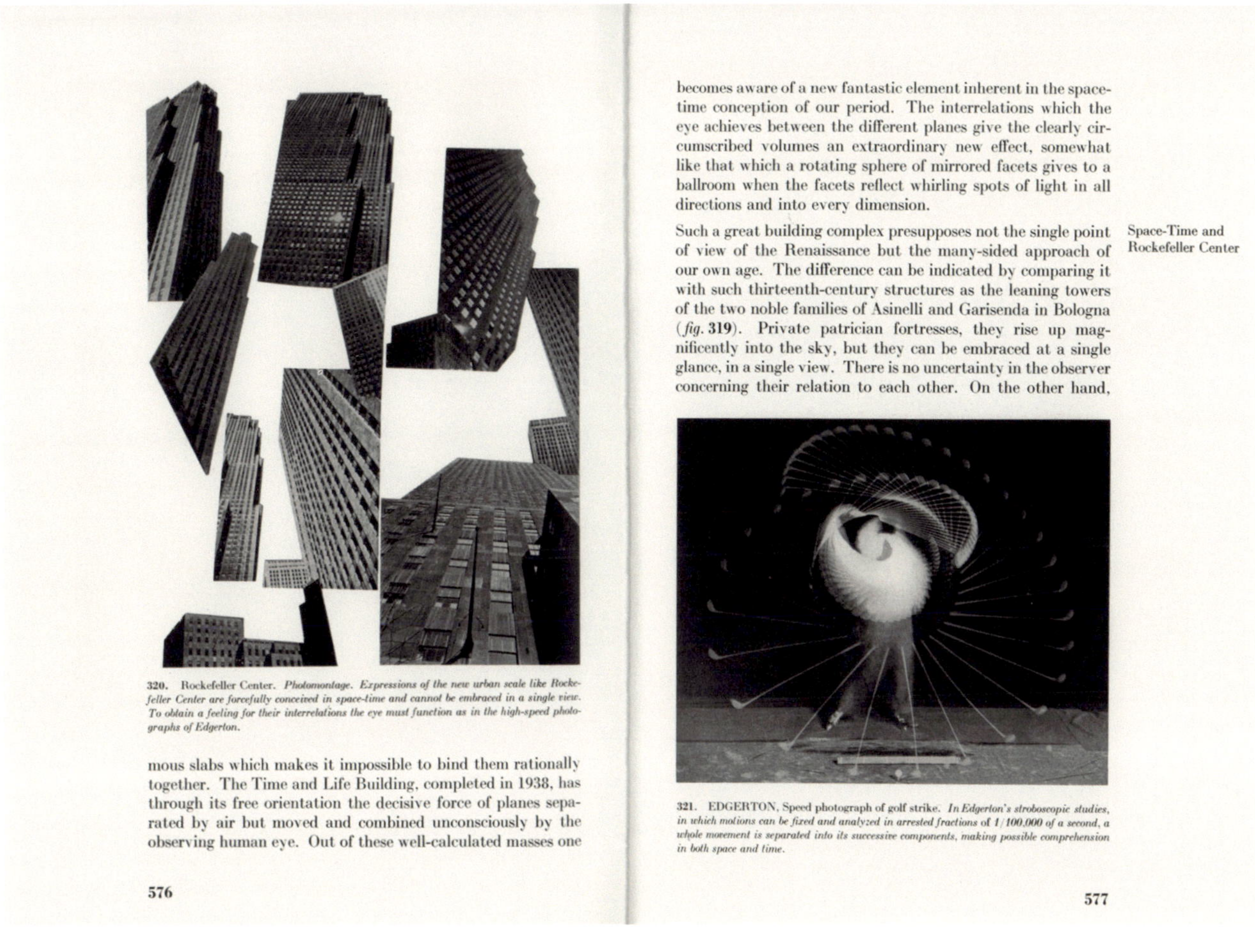

becomes aware of a new fantastic element inherent in the space-time conception of our period. The interrelations which the eye achieves between the different planes give the clearly circumscribed volumes an extraordinary new effect, somewhat like that which a rotating sphere of mirrored facets gives to a ballroom when the facets reflect whirling spots of light in all directions and into every dimension.

Space-Time and Rockefeller Center

Such a great building complex presupposes not the single point of view of the Renaissance but the many-sided approach of our own age. The difference can be indicated by comparing it with such thirteenth-century structures as the leaning towers of the two noble families of Asinelli and Garisenda in Bologna (*fig.* **319**). Private patrician fortresses, they rise up magnificently into the sky, but they can be embraced at a single glance, in a single view. There is no uncertainty in the observer concerning their relation to each other. On the other hand,

320. Rockefeller Center. *Photomontage. Expressions of the new urban scale like Rockefeller Center are forcefully conceived in space-time and cannot be embraced in a single view. To obtain a feeling for their interrelations the eye must function as in the high-speed photographs of Edgerton.*

mous slabs which makes it impossible to bind them rationally together. The Time and Life Building, completed in 1938, has through its free orientation the decisive force of planes separated by air but moved and combined unconsciously by the observing human eye. Out of these well-calculated masses one

321. EDGERTON, Speed photograph of golf strike. *In Edgerton's stroboscopic studies, in which motions can be fixed and analyzed in arrested fractions of 1/100,000 of a second, a whole movement is separated into its successive components, making possible comprehension in both space and time.*

576

577

5 _ Comparison of a collage by Sigfried Giedion with the chronophotograph of a golf player by Harold Edgerton, repro of a double page from: Sigfried Giedion, *Space, Time and Architecture. The Growth of a New Tradition*, 1944

Soon after completion some observers reacted to the size of the building's North and South fronts, to its unbroken mass and extraordinary thinness by giving it the nickname "The Slab".[12] The success of the implied concept was resounding. In the quarter century after World War II, whenever companies, brands, or governmental offices took to the stage of the city and thus the world, the slab seems to have been the most obvious formula. True, by reducing the slab to its stereometric quintessence, i.e. ignoring the stepped endings of the elevator shafts, architects partly undid the very legibility of its genesis that the RCA Building with its stepped sides had so clearly emphasized. For indeed, with the International Style[13], or rather its fascination for the aesthetic of the steel skeleton, what counts is the expression of structure; the dynamics of mobility play only a secondary role in formgiving. Such had already been the case around 1928, by the way, when the "high-rise virus"[14] first spread to residential architecture. As the coordinator of CIAM (International Congress of Modern Architecture), Giedion was one of the first witnesses of this trend – and one of its early historiographers.

Approaching Rockefeller Center from Fifth Avenue, one enters a narrow symmetrical enclosure framed by two massive six-storey blocks on the left and the right and confronts the edge of the central RCA Building as a steeply rising, adventurously slender tower – reminding one of a cathedral (see fig. 4).[15] Only the bird's-eye view reveals the "open" composition of the windmill-like grouping of the buildings. That is the view that is of interest from the perspective of post-war modernism. Not by chance, the Rockefeller Center is key in Giedion's elucubrations on modernism's "space-time" syndrome (the classicist overall concept of the complex as a whole interested him just as little as the "gothicism" of Hood's stepped tower that dominates the plaza). The city here found a "new order," Giedion says, based on "the radically new form" developed in response to the unusual height of contemporary office buildings and its effects on the inner organization.[16] There was no way a complex like Rockefeller Center could be grasped from "a single viewpoint," we read in *Space, Time and Architecture*. It is only by walking through the complex that one experiences space. A collage made of views seen in temporal sequence illustrates the idea (fig. 5).[17]

Giedion coined his "stroboscopic" image of Rockefeller Center at a time when architects elsewhere in the world had already begun turning Hood's scenographically-charged "gothic" vista of the slab by 90 degrees, thus giving it a different, rather "billboard"-like effect. The key example is the

6 _ Lúcio Costa, Oscar Niemeyer, Jorge Moreira, Affonso Eduardo Reidy, et al; consultation: Le Corbusier, Ministry for Education and Health (1936-43), Rio de Janeiro, from: Le Corbusier, *New World of Space,* 1948

Brazilian Ministry for Education and Health in Rio de Janeiro (Lúcio Costa, Oscar Niemeyer, Jorge Moreira, Affonso Eduardo Reidy, et al.; consultant: Le Corbusier; built from 1939 to 1943). Majestically raising from the center of a public plaza and supported by a forest of pilotis, the slab here acquires an aura of democratically legitimated state authority – all the more so as it is surrounded by a cluster of ministries built more or less at the same time, but in a variety of traditional idioms. In 1942, Philip Goodwin praised the building as the "most beautiful government building in the Western world,"[18] thus placing it at the focus of the then emerging interest in the "new monumentality."

More convincingly than any government building previously realized, the ministry put the language of international modernism at the service of a distinctly monumental purpose (fig. 6). The much larger UN Secretariat Building, rising a few years later on the banks of the East River in New York (1948–1952), was built on a similar agenda. Symptomatically, however, its colossal size is not characterized as classicizing in the way the Rio building is due to its magnificent peristyle. On the other hand, since "monumentality" was here not limited to the horizon of a single nation, all prerequisites seemed in place in order to successfully launch the slab alone, set free from any "urban" context, as an architectural password for international collaboration in the service of peace and progress (fig. 7). One may note in passing that, as already in Rio, Le Corbusier played a key role in determining the building's layout.[19]

As an office complex and shopping center, Europa-Center is no equivalent to such examples. And yet the UN Secretariat Building was undoubtedly one of the buildings that Helmut Hentrich, the leading architect of the Center, studied closely during his 1954 trip to New York, even though a different building plays the starring role in his memoirs: the Lever House, on Park Avenue, diagonally across from the Seagram Building (which, however, did not yet exist at the time [fig. 8]). Lever House was built from 1949 to 1952 by SOM (Skidmore, Owings and Merrill). The vertical office slab is here demonstratively combined with a similarly slab-shaped horizontal element at its foot – a combination that is, in fact, rather un-elegantly echoed in the Europa-Center (see fig. 3). Note that Gordon Bunshaft, who had been responsible for the design of Lever House, later played a key role in consulting for the Thyssen Building in Düsseldorf (designed by Hentrich, Petschnigg & Partner, HPP). There can be no doubt, on the other hand, that the spectacular three-slab building in Düsseldorf had its share in Karl-Heinz Pepper's choice of the architect of his prestigious Berlin project.[20]

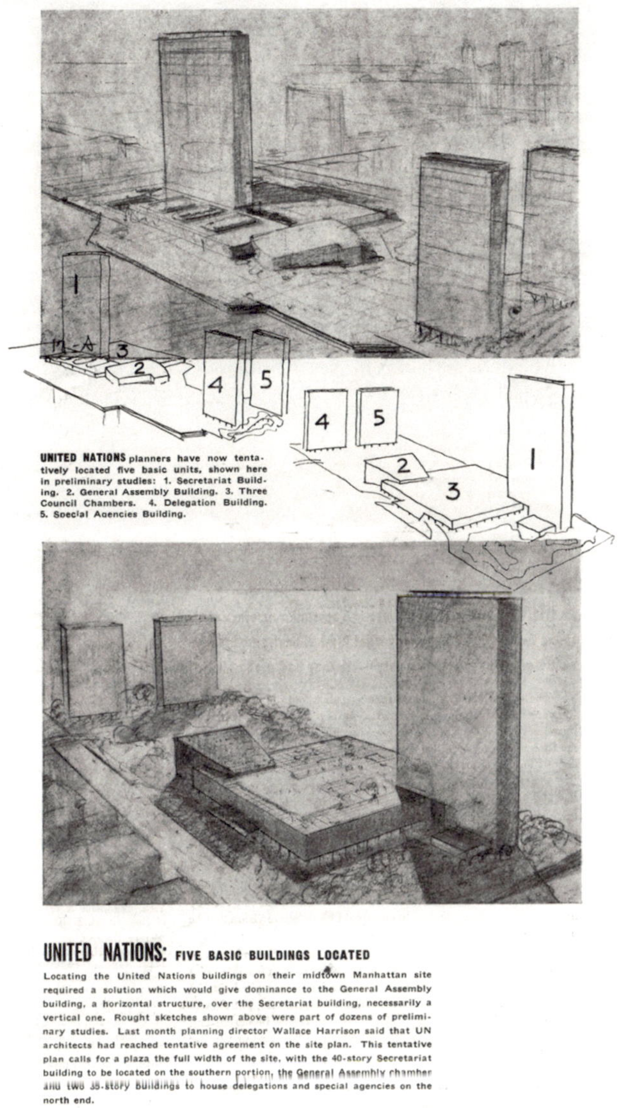

UNITED NATIONS planners have now tentatively located five basic units, shown here in preliminary studies: 1. Secretariat Building. 2. General Assembly Building. 3. Three Council Chambers. 4. Delegation Building. 5. Special Agencies Building.

UNITED NATIONS: FIVE BASIC BUILDINGS LOCATED

Locating the United Nations buildings on their midtown Manhattan site required a solution which would give dominance to the General Assembly building, a horizontal structure, over the Secretariat building, necessarily a vertical one. Rought sketches shown above were part of dozens of preliminary studies. Last month planning director Wallace Harrison said that UN architects had reached tentative agreement on the site plan. This tentative plan calls for a plaza the full width of the site, with the 40-story Secretariat building to be located on the southern portion, the General Assembly chamber and two 35-story buildings to house delegations and special agencies on the north end.

7 _ Wallace K. Harrison, Le Corbusier and Oscar Niemeyer, Studies with respect to the offices and parliamentary chamber of the United Nations, New York, 1947, from: *Architectural Forum,* April 1947

8 _ Ezra Stoller, Seagram Building (1956–58), New York City, architects: Ludwig Mies van der Rohe, Philip Johnson, 1958

The core part of the Europa-Center, at least from the investor's perspective, was the shopping center complex at the foot of the tower, including also an entire wealth of attractions and amenities. Though often presented as the European counterpart to the skating rink at Rockefeller Center, the covered rink in the second courtyard can hardly be compared to its model at Rockefeller Center, being, after all, a mere appendix to the fully air-conditioned "ladies' shopping paradise," as the *Tagesspiegel* called it. Furthermore, lacking both the Rockefeller Center's and the Lever House's main attraction – its open plaza – the shopping center was subsequently marketed as an adaptation of the shopping arcades of Bern. In reality, the only plausible model was the shopping centers and malls that Victor Gruen began erecting in 1950 throughout the United States. – Rockefeller Center and the Old Town of Bern were mere smoke screens of marketing mystique.[21]

Smoke Signals in the Cold War

In the world of consumer goods, "symbolic value" is most aggressively marketed when the price is high. Similarly, in architecture, "meaning" and "symbolism" tend to become an issue when there is a contradiction that needs to be bridged between the planned structure and the costs involved. In these circumstances, there is a special need for convincing. Lever House is a good example in this context. In terms of structural economy or elegant office space, flooded with daylight, the slab seems like the best possible solution. As to the rent yields, however, it is hard to defend in one of the most expensive locations worldwide – especially so when it comes in combination with an open plaza. To assuage the skepticism of his board members, Charles Luckman, the president of Lever and himself an architect, argued that open space at the foot of the building that would result from the sacrified office space would make people feel "part of Lever."[22] The plaza would contribute a "very human feeling" on the level of the street to the transparent and polished surface of the curtain-wall façade, the purity of which symbolized the soap company (see fig. 3).[23]
Apart from the positive effects on the company's "image", Luckmann argued, all this would also promote what he called the "humanation of cities."[24] For people need "freedom of space" to dedicate themselves to the "pursuit of happiness" in a life of freedom.[25]
Luckman was clever enough not to submit a project himself, but to assign the task to one of the leading architectural firms in New York, Skidmore, Owings and Merrill. SOM's aura must have contributed to convincing Lever to massively invest in the symbolic function of its headquarters. In fact, the elementary stereometrics of the box form made the building a unique sculptural presence in the city, thus providing a striking trademark for the company.
As Luckman's diatribes suggest, the neuroses of McCarthyism didn't stop at architecture's doorstep: the chairman even wanted the building to be seen as a symbol of "American values" in the face of the malignancies of socialism and communism.[26] Thus even in New York, socialism appears to have been perceived as an imminent threat. In Berlin, where the founding of the GDR and the currency reform in West Germany (1949) practically charged all realms of life, the way buildings looked inevitably became part of the political conversation. Slabs turn out to have been at the core of this scenario. No wonder, in any case, that the Europa-Center played a "key role in the press" as a beacon of the West in the face of the Wall.[27]
Matchboxes can be used to send smoke signals or even result in a dangerous fire. When the publisher Axel Springer decided to move his company headquarters from Hamburg to Berlin and to build an office tower in the old newspaper district of Kochstraße, right on the sector border, his intention to use architecture to send a political signal was instantly clear to everybody.[28] It is not worth building "high-rises for newspapers without an idea that is greater than ourselves. An idea, that means: freedom for all Germans in one fatherland with the legal capital of Berlin in the midst of a Europe at peace."[29] The Springer building, 78 meters high, built 1959-1962 at a right angle to Kochstraße, shimmering festively with its golden aluminum coating, was to be understood as a "scream against the wind," indeed a "powerful architectural exclamation point ... of the belief that Berlin and Germany would soon ... be reunited."[30] The location directly on the sector border provided the necessary visibility to this program and Müller and Sobotka's architecture even gave it a somewhat sleazy appearance of luxury.
Just two years after construction, the sector border was sealed off by the Wall (fig. 9). Countless photographs document the situation, among them a picture taken by Rem Koolhaas in 1971 that shows the Springer Building towering in the evening twilight over the wall (fig. 10).[31] In the mid-1960s, Oskar Kokoschka had captured the desolation of East Berlin from the commanding perspective of Axel Springer's penthouse in a painting.[32] In the area just beyond the wall, reconstruction had in fact hardly begun. As a result, the Springer building, with its neon sign installed on the roof in 1963, could be seen from a great distance day and night. Even from Berlin-Mitte! – At about the same time, yet another neon sign blinking towards the east was in-

9 _ Rem Koolhaas and Madelon Vriesendorp, "Exodus or the Voluntary Prisoners of Architecture," Collage, 1972

10 _ Rem Koolhaas, View along the Berlin Wall to the Axel Springer high-rise building, 1971

stalled on the nearby GSW Tower (built in 1958), this one being directly fed with propaganda by the West Berlin Senate. In the Ministry for State Security of the GDR, this caused considerable nervousness: at any event, Albert Norden, the secretary of the Central Committee for Agitation and Propaganda, had a report prepared on how to limit the effect of this double enemy act. The proposals made included blocking the view of the writing with the help of screens or making the signs illegible by shining light on them.[33]

To put an end to the problem, East Berlin seemed to have no other choice than to block the devil of capitalist office buildings with the Beelzebub of socialist housing, which, due to central planning in the East also succeeded.[34] Soon enough – in the 1980s both the office buildings at Kochstraße and the nearby housing blocks at Leipziger Straße were caught up by the then fashionable critique of functionalism, but by the year 2000, a younger generation of architects finally began to view the buildings that marked the "high-rise war" in the 1950s and those that tried to neutralize it after 1970 as part of a coherent urban landscape (fig. 11).[35]

11 _ Sauerbruch Hutton, *Dialogue across the Wall*, 1991, right: View along Kochstraße with the projected extension of the GSW head office (Sauerbruch Hutton), left: residential blocks along Leipziger Straße, in the background the Axel Springer "slab"

12 _ Announcement by Harvard University Press of Sigfried Giedion's, *Architecture, You and Me* (1958) with the model of the headquarters of Prudential insurance planned for the Back Bay Center (1954) by Walter Gropius and Pietro Belluschi, Boston, MA, circa 1958

"Überholen, ohne Einzuholen" ("Overtaking without Catching Up")

As teaching was resumed at schools of architecture after 1945, modernism was the accepted rule almost everywhere in both East and West. A few years later, after the division of Germany had become cemented, the cultures developed differently, at times even in radically opposite directions. For a time it seemed that German architecture East and West of the "Sektorengrenze" was all about incompatibility of form, style and social role. Granted the friction of the systems, the display of incompatibility appears to have reached its climax at the time the inner-German border was still passable, at least for large parts of the population, i.e. when East Berlin's Stalinallee and West Berlin's new Hansa Viertel marked the span between the "extremes."[36] By 1961, at a point in time when, due to the Wall, the overwhelming majority of Berlin residents were no longer in the position of experiencing "live" the contrast between "here" and "there," the architectural and planning cultures in both states had moved considerably closer. Since socialist land reform in the GDR made implementing modern planning goals in the city centers possible to an extent that was unthinkable in the West, the East naturally had a much stronger record in that area. The chances for an architect like Hermann Henselmann to unfold a brilliant activity in the field of urban design were all the more real. After pleasing the regime with the triumphalist mise-en-scène at the service of the "national tradition" at Strausberger Platz and Frankfurter Tor, he now returned to architectural modernism, of which he had so emphatically declared himself a proponent after 1945.[37] It comes as no surprise that the West's lead in this realm suffered from significant structural lacks in his eyes. Long before Europa-Center was in planning, he complained about how West Berlin was putting the icing on the cake of the city's division "with a veritably sadistic pleasure." What was happening in the Zoo area in terms of "urban design" could "easily turn into a tragedy," he writes. Everything here was going wrong: high-rises are placed randomly and without adequate space along existing streets, while banks, insurance companies, and business headquarters "that should be located in the city center" were placed in the realm of Breitscheidplatz, etc.[38] Bruno Flierl was even more vigorous in his critique: the "power aims of certain companies, the business interests of shopkeepers as well as restaurant and cinema owners, not least the church's ideological determination to join the others in representing the beautiful, 'free' Western world ... has here resulted in a virtually unique chaos of urban design."[39] At least, it was clear what kind of sins needed to be avoided in planning Berlin-Mitte.

The planning of that was already fully underway at the time. Once it had conquered the West after 1945, be it in terms of simple economic expediency or with the pathos of *noblesse oblige* (see fig. 8),[40] the slab-shaped office building now began its victorious march in the world of real existing socialism. Since when it came to "overtaking without catching up,"[41] it was the U.S. that provided the criteria, the process can be understood as a kind of parallel recycling of international high-rise modernism under different premises. Once again, Rockefeller Center came into view. When Gerhard Kosel, president of the Deutsche Bauakademie, proposed his "central building" in Berlin Mitte (with 150 meters, it would have been almost twice the size of Europa-Center), he surely had in mind one of the projects for the never-realized Soviet Palace in Moscow.[42] While the shape of an office building facing Lustgarten with a rhomboid forecourt lined by colonnades may almost have been dictated by the recently dethroned imperatives of adherence to the "national tradition,"[43] it also resonated with the classicist layout of Rockefeller Center.[44]

Meanwhile, American architects had developed their own updates of the mythic model from Midtown New York, for instance in the once famous project for the Back Bay Center in Boston, Massachusetts (1953). An elegant, lentil-shaped slab resting on high stilts forms the core of the project by Walter Gropius and TAC (The Architects Collaborative; in collaboration with Pietro Belluschi, Hugh Stubbins, and other architects from the Harvard / MIT circle). A large hall

13 _ Luckman & Pereira, Rendering of the Prudential Insurance Headquarters in Boston (1957/58). Prudential Center was built 1957–65

14 _ Gerhard Kosel with Hanns Hopp and Hans Mertens, Marx-Engels-Forum with central building. Competition proposal towards a "socialist re-design of the center of the capital of the GDR – Berlin," 1959

covered by a flat vaulted roof is linked to the slab by way of a system of asymmetrically grouped, rather narrow squares and promenades (fig. 12).[45] The project was commissioned in 1952/53 by the investor Roger Stevens and was later frequently referred to as a summary of sorts of the ideas discussed at the CIAM congress on *The Heart of the City* (Hoddesdon, 1951).[46] But when Prudential, the giant among American insurance companies, decided to move to Boston in 1957 and to establish its headquarters on the location of the proposed Back Bay Center, the company had no use for the project. Luckman, who had become the company's architect, subjected the large superblock to a much simpler overall plan, with a high tower based on a square plan as central element that has left its stamp on the Boston Back Bay area since the early 1960s (The Prudential Center was built from 1957 to 1965). Gropius' and TAC's system of loosely meandering promenades was replaced by a palatial, two-winged free standing stairway connecting the wide open plaza to street level, all perfectly symmetrical. Thus *humanization* here once again followed the lead of absolutist representation. The cost-benefit analysis seemed to justify the choice (fig. 13).[47]

Gerhard Kosel's similarly organized project for the "Zentrales Gebäude" remained unbuilt. Berlin's head architect at the time, Hermann Henselmann, rejected the plan as a "leveling of the art of building." To propose an office building as a monument to socialism is a "serious mistake," he argued. Such might be possible for a "capitalist downtown," but not for a "socialist city center."[48] Is it a coincidence that Henselmann's counter proposal in the form of a "German Pantheon" ("Pantheon der Deutschen") on Alexanderplatz recalls the Congress Rotunda in Gropius and Belluschi's Back Bay Center project (fig. 12)? In a somewhat later revision of his project,[49] Kosel himself not only simplified the volumetrics of his tower but also added two lower side wings that form a forecourt closed off by a colonnade reflected in a plateau d'eau at its base. And finally he, too, added a rotunda at the rear (1959; fig. 14).

15 _ René Burri, Office building by Oscar Niemeyer (1957–60), National Congress, Brasília, 1960

Haus des Lehrers and Artistic Autonomy

"The very fact that West German companies were erecting high-rises in West Berlin" is enough to refute the idea that "representative buildings of our worker and peasant state cannot be made visible from afar in the skyline of the city." Such was State Council Chairman Walter Ulbricht's rather contorted verdict in 1960. Subsequently, even Henselmann began to entertain the idea of a "Stadtkrone" in the form of an office skyscraper. He did so all the more seriously, as the just completed and widely publicized government center complex in Brasilia, designed by Oscar Niemeyer (1957–1960; fig. 15), seemed to offer a particularly promising model in that context.[50] Long before Brasilia, Niemeyer, the Communist star architect, had already played a decisive part in the planning of the UN Secretariat Building. No wonder that he soon became a living myth in the GDR. What better model could there be for any attempt to finally checkmate West Berlin's uncoordinated efforts to control the cityscape by ways of slabs than the twin towers of Brasilia's Capitol Complex? – Alas, the Brazilian temptation and Henselmann's dream of an East Berlin city crown remained just a brief flash in the pan.

Instead, the Brazilian spark spread to his most important project for the city center: the Haus des Lehrers (Building of the Teacher) on Alexanderplatz (1961–1964; fig. 16). Ten years before, Henselmann had used an architectural idiom based on the Baroque and on the historicism of the Wilhelminian era in order to satisfy the national leadership's desire for magnificence. The result was Frankfurter Tor in the East of Stalinallee and Strausberger Platz as its preliminary western end. This time the ambition was to connect the recently completed western end of the Grand Boulevard and Alexanderplatz to international modernism.[51] Gendarmenmarkt with its two majestic domes from the era of Friedrich the Great, the classicism of the Schinkel era, and the architecture of the new Moscow had been the points of reference for Henselmann's earlier projects. Now the models were Brasília's National Congress and New York's Seagram Building (fig. 8; 15). For GDR architecture, an age of frenetic internationalization had begun, as in other Eastern bloc countries, too. Typically, the attention was often emphatically directed beyond the Federal Republic – including especially the Netherlands and Switzerland.[52]

In comparison to Brasília, Henselmann's elegant coupling of an office slab cum library with a domed hall is a miniature. The nearby muscular buildings by Peter Behrens that frame the entrance to Alexanderplatz from the West make Haus des Lehrers appear almost delicate. At the height of the library floors, the slab is decorated with a mural of socialist-heroic content – an idea borrowed from Mexico City's University Campus. Inspired by the Byzantine mosaics of Basilica Sant'Apollinare in Classe (and perhaps also by Léger), Walter Womacka created a rather schoolbook-like didactic broadsheet covering part of the lower third of the slab.[53] Henselmann went along with the idea, thus accepting that the pathos of the Miesian curtain wall was now reduced to the role of a mere backdrop for "art."

Naturally, there were and are other ways in architecture and urban design to achieve, as Abbé Laugier famously put it, *du tumulte dans l'ensemble, de l'uniformité dans le détail* (tumult in the overall impact, uniformity in detail) as those used in 1960s residential construction in the GDR. It is enough to think of Le Havre by Auguste Perret. A small 1959

16 _ Hermann Henselmann, Haus des Lehrers with monumental natural stone mosaic by Walter Womacka, circa 1964

17 _ Juan O'Gorman, Universidad Autónoma de Mexico, central library with monumental mural painting by the architect, 1954–59

sketch by Hans Schmidt, then director of the Institut für Theorie und Geschichte at Berlin's Bauakademie, may stand for Schmidt's fascination with Perret. At a point in time when he could not even know Henselmann's project, Schmidt experimented with alternative formal possibilities for that building.[54] We do not know what might have resulted if these ideas had been further developed.

As it was built, the Haus des Lehrers remained unique in East Berlin. Slightly out of scale considering the context and idiosyncratic with its curiously illustrated body-belt, not to mention the playfully ornamental interior of the plenary hall, it points to a symptomatic break in the architectural culture of the GDR. Fighting for the right to artistic autonomy could mean questioning the rationalization of construction and vice-versa. "We have to build better, faster, and more cheaply than capitalism can," Bruno Flierl, speaking more or less on behalf of the Deutsche Bauakademie, summed up the tasks of GDR architecture in 1960.[55] In the terms of the period, this could only be achieved by typification. Meanwhile, the "star architects," a breed not only known in the West, tried to call in a certain degree of autonomy with respect to the administration's logic of "merciless norming and typification" (Henselmann) in the realm of residential construction. The "social buildings" ("Gesellschaftsbauten") in the urban centers at least offered some promising escapes in this context. Scharoun, Mies, Le Corbusier – or indeed Niemeyer – had shown the way. In any case, once Kosel's proposals for a "central building" were given up, the leadership turned to Henselmann: his Haus des Lehrers is, besides the Television Tower, the outstanding example in this context. Although itself based on a strict logic of modular seriality, it wants to be seen as a critique of the frenzy of universal typification that Henselmann considered "distressing enough."[56] Not surprisingly, the Bauakademie complained that the building should not have been realized as an individualized design, but rather based on one of the customarily used systems of prefabrication so as to reduce costs. Henselmann later responded with the tautological, yet objectively plausible argument, that prefabrication was not worthwhile for individual projects.[57]

NOTES

1 _ On Kaiser-Wilhelm-Gedächtniskirche and the controversy on whether to maintain or demolish the building (they reach back to the 1920s), see Vera Frowein-Ziroff, *Die Kaiser Wilhelm-Gedächtniskirche. Entwicklung und Bedeutung* (Berlin, 1982), especially pp. 333–340 ("Vom Nationaldenkmal zum Wahrzeichen für West-Berlin") and Stephanie Warnke, *Stein gegen Stein: Architektur und Medien im geteilten Berlin 1950–1970* (Frankfurt am Main, 2009), pp. 220–231.
This essay is part of a broader study on the history of post WW II reconstruction of Europe. My thanks to Bruno Flierl and Rainer Laabs for their helpful conversations. I am also grateful to Teresa Fankhänel (Kunsthistorisches Institut, Universität Zürich) for her comments on an early draft of the text.

2 _ Frowein-Ziroff, *Die Kaiser Wilhelm-Gedächtniskirche*, see note 1, p. 340.

3 _ The key texts on the "New Monumentality" are Sigfried Giedion, "The Need for a New Monumentality," *New Architecture and City Planning*, ed. Paul Zucker (New York, 1944), pp. 549–568 and Sigfried Giedion, Josep Lluís Sert, Fernand Léger, "Nine Points on Monumentality," *Architecture Culture: A Documentary Anthology*, ed. Joan Ockman (New York, 1993).

4 _ Karl H. Pepper, the initiator and builder of Europa-Center, thus has a point when he writes that church and monument only became the center of the square once the skyscraper was complete. See Karl H. Pepper, "Erfüllter Traum," *Der Tagesspiegel* (April 2, 1965).

5 _ "Mensch, Pepper," *Der Spiegel* (1963) 39, pp. 97–100. "The realization of project ... seeks to demonstrate a faith in the future of the city and the achievements of free enterprise, in particular vis à vis the communist system," according to Berlin's *Tagesspiegel* (quoted in "Mensch, Pepper"). For more on the details of how the project was financed, see ibid. and Egbert Steinke, "Peppers großer Coup im 'Pfefferhaus'," *Handelsblatt* (March 30, 1965).

6 _ On the history of the reconstruction of Breitscheidplatz, see Adrian von Buttlar, Kerstin Wittmann-Englert, and Gabi Dolff-Bonekämper, eds., *Baukunst der Nachkriegsmoderne: Architekturführer Berlin 1949–1979* (Berlin, 2013), pp. 182–189.

7 _ Maria Sack, "Erster Spatenstich im Juni 1963. Zwischen dem ersten Projekt und dem letzten Hammerschlag," *Der Tagesspiegel* (April 2, 1965). Felix-Erik Laue even calls it one of the "largest built volumes on the continent," See "Anatomie eines Giganten. Summe konstruktiver Möglichkeiten und Umfang einer Stadt," *Der Tagesspiegel* (April 2, 1965).

8 _ Peter Meyer, "Monumentale Architektur?," *Das Werk* (1937) 3, pp. 66–73; see also Meyer, "Diskussion über Monumentalität," *Das Werk* (1940) 27, pp. 189–195.

9 _ See Giedion et al, "Nine Points," and Sigfried Giedion, "The Need for a New Monumentality," *New Architecture and City Planning*, ed. Paul Zucker (New York, 1944).

10 _ For a brief discussion, see Reinhold Martin, *The Organizational Complex: Architecture, Media, and Corporate Space* (Cambridge, Mass., 2003), especially pp. 88–90.

11 _ For more on Rockefeller Center, see in particular Manfredo Tafuri, "La montagna disincantata. Il grattacielo e la City," *La città americana dalla guerra civile al New Deal*, eds. Giorgio Ciucci, Francesco Dal Co, Mario Manieri-Elia, and Manfredo Tafuri (Bari, 1973), pp. 417–550 (especially pp. 496–526); Alan H. Balfour, *Rockefeller Center. Architecture as Theater* (New York, 1978), and Robert A. M. Stern, Gregory F. Gilmartin, and Thomas Mellins, *New York 1930: Architecture and Urbanism between the two World Wars* (New York, 1987), pp. 638–671 (for Hood's "functionalist" discussion of the RCA Building, referred to above, see p. 650).

12 _ Sigfried Giedion, *Space, Time and Architecture* (Cambridge, Mass., [1941] 1967), p. 848.

13 _ The canonic definition of the "International Style" is by Henry-Russell Hitchcock and Philip Johnson, *The International Style: Architecture since 1922* (New York, 1932). Alexander Sedlmaier is certainly correct when he suggests that Europa-Center must be seen in this context; see "Berlin's Europa-Center (1963–1965): Americanization, Consumerism, and the Uses of the International Style," *Historical Bulletin Supplement* (2005), pp. 87–100.

14 _ "Hochhaus-Bazillus", as put by Ernst May; see Kees Somer, *The Functional City: The CIAM and Cornelis van Eesteren, 1928–1960* (Rotterdam, 2007), pp. 38–47.

15 _ Rockefeller Center owes its symmetrical layout to the Beaux-Arts tradition of American civic centers. See in this context Werner Hegemann and Elbert Peets, *The American Vitruvius: An Architect's Handbook of Civic Art* (New York, 1922).

16 _ Giedion, *Space, Time and Architecture*, see note 12, pp. 845–856.

17 _ Ibid., pp. 850–851.

18 _ According to Goodwin, "the capitals of the world in need of rebuilding after the war cannot choose a better model than the modern buildings of the Brazilian capital"; quoted in Zilah Quezado Deckker, *Brazil Built: The Architecture of the Modern Movement in Brazil* (London, 2001), p. 148. The planning history, building, and international reception of the Ministry for Education and Health are now documented comprehensively in Roberto Segre, *Ministério da Educação e Saúde: Ícone urbano da modernidade brasileira* (1935–1945) (Sao Paulo, 2013). On the international reception of the building see in particular pp. 471–480. Le Corbusier, who went so far as to claim the work as his own (see Willy Boesiger, ed., *Le Corbusier. Œuvre complète, 1938–1946* [Zurich 1946], pp. 82–89), realized his own exemplary "monumental" use of a slab in a design for the government center of Bogotá (1949). See Willy Boesiger, ed., *Le Corbsier: Œuvre complète, 1946–1952* (Zurich 1953), pp. 42–45.

19 _ See in this context Stanislaus von Moos, *Le Corbusier: Elements of a Synthesis* (Rotterdam, 2009), especially pp. 236–244.

20 _ Helmut Hentrich, *Bauzeit: Aufzeichnungen aus dem Leben eines Architekten* (Düsseldorf, 1995), p. 224. The opening of Lever House was celebrated by the architectural press around the world. See "Skidmore, Owings and Merrill, Lever House à New York," *L'Architecture d'Aujourd'hui* (1953), pp. 34–38. On Lever's world-wide impact on office building see Jürgen Joedicke, *Geschichte der modernen Architektur: Synthese aus Form, Funktion und Konstruktion* (Stuttgart, 1958), especially pp. 82ff. Sara Stroux rightly emphasizes that the European fascination for the American model of the slab-shaped office high-rise was by no means limited to questions of "form" and "style," but involves "the entire complexity of the actual process of planning and building." See Sara Stroux, "Rezept Lever House? Planungsprozesse und Bauherrenentscheide beim Bau westdeutscher Konzernhochhäuser in der Nachkriegszeit," *Building America: Eine große Erzählung*, eds. Anke Köth, Kai Krauskopf, and Andreas Schwarting (Dresden, 2008), pp. 305 and 307.

21 _ See especially Gruen's project for renewing downtown Fort Worth, Texas, in Victor Gruen, "Urban Design of Today: Fort Worth," *Progressive Architecture* (1956), pp. 110-111 and Victor Gruen and Larry Smith, *Shopping Towns USA: The Planning of Shopping Centers* (New York, 1960).

22 _ Elihu Rubin, *Insuring the City: The Prudential Center and the Postwar Urban Landscape* (New Haven, 2012), p. 181. On the importance of Lever House in American architecture of the 1950s, see Gwendolyn Wright, *USA: Modern Architectures in History* (London, 2007), pp. 156-161.

23 _ "To their everlasting credit, they gave me exactly what I asked for . . . The final straw that broke the back of their belief in my sanity was when I said that I wanted the entire ground floor at Park Avenue left open so that people could walk in and feel part of Lever; so that there might be a very human feeling at the ground level to contrast with the kind of slick and gleaming tower which I felt would properly reflex a soap company" (Rubin, *Insuring the City*, see note 22, p. 181).

24 _ Ibid., pp. 180ff. Luckmann's use of the word "humanation" appears to allude to the CIAM debates on the "Humanization of Urban Life", such as in Jacqueline Tyrwhitt et al., *The Heart of the City: Towards the Humanization of Urban Life* (New York, 1952).

25 _ Rubin, *Insuring the City*, see note 22, p. 182.

26 _ Ibid.

27 _ Warnke, *Stein gegen Stein*, see note 1, p. 353.

28 _ See Hans-Peter Schwarz, *Axel Springer: Die Biografie* (Berlin, 2008); see also Axel Springer, *Von Berlin aus gesehen: Zeugnisse eines engagierten Deutschen* (Stuttgart, 1972).

29 _ Felix Henseleit, *... und doch ist dies der alte Schauplatz noch. Das Berliner Zeitungsviertel damals und heute* (Berlin, 1965).

30 _ Schwarz, *Axel Springer*, see note 28, p. 296 (the quotation is slightly shortened here). For more on the architecture of the Springer printing plant and office high-rise, which are not at stake in this context, see Lucie Schauer, "Architektur und Stil des Axel-Springer-Hauses," *Berlin, Kochstraße*, ed. Hans Wallenberg (Berlin, 1966), pp. 13-20 and Ulrich Conrads, "Die technischen Probleme und ihre Lösung," *Berlin, Kochstraße*, pp. 21-29. As the guest list reveals, the very dedication of the building was a political event: Heinrich Lübke, President of the German Confederation was present; so was Defense Minister Franz Josef Strauß along with Herbert von Karajan and Günter Grass. West Berlin's mayor Willy Brandt and the vice-chancellor Erich Mende celebrated the building in their speeches: see Schwarz, *Axel Springer*, see note 28, p. 383.

31 _ The photograph was first shown at the 2010 Architecture Biennial in Venice. It was part of the documentation brought home from Koolhaas' 1971 "field trip" to Berlin. See Rem Koolhaas, *Field Trip: [A] A Memoir. The Berlin Wall as Architecture* (1971); later published in Rem Koolhaas and Bruce Mau, *S, M, L, XL* (Rotterdam, 1995), pp. 212-233.

32 _ Sven Simon (aka Axel Springer, jun.), *Kokoschka malt Berlin* (Berlin, 1966).

33 _ Jochen Staadt, Tobias Voigt, and Stefan Wolle, *Feind-Bild Springer: Ein Verlag und seine Gegner* (Göttingen, 2009), pp. 8-9.

34 _ The *Städtebauliche und architektonische Direktive für den Investitionskomplex Leipziger Straße inklusive Spittelmarkt* (Urban Planning and Architectural Directive for the Investment Complex Leipziger Straße including Spittelmarkt) was decreed in January 1969. This was the premise for the four large residential twin-towers rowed up at a right angle to Leipziger Straße; they have formed the southern horizon of Berlin-Mitte since the 1970s. The culmination of the project was to be a "ca. 30 story office tower" at Spittelmarkt. This high-rise, according to the directive "dominates the axis Hans-Beimler-Straße-Alexanderplatz-Grunerstraße-Leipziger Straße, and blocks the view of the Springer Building," quoted in Staadt/Voigt/Wolle, *Feind-Bild Springer*, see note 33, p. 10. For a summary of these events, see Bruno Flierl, *Hundert Jahre Hochhäuser. Hochhaus und Stadt im 20. Jahrhundert* (Berlin 2000), p. 193.

35 _ See here the documentation of the urban context in GSW Hauptverwaltung Berlin: *Sauerbruch Hutton Architekten* (Baden, 2000), pp. 28-35. See also "GSW Hauptverwaltung Berlin – Wettbewerb," *Sauerbruch Hutton Archive* (Baden, 2006).

36 _ See the excellent overview by Francesca Rogier, "The Monumentality of Rhetoric: The Will to Rebuild in Postwar Berlin," *Anxious Modernisms: Experimentation in Postwar Architectural Culture*, eds. Sarah Williams Goldhagen and Réjean Légault (Montreal/Cambridge, Mass. 2000), pp. 165-189.

37 _ See Elmar Kossel, *Hermann Henselmann und die Moderne. Eine Studie zur Modernerezeption in der Architektur der DDR* (Königstein im Taunus, 2013), pp. 54-88; on post-war modernism in the Soviet Zone and later the GDR, see Andreas Butter, *Neues Leben, neues Bauen. Die Moderne in der Architektur der SBZ/DDR 1945-1951* (Berlin, 2006), pp. 11-33.

38 _ Hermann Henselmann, "Wie wir wohnen wollen," *Neues Deutschland* (June 15-16, 1957); reprinted in Henselmann, *Vom Himmel an das Reißbrett ziehen: Ausgewählte Aufsätze* (Berlin, 1982), pp. 43-51, 50-51. Henselmann was referring to the Telefunken-Wohnhochhaus and the five-story block of the Bikini-Haus that separates the square from Tiergarten. This simply "chaotic" development (see note 41), has more recently been seen in a much more positive light: See for example "Mohsen Mostafavi in Conversation with Sauerbruch and Hutton," *What You See Is What You Get: Sauerbruch Hutton Architects* (London, 1999), pp. 13-14.

39 _ Bruno Flierl, "Über unser Verhältnis zur Architektur und zum Städtebau kapitalistischer Länder," *Deutsche Architektur* (1961) special supplement, pp. 8ff.; quoted in Kossel, *Hermann Henselmann und die Moderne*, see note 37, p. 146.

40 _ On New York's Seagram Building by Ludwig Mies van der Rohe and Philip Johnson see Phyllis Lambert, "Mies van der Rohe's Ur-Building," *Building Seagram* (New Haven, 2013), pp. 38-87.

41 _ The semi-official maxim used in the GDR for the cultural policy introduced by Khrushchev: quoted in Kossel, *Hermann Henselmann und die Moderne*, see note 37, p. 147.

42 _ See for example Selim O. Chan-Magomedow, *Pioniere der sowjetischen Architektur: Der Weg zur neuen sowjetischen Architektur in den zwanziger und zu Beginn der dreißiger Jahre* (Dresden, 1983), especially pp. 403-404, 405, 418-423. See also Harald Bodenschatz and Christiane Post, eds., *Städtebau im Schatten Stalins: Die internationale Suche nach der sozialistischen Stadt in der Sowjetunion 1929-1935* (Berlin, 2003), especially pp. 170-175, 212-222.

43 _ On the discussions about the "central building," see in particular Bruno Flierl, "Der Zentrale Ort in Berlin – zur räumlichen Inszenierung sozialistischer Zentralität," *Gebaute DDR: Über Stadtplaner, Architekten und die Macht* (Berlin, 1998), pp. 121-171; cf. also Kossel, *Hermann Henselmann und die Moderne*, see note 37, especially pp. 141-144.

44 _ Kosel's interest in classicism should perhaps come as no surprise, considering his erstwhile career as one of few German architects in Soviet exile who had turned neoclassical under Stalin.

45 _ See Walter Gropius et al., *The Architects Collaborative* (Teufen AR, 1966), pp. 78-83; see also Giedion, *Architektur und Gemeinschaft*, see note 3, pp. 106-107 (fig. 49). On the history of the project, see Rubin, *Insuring the City*, see note 22, pp. 167-172.

46 _ Tyrwhitt et al., eds., *The Heart of the City*, see note 24.

47 _ Rubin, *Insuring the City*, see note 22, pp. 106-204.

48 _ "I cannot accept that socialism should make this building type the central point of its capital as a monument of its great liberating and universally progressive idea. Comrade Ulbricht, if we do that, we would be making a great mistake," according to Henselmann in a letter to Ulbricht on Gerhard Kosel's proposed "central building." See Kossel, *Hermann Henselmann und die Moderne*, see note 37, p. 136.

49 _ 1959; see Flierl, *Der Zentrale Ort in Berlin*, see note 43, pp. 135ff.

50 _ Ibid., p. 143.

51 _ See my essay „No fear of Monotony" in this context, pp. 138-147 in this book (in particular p. 140).

52 _ See for instance Haus des Reisens (House of Travel) on Alexanderplatz, roughly contemporary to Haus des

Lehrers, which was clearly inspired by the Zurich high-rise Zur Palme (architects Max Ernst Haefeli, Werner Max Moser, Rudolf Steiger, with André M. Studer; built 1955–59). See von Buttlar et al., *Baukunst der Nachkriegsmoderne*, see note 6, pp. 209–210. In subsequent years, GDR architecture became even more "cosmopolitan". Apart from its obvious analogies with the reconstruction plan for Rotterdam, Peter Sniegon's master plan for Prager Straße in Dresden also adopts elements of W. Vetter's project for the city center of Lausanne (1951). See Peter Sniegon, "Die Planung des Gebiets Prager Straße in Dresden," *Deutsche Architektur* (1965), pp. 9–13; on Rotterdam, see Hans Schmidt, "Rotterdam, der Neubau einer Stadt," *Deutsche Architektur* (1961), pp. 572–575, and on W. Vetter's project, see Tyrwhitt et al., eds., *The Heart of the City*, see note 24, pp. 143–145.

53 _ See André Meier, "Preisen will ich... Oder wie man von Womacka über Malewitsch und Rockefeller nach Byzanz kommt," *Model Map: Zur Kartographie einer Architektur am Beispiel Haus des Lehrers in Berlin*, eds. Bettina Allamoda et al. (Frankfurt am Main, 2003), pp. 18–32 and Peter Krieger, "El mural sobre la fachada del Haus des Lehrers (Casa del Maestro) en Berlin. Aplicación plástica de una iconografia politica y sus contextos," *Crónicas* (2006), pp. 124–125.

54 _ The sheet from the sketchbook is dated April 27, 1959: building began in 1961. Hans-Schmidt-Archiv, Institut gta, ETH-Zürich.

55 _ Quoted in Kossel, *Hermann Henselmann und die Moderne*, see note 37, p. 147.

56 _ On Haus des Lehrers, see Kossel, *Hermann Henselmann und die Moderne*, see note 37, pp. 148–165. On Henselmann's reference to the "merciless norming and typification" ordered by the Deutsche Bauakademie, that are "deterrent enough in residential construction," see p. 155.

57 _ Ibid.

PICTURE CREDITS

Fig. 1 _ Bert Sass, Ruins of Kaiser Wilhelm Memorial Church, September 1949, Berlin State Archive, F Rep. 290 no. 0004301 © Berlin State Archive

Fig. 2 _ Breitscheidplatz with Europa-Center and Kaiser Wilhelm Memorial Church, postcard, photography: unknown author, 1975 © holder of rights unknown

Fig. 3 _ Skidmore, Owings & Merrill Model of Lever House, New York, slab high-rise block on the southern side of the plot, 1949 © Ezra Stoller/Esto

Fig. 4 _ RCA (Radio Corporation of America) Building, Rockefeller Center, New York City, postcard, photography: unknown author, circa 1940, Archive Stanislaus von Moos © holder of rights unknown

Fig. 5 _ Comparison of a collage by Sigfried Giedion with the chronophotograph of a golf player by Harold Edgerton, repro of a double page from: Sigfried Giedion, *Space, Time and Architecture. The Growth of a New Tradition* (Cambridge/Mass. 1944), pp. 576-577.

Fig. 6 _ Lucio Costa, Oscar Niemeyer, Jorge Moreira, Affonso Eduardo Reidy, et al; consultation: Le Corbusier, Ministry for Education and Health (1936-42), Rio de Janeiro, repro from: Le Corbusier, *New World of Space* (New York 1948), pp. 84–85.

Fig. 7 _ Wallace K. Harrison, Le Corbusier and Oscar Niemeyer, studies with respect to the offices and parliamentary chamber of the United Nations, New York, 1947, repro from: *Architectural Forum*, April 1947.

Fig. 8 _ Ezra Stoller, Seagram Building (1956-58) by Ludwig Mies van der Rohe and Philip Johnson, New York City, 1958 © Ezra Stoller/Esto

Fig. 9 _ Rem Koolhaas, Madelon Vriesendorp, *Exodus, or the Voluntary Prisoners of Architecture. The Reception Area*, "Minimal training for new arrivals: overwhelming previously undernourished senses", project 1972, 26.7 x 36.8 cm, silver gelatin paper with colored inks, Patricia Phelps de Cisneros Purchase Fund, Takeo Ohbayashi Purchase Fund, and Susan de Menil Purchase Fund. Acc. n.: 364.1996 © Office for Metropolitan Architecture; repro © 2015 digital photograph, The Museum of Modern Art, New York/SCALA, Florence

Fig. 10 _ Rem Koolhaas, View along the Berlin Wall to the Axel Springer high-rise building, 1971, Office for Metropolitan Architecture © Rem Koolhaas/Office for Metropolitan Architecture

Fig. 11 _ Sauerbruch Hutton, *Dialogue across the Wall*, architectural rendering, 1991 © Sauerbruch Hutton

Fig. 12 _ Announcement by Harvard University Press of Sigfried Giedion's, *Architecture, You and Me* (1958) with the model of the headquarters of Prudential insurance planned for the Back Bay Center, (1954) by Walter Gropius and Pietro Belluschi, Boston, MA, circa 1958 © gta Archiv/ETH Zurich, estate of Sigfried Giedion

Fig. 13 _ Luckman & Pereira, Rendering of the later realised headquarters of Prudential Insurance (1957/58, realized 1957-65), Boston, circa 1957 © Archive Elihu Rubin, New Haven

Fig. 14 _ Gerhard Kosel, Hanns Hopp, Hans Mertens, Urban-developmental study for the "central building" on Marx-Engels-Forum, produced outside the competition for ideas for the "Socialist re-design of the center of the capital of the GDR – Berlin", photograph: Gisela Dutschmann, 1959, repro from negative, Berlinische Galerie BG-AS 1436.001758_B19725 © Gisela Dutschman/Berlinische Galerie

Fig. 15 _ René Burri, Office building by Oscar Niemeyer (1957-60), National Congress, Brasília, 1960 © René Burri/Magnum Photos/Agentur Focus

Fig. 16 _ Hermann Henselmann, Haus des Lehrers (1961-64) with monumental natural stone mosaic by Walter Womacka, photographer unknown, circa 1964 © Berlinische Galerie

Fig. 17 _ Juan O'Gorman, Universidad Nacional Autónoma de Mexico, central library with monumental mural painting (1952–54) by Juan O'Gorman, architectural design: Gustavo Maria Saavedra, Juan Martínez de Velasco, Juan O'Gorman, 1954-59 © Wayne Andrews/Esto

Urban Spaces/ Urban Dreams

Breitscheidplatz and the New Kaiser Wilhelm Memorial Church, circa 1965

Alexanderplatz with Haus des Lehrers, 1969

Helmut Hentrich, Hubert Petschnigg, Europa-Center, postcard, circa 1968

Engelbert Kremser, Europa-Center, photomontage, 1969 (not built)

Heinz Lieber, Panorama Alexanderplatz, 1972

View along Karl-Marx-Allee from the corner of Grunerstraße, 1964

Rem Koolhaas, View along the Berlin wall towards the Axel Springer high-rise, 1971

Large pub-restaurant “Ahornblatt” (1971-73, demolition 2000) with housing on Leipziger Straße, circa 1986

Bruno Flierl in Conversation
with Ursula Müller

The New Alexanderplatz in East Berlin's City Center

1 _ Alexander Naumov, Sergey Speransky, Design for the "Competition for ideas for a socialist re-design of the center of the capital of the GDR – Berlin" 1958

2 _ Josef Kaiser, Hans Gericke, Peter Schweizer, Design for the "Competition for ideas for a socialist re-design of the center of the capital of the GDR – Berlin," stage 2 with central building, 1960

Bruno Flierl, born in 1927, is renowned not just among experts. After studying architecture, he took a post in architectural studies at East Berlin's Deutsche Bauakademie in 1952, in 1962 becoming editor-in-chief of the journal *Deutsche Architektur*, later renamed *Architektur der DDR*. Beginning in 1965, he worked in the office of the head architect of East Berlin, at the Institut für Städtebau und Architektur (Institute for Urban Planning and Architecture), of the Bauakademie der DDR. He began teaching at Berlin's Humboldt-Universität in 1981. In 1984, Flierl began work as a freelancer, and is today considered an expert on architecture and urban planning in the former GDR.

Your professional interest in Berlin began in the late 1950s, when in both the West and East of the divided city competitions were held for the urban rebirth of the historical city center, destroyed in the war. In the competition held in the East, you were part of the team of Hans Schmidt. Here, outstanding designs were submitted that in terms of architectural style and spatial structure no longer were oriented to the GDR's official line of an architecture of "national traditions," but from so-called modernism. How did this sudden change take place, which had an impact above all between Kupfergraben and Alexanderplatz, and which was pioneering for the further development of architecture in the GDR?
The *Ideenwettbewerb zur sozialistischen Umgestaltung des Zentrums der Hauptstadt der DDR, Berlin* (Competition for the Socialist Re-design of the Center of the Capital of the GDR, Berlin) held in East Berlin in 1958/59 in fact turned away from an authoritarian Stalinist theory and practice in society and architecture to a democratic socialism and a modern notion of architecture that had begun in the Soviet Union and then spread to the GDR. Notably, this shift was more successful in architecture than it was in society in general. This is the only way to explain how in the East Berlin competition there was a whole series of projects that instead of the requested "Central Building" proposed, as if self-evident, but still provocative, a governmental high-rise using a strikingly modern architecture for Marx-Engels-Platz, a building housing the Volkskammer, the GDR's parliament. Two submissions, a Soviet one and a German one, demonstrate this concept in an especially impressive way: one by Alexander Naumov and Sergey Speransky from Leningrad (figs. p. 7 and fig. 1) and the design by Hermann Henselmann from Berlin (fig. p. 73). Their designs followed a second, internal competition in 1960, the project of the Stadtbauamt Berlin-Ost, where Josef Kaiser proposed a 90-meter-high glass dome for the plenary hall of the Volkskammer, transparent in the city space and at the same time a symbol for transparency in politics, virtually anticipating Gorbachev's popularized, but never realized dream of "glasnost" (fig. 2).

Were the competition entries discussed in public? What was the response?
The designs were shown publicly in 1959 and were praised in particular for their modern architecture. Special interest was paid to the proposals of Naumov and Henselmann, because they demonstratively refused the statist-authoritarian high-rise preferred by the political leaders holding the competition. Henselmann was especially praised for his idea to build a "tower of signals" as a symbol of scientific-technological progress – even using a cosmic iconography.

And how did the competition jury react to the submitted proposals?
The jury, as would be expected, shared the opinion of those holding the competition. It rejected all designs that differed from the call for submissions and criticized them, but did not award a first prize, and so kept everything open for future planning. But it did not condemn the designs submitted, almost all of them strikingly new, giving modern architecture in the GDR a chance for the future, if not yet realized.

How did things continue with planning the city center?
The urban planning office of the East Berlin government (which was officially still called Magistrate of Greater Berlin) developed a construction plan under the direction of Peter Schweizer, decided by the Chamber of Deputies on April 21, 1961. This plan still included the Central Building as a

government high-rise east of Marx-Engels-Platz, but no longer with a fixed architectural style. In contrast, there were clear choices in terms of the traffic system in the city center, with Alexanderplatz as a main traffic hub, and west of that, for the erection of a central shopping zone from S-Bahnhof Alexanderplatz to the Rathaus and Marienkirche and for reconstruction and new construction in modern style along Unter den Linden, Leipziger Straße, and Friedrichstraße.

New in the street plan was that Prenzlauer Allee was continued from the north, meeting Karl-Liebknecht-Straße at Marienkirche. Similarly, Greifswalder Straße was no longer to end in Rathausstraße from the north, but would lead via Grunerstraße into Leipziger Straße. In this way, two new thoroughfares were created that cross the old city center, and it was also possible to enlarge Alexanderplatz to fill the space between the two.

For example, since the early 1960s the new Alexanderplatz became the main traffic hub of East Berlin, not only in light of the existing subway, city rail, and long distance rail lines, but also in terms of modern street traffic. But it had not yet become an urban square with intense pedestrian presence and attractiveness. The step in this direction was only taken in 1964 (figs. 3.1 and 3.2)

Did the building of the wall on August 13, 1961 put the building plan in question?

Basically, no, and yet there were of course corrections. For example, the highways planned for the city center since 1948 in undivided Berlin and confirmed in the city competitions held in divided Berlin of the late 1950s were still included in planning in both East and West, but now were led around the city center in both sectors. The most important urban planning task for East Berlin in the context of the division of Berlin in occupation zones in 1945, namely creating an inner-city connection – in both directions – with a functionally and spatially optimal city center, decentrally located with respect to the GDR zone, was not hampered, but still needed to be solved. Not least, it was necessary to create a new Alexanderplatz as the most important hub in this city center axis that since 1950 was called the "Central Axis" in

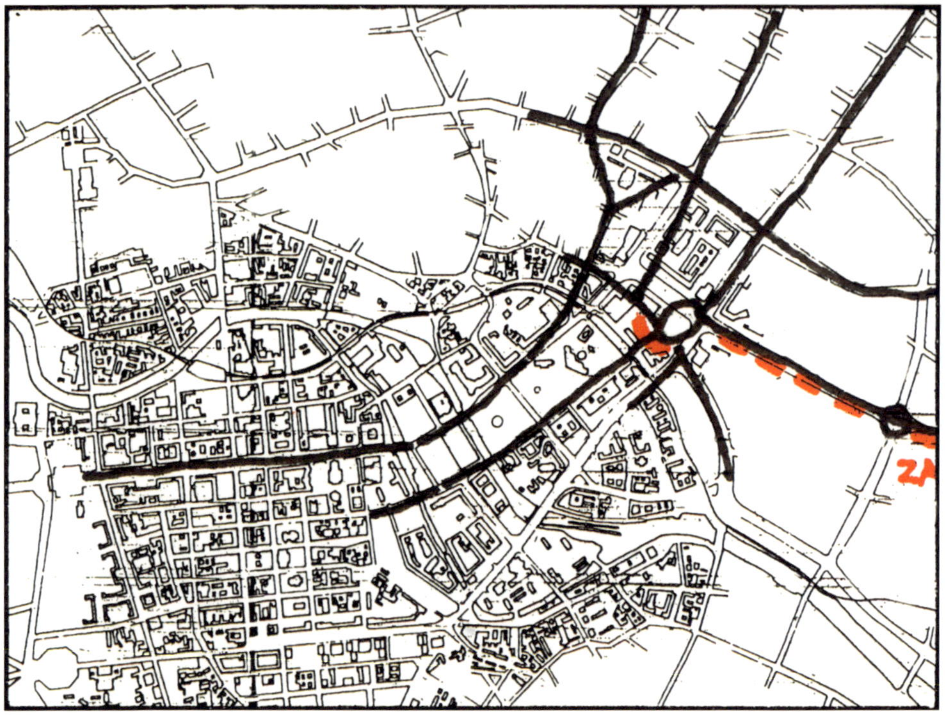

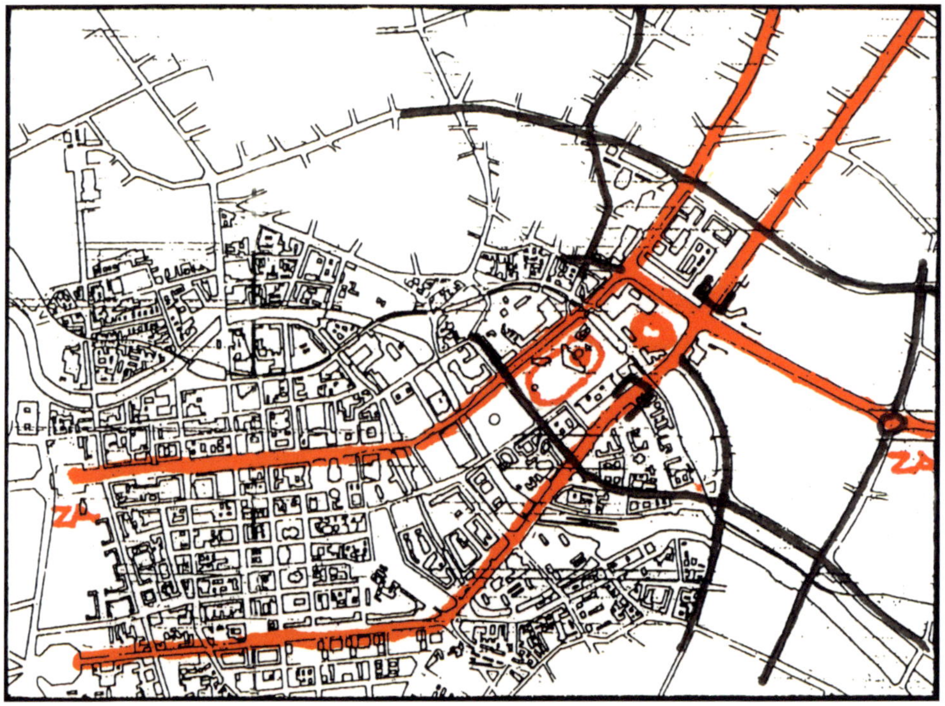

3.1 _ Main road network with traffic rotary on Alexanderplatz, situation in 1951, city map with annotations drawn by Bruno Flierl, 2015

3.2 _ Traffic planning with axial traffic network and city square from 1964, city map with annotations drawn by Bruno Flierl, 2015

4 _ Redevelopment of the TV tower with view to the Marienkirche (Church of Our Lady), circa 1970

the lingo of urban planners and that had already been realized along Stalinallee – renamed Karl-Marx-Allee in 1961 – from the East to Alexanderplatz and which had been strikingly concluded with the Haus des Lehrers along with its Congress Hall, designed by Hermann Henselmann and built from 1961–1964. (figs. p. 47 and 186/187).

And how did the Television Tower end up in the city center?
In brief, to replace the non-realizable central high-rise. To go into more detail, since 1954, with an international agreement among the four victor powers in the Control Council of the divided Berlin of the Anti-Hitler Coalition from the Second World War, the erection of a television tower was deemed neccessary. The planned location in the Müggelberge in Berlin-Köpenick proved unfavorable, since it was located in the approach to the planned airport Berlin-Schönefeld. This led to the idea of placing the tower, planned to be 365 meters high, in the middle of the city, symbolically guaranteeing it great importance in Berlin and the GDR, since it had become increasingly realized that the originally planned government high-rise, despite repeated new projects, was considered economically unfeasible and politically unnecessary. So in 1962, the public commissioners charged with choosing a fitting design of the capital of the GDR – led by Walter Ulbricht as chairman of the State Council – warmed to the idea to use the existing funds on the one hand to build a new Alexanderplatz as a urban city space, with intense pedestrian traffic and attractive amenities, and on the other hand for the erection of a Television Tower in the middle of the city, which would have a profound impact on the cityscape. In so doing, the leadership rebooted Hermann Henselmann's competition entry with the "Tower of Signals."

Who was actually behind the design of the Television Tower?
To be clear about this, there was a proper controversy over authorship, an unusual event in the GDR, since things clearly did not operate as collectively as was often claimed but not believed. When a location was chosen for the erection of the Television Tower, at first on the boundary of Volkspark Friedrichshain, later West of Alexanderplatz, experts from the Industrieprojektierungsbüro Berlin (IPRO I) received the commission for planning, without the input of Hermann Henselmann: Günter Franke was responsible for the concrete tower and Fritz Dieter for the top of the tower – a metal ball thirty meters in diameter with an observation platform and a rotating restaurant. To acknowledge his initial idea of a "Tower of Signals," Henselmann was named consultant. As of 1962, Gerhard Kosel, in the 1950s State Secretary in the Construction Ministry and at the end of

1961 president of the Deutsche Bauakademie, actively supported a Television Tower to crown the city skyline, and served as of 1964 as project manager, appointed by Walter Ulbricht himself. By making sketches in his journal he tried to generate the impression that he was the creator of the Television Tower, until Günter Mittag, the top GDR economics party functionary accused him of overspending before the completion of the Tower and he fell from grace. All the same, the Television Tower became a significant, modern, technoid structure of great quality. This is true especially of the two-floor foot of the tower with its amenities and an interesting, folded, sharply angled concrete shell construction, that Walter Herzog and Rolf Heider designed, taking into account the nearby Gothic Marienkirche in form and dimensions (fig. 4).

5 _ Collective Urban Development Office: Peter Schweizer, Dorothea Tscheschner, Hubert Martinetz, Central area with TV tower in its final position and cubist low-level building, December 1964

According to an anecdote, Walter Ulbricht is supposed to have personally chosen the location of the Television Tower. Is that true?

In fact, what Walter Ulbricht said was not the original impetus. Instead, it was information he received about the sandy subsoil near Marienkirche that was better suited to building such a tower than the marshy location in the glacial valley vis-à-vis Marx Engels Platz that Gerhard Kosel had originally suggested without knowing anything about the subsoil.

What is the link between planning for the Television Tower and the new Alexanderplatz?

Both plans were decided and implemented at the same time. For Alexanderplatz, preliminary planning was begun with an internal competition in 1964. Including the extant buildings by Peter Behrens – Alexander Haus and Berolina Haus – the new Alexanderplatz was to emerge as a pedestrian square with the new construction of a hotel and a large department store, separated from the street traffic around it, but freely linked to the entrances of surface and underground rail transportation. To do this, once again the streets were changed: the circle in the middle of the square was removed and replaced with a ground-level intersection with an underground street tunnel for Greifswalder Straße and Grunerstraße. This created the link that had been already striven for since 1951, connecting the eastern radial Karl-Marx-Allee to the central boulevard Unter den Linden, a solution that still works today. The plans for Alexanderplatz and for the space around the Television Tower were basically decided by August 1964. They included initial ideas for the buildings bordering on the two spaces, including the building of a congress hall and Volkskammer building between Spandauer Straße and the Spree. As of 1965, the planning was implemented. Everything except for the congress building was to be completed by 1969, to mark the twentieth anniversary of the founding of the GDR, or briefly thereafter. The congress building was erected beginning in 1973 on Marx-Engels-Platz and opened in 1976 as Palast der Republik (fig. 5).

To return to Alexanderplatz. What was built after the 1964 decision?

The new buildings emerged as an urban ensemble, in coordination with the architectural collectives responsible for the individual buildings. Everything that was built was modern in the best sense of the word – in the GDR of the 1950s even radically modern – for the purposes of living in a socialist society, with an orientation towards contemporary international modernism. This is shown by the new buildings on the square, the department store Centrum with its strik-

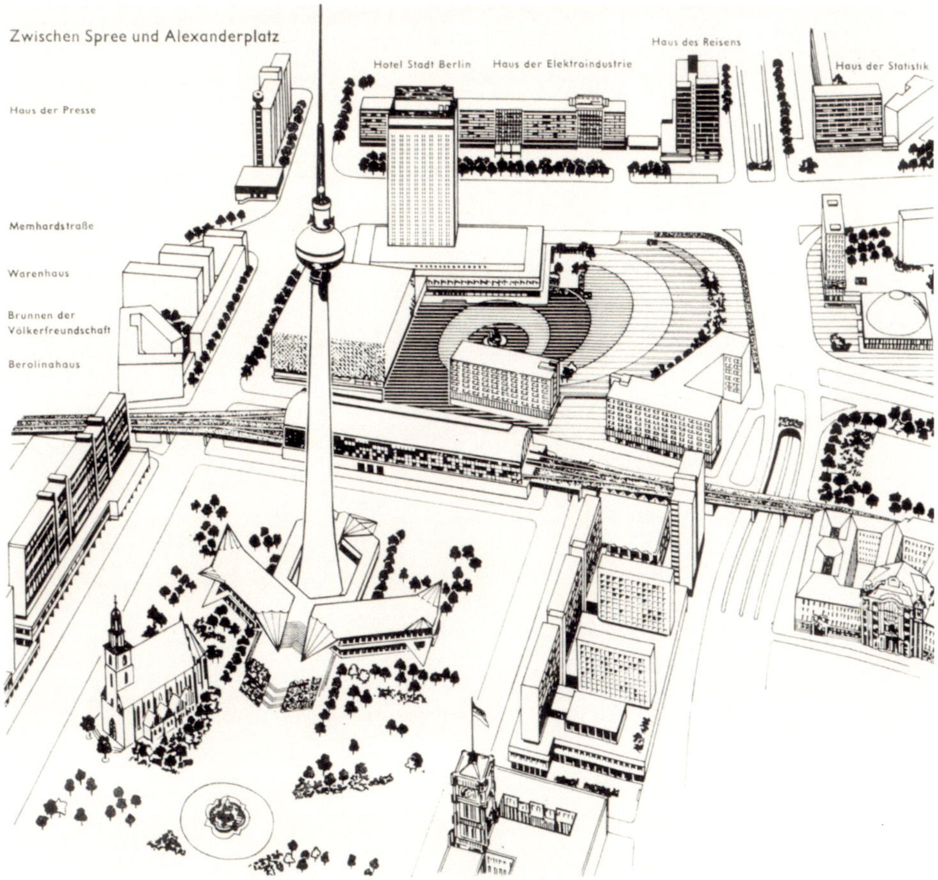

6 _ Drawing of Alexanderplatz with TV tower as realized, 1978

ing honeycomb structure on the façade (architectural collective Josef Kaiser, today rebuilt as Galerie Kaufhof) and the 124 meter high Interhotel Stadt Berlin with a two-story flat base (architectural collective Roland Korn, renovated and used by the Hotel Park Inn today). The external buildings surrounding the square were also highly modern at the time: Haus der Elektroindustrie (Roland Korn collective) and Haus des Reisens (Manfred Körner collective). The Berliner Verlag headquarters, located on the corner of Karl-Liebknecht-Straße, or the northwest corner of Alexanderplatz, with a striking façade and the Presscafe (Karl-Ernst Swora collective) was only finished in 1972. All of these buildings shaped or continue to shape the cityscape, sometimes amplified by the artistic designs of their façades. Today, all these buildings, including Haus des Lehrers, have been renovated and are used effectively. The Congress Hall has become Berlin Congress Center, bcc (fig. 6).

One striking element about Alexanderplatz is the inclusion of artists and designers in architectural planning. How did this come about?

In fact, in the GDR a unity of architecture, art, and design was the idea, intended to make places in the lives of people unmistakable in their function and effect, especially when it came to rebuilding the cities destroyed during the war. Alexanderplatz here provided the grounds for experimentation, and later, since some of it was a success, it even served as "model" in designing large ensembles of buildings elsewhere in the GDR. The spark for Alexanderplatz was the design of the first modern building there, Haus des Lehrers, with a large mosaic frieze on the subject of "education in socialism," which Hermann Henselmann insisted that the painter Walter Womacka create. Two other buildings were also given large format images on their façades, the Berliner Verlag building with the Presscafé featured a two-sided mural by Willi Neubert on the subject of "Press in Socialism" and Haus des Reisens was provided with a large metal bas relief by Walter Womacka on the subject of "Travel in Socialism." This schematic choice of art for buildings based on their function and significance was later abandoned in the GDR in favor of a thematic treatment of built space as the space of human life. The most effective artistic treatment, however, was the temporary arrangement of enlarged children's pictures behind the glass panels of the horizontal line of windows on the first floor of the Alexander and Berolina Haus to mark the 10th World Festival of Youth and Students in East Berlin in August 1973, visible over the heads of the participants as an almost 200 meter long horizontal image on the edge of the square.

7 _ Karl-Ernst Swora, Rainer Hanslik, Gunter Derdau, Haus der Berliner Verlage (Berlin Publishers' House) with mural of Willi Neubert, circa 1980

8 _ Urania World Clock and Interhotel Stadt Berlin, Alexanderplatz, circa 1970

But the new Alexanderplatz also hosted other popular art works that are half-sculpture, half design, that have their own importance and impact on the urban space as a place of urban living. There's the fountain designed by Walter Womacka, Brunnen der Völkerfreundschaft, and then there's the Urania-Weltzeituhr, which are still very popular today. The large fountain, planned to be visible from the Television Tower in mind, was located in a design by Walter Womacka as the starting point of a spiral that filled the entire square, marked in the ground and accompanied by a series of trees. Both no longer exist today.

At the end of the 1960s and early 1970s, Alexanderplatz was still marked by the reticent colors used for the buildings: not artistic in nature, but rather structured according to significance. Only the hotel was given a light blue, all other buildings remained white, if only to preserve the effect of all the colorful images. Striking was the sparse use of advertising on the buildings of the square, making the mobile advertising on the front of Berliner Verlag all the more prominent.

From the very beginning, the recreation of the now worldwide renowned "light architecture" was a marvel, with the light columns on the fronts of the two Peter Behrens buildings that virtually served as a gateway of light at the entrance from and exit towards Rathausstraße, on the edge of the historical city center. It all was part of a complex design of the urban environment (figs. 7 and 8).

What was the importance of the new Alexanderplatz for the development of East Berlin's city center and the later architecture in the GDR?

The new Alexanderplatz sent out powerful impulses for the later urban-architectural design of East Berlin and the centers of other cities in the GDR. Already in the 1960s, modern architecture was erected that lastingly changed the cityscape, with the buildings for the Foreign Ministry and the State Council Building on Marx-Engels-Platz, the new buildings in gaps left by bombing on Unter den Linden and Breite Straße, most importantly the reconstruction of the Berlin City Library and at the end of the 1960s and early 1970s with larger residential ensembles in the city center – along Leipziger Straße and at Leninplatz (today's Platz der Vereinten Nationen).

It was only in the mid-1970s and mid-1980s, with the Palast der Republik and the Marx-Engels-Forum, highlighted by the Marx-Engels Monument, that the political-social center of the city sought since the 1950s came to fruition, not in a state authoritarian form, but in a function that was closer to the citizens and more modern. The creation and design of a new Alexanderplatz was a decisive step on the way there.

Today, in united Berlin, the function and urban-architectural shape from the 1960s of the new Alexanderplatz remains intact, whereby individual buildings are used more intensely than they were earlier. The tangential position of the main streets around the square has proved its value, helping to develop and preserve the pedestrian square. By way of its connection to the tram lines, it has even gained in terms of its urban attractiveness and quality. The new Alexanderplatz is now one of the most popular squares in Berlin, for Berlin residents and Berlin's visitors from all over the world. The planners should keep this in mind when discussing the future development of the city.

NOTE

The content of this conversation is based on the author's studies on developing a city center in East Berlin and texts by Dr. Dorothea Tscheschner, who worked on planning the capital of the GDR and the development of a new Alexanderplatz in East Berlin. in the urban planning division of the East Berlin city government.

SELECTED LITERATURE (IN CHRONOLOGICAL ORDER)

1 _ Bruno Flierl, "Vom Münzturm zum Fernsehturm. Höhendominanten in der Stadtplanung von Berlin," *Studien zur Berliner Kunstgeschichte*, ed. Karl-Heinz Klingenburg (Leipzig, 1986), pp. 11ff.

2 _ Dorothea Tscheschner, "Der Wiederaufbau des historischen Zentrums in Ost-Berlin," *Hauptstadt Berlin. Internationaler städtebaulicher Ideenwettbewerb 1957/58*, ed. Berlinische Galerie (Berlin, 1990), pp. 217ff.

3 _ Dorothea Tscheschner, "Der Alexanderplatz: Seine Entwicklung nach 1945," *Alexanderplatz: Städtebaulicher Ideenwettbewerb*, ed. Entwicklungsgemeinschaft Alexanderplatz (Berlin, 1994), pp. 30ff.

4 _ Bruno Flierl, *Gebaute DDR: Über Stadtplaner, Architekten und die Macht. Kritische Reflexionen 1990–1997* (Berlin, 1998), especially: "Der Zentrale Ort in Berlin: Zur räumlichen Inszenierung sozialistischer Zentralität," pp. 121ff. and "Hermann Henselmann: Bauen in Bildern und Worten," pp. 172ff.

5 _ Peter Müller, *Symbolsuche: Die Ost-Berliner Zentrumsplanung zwischen Repräsentation und Agitation* (Berlin, 2005).

6 _ Harald Bodenschatz, Jörn Düwel, Niels Gutschow, Hans Stimmann, *Berlin und seine Bauten. Teil 1: Städtebau* (Berlin, 2009).

7 _ Bruno Flierl, "Hauptstadtplanung im geteilten und vereinten Berlin," *Berlin plant. Plädoyer für ein Planwerk Innenstadt Berlin 2.0*, eds. Harald Bodenschatz and Thomas Flierl (Berlin, 2010), pp. 38ff.

8 _ Adrian von Buttlar, Kerstin Wittmann-Englert, Gabi Dolff-Bonekämper, eds., *Baukunst der Nachkriegsmoderne. Architekturführer Berlin 1949–1979* (Berlin, 2013).

9 _ Elmar Kossel, *Hermann Henselmann und die Moderne. Eine Studie zur Modernerezeption in der Architektur der DDR* (Königstein im Taunus, 2013).

10 _ Bruno Flierl, "Stadtzentrum Berlin-Ost," *Stadtplanung im doppelten Berlin*, ed. Stiftung Gedenkstätte Berliner Mauer (Berlin, 2014), pp. 40ff.

PICTURE CREDITS

Fig. 1 _ Alexander Naumov, Sergey Speransky, Design for the "Competition for ideas for a socialist re-design of the center of the capital of the GDR – Berlin" 1958, photograph of the model: Gisela Dutschmann, 1959, repro from negative, Berlinische Galerie BG-AS 1436.001635 © Gisela Dutschmann/ Berlinische Galerie

Fig. 2 _ Josef Kaiser, Hans Gericke, Peter Schweizer, Design for the "Competition for ideas for a socialist re-design of the center of the capital of the GDR – Berlin", stage 2 with central building, photograph of the model: Gisela Dutschmann, 1960, repro from negative, Berlinische Galerie BG-AS 1436.001787, neg. no. 428 © Gisela Dutschmann/Berlinische Galerie

Fig. 3.1 _ Main road network with traffic rotary on Alexanderplatz, situation in 1951, city map with annotations drawn by Bruno Flierl, 2015 © Bruno Flierl

Fig. 3.2 _ Traffic planning with axial traffic network and city square from 1964, city map with annotations drawn by Bruno Flierl, 2015 © Bruno Flierl

Fig. 4 _ Redevelopment of the TV tower with view to the Marienkirche (Church of Our Lady), photographer unknown, circa 1970, 18 x 24 cm, silver gelatin paper, Berlinische Galerie © Berlinische Galerie

Fig. 5 _ Collective Urban Development Office: Peter Schweizer, Dorothea Tscheschner, Hubert Martinetz, Central area with TV tower in its final position and cubist low-level building, model of the state of planning, December 1964, photographer unknown, silver gelatin paper, Berlinische Galerie © Berlinische Galerie

Fig. 6 _ Martha-Luise Gubig, Drawing of Alexanderplatz with TV tower as realized, 1978, reproduction from: Waltraud Volk, *Berlin, Hauptstadt der DDR. Historische Straßen und Plätze heute* (Berlin, 1978), p. 219 © Legal successor Martha-Luise Gubig

Fig. 7 _ Karl-Ernst Swora, Rainer Hanslik, Gunter Derdau, Haus der Berliner Verlage (Berlin Publishers' House), photographer unknown, circa 1980, repro from a slide, Berlinische Galerie © Berlinische Galerie

Fig. 8 _ Urania World Clock and Interhotel Stadt Berlin, Alexanderplatz, photographer unknown, circa 1970, color print, Berlinische Galerie © Berlinische Galerie

Adrian von Buttlar

New Urban Spaces in West Berlin: Breitscheidplatz and Kulturforum

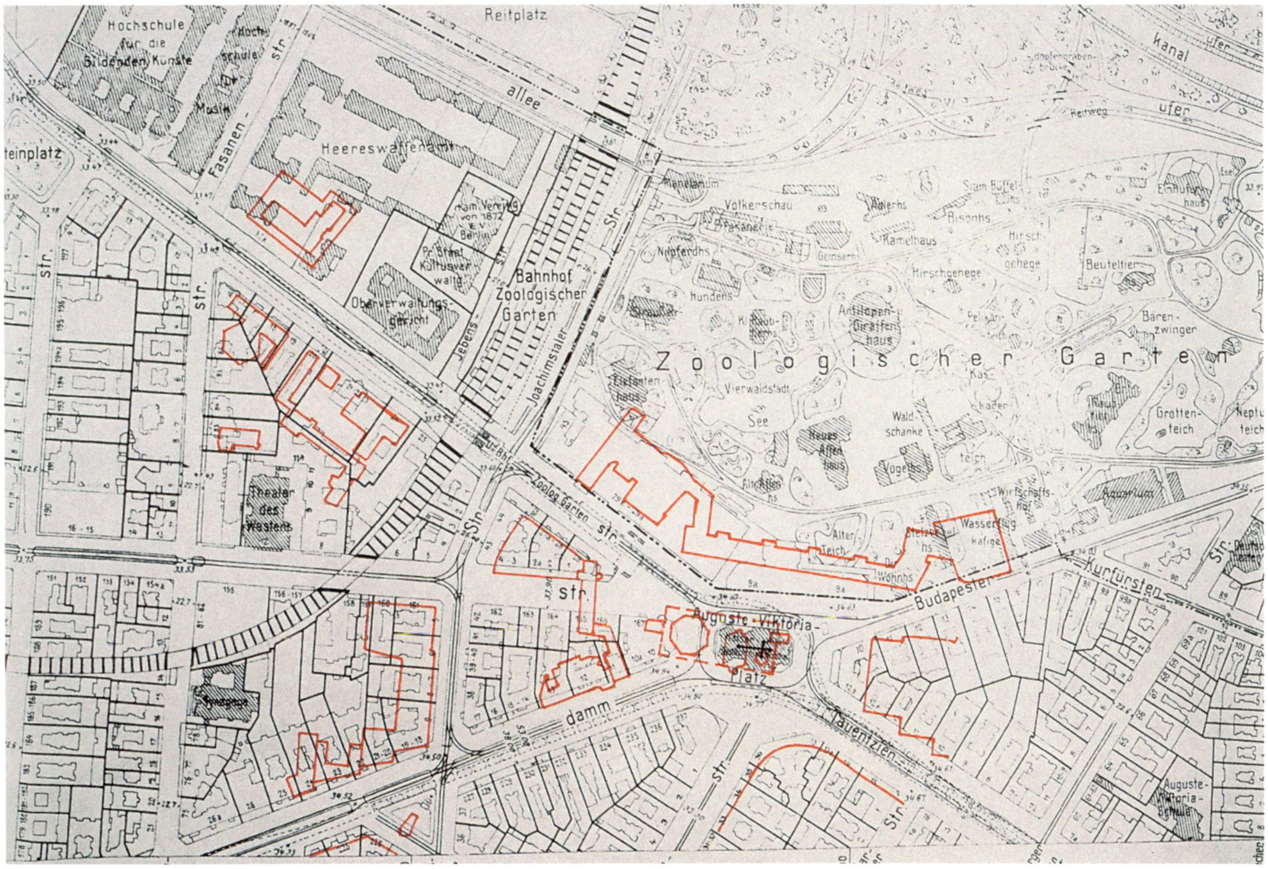

1 _ Christine Hoh-Slodczyk, Synopsis of Auguste-Viktoria-Platz and post-war building on Breitscheidplatz, 1990

Breitscheidplatz – the center of West Berlin, rebuilt from 1954 to 1965 – and Kulturforum, erected not far from Postdamer Platz beginning in 1960, are considered characteristic, if not fully contrary implementations of Hans Scharoun's now rejected urban concept of the "urban landscape."[1] Both urban spaces, created from the ruins of the post-war period, have recently been called into question – re-planned, fragmented, and altered. Even more than the self-confident architectural monuments of functionalism and brutalism, the free-flowing, luscious complementary greenery in the urban landscape has met with rejection among urban sociologists and urban planners since the 1980s. The loosening and liberation of the compact, urban spatial body proposed by the protagonists of "organic architecture" and the "structured and loosened city"[2] since the 1930s was now as lacking in "urbanity" with all the suffering that supposedly involves. Instead, the pre-modern paradigm of the "old European city" was declared the new model. On the basis of the Berlin *Planwerk* from the 1990s, the city landscape has been rebuilt along these lines.[3]

The starting point for planning Breitscheidplatz[4] was a futuristic competition to redesign the hub around Bahnhof Zoo, which after the city was divided was forced to serve as West Berlin's main railway station. Even if the station hall was only modernized in the end, the optimism of the design radiated towards the east and west, where on Hardenbergstraße in the direction of Ernst-Reuter-Platz the West Berlin's economic center was created. At the same time, the reconstruction of the neighboring Auguste-Viktoria-Platz began, renamed after Rudolf Breitscheid, a Social Democrat who died in 1944 in the Buchenwald concentration camp.

Comparing the prewar construction with the redesign of the 1950s and 1980s (fig. 1), despite the radically altered appearance there is a surprising similarity in terms of the spatial arrangement around the Memorial Church, which originally formed an island in the midst of a lively network of streets. From the West, Hardenbergstraße, Kantstraße, and Kurfürstendamm met here, from the east Budapester Straße and Tauentzien, which ends with Rankestraße. The neo-Romanesque style of the Kaiser-Wilhelm-Gedächtniskirche (1891–1895) by Franz Schwechten also set the tone for the Romanisches Forum office buildings on the east and west side, with the legendary Romanisches Café and the Carl Gause exhibition halls on the north side. In 1925 and 1926, these halls, which also housed UFA Palasttheater am Zoo, were complemented in the east by a radically modern steel skeleton building along the Zoologischer Garten, designed by Hans Poelzig. This row of stores anticipated the stretched dimensions of the later Bikini-Haus as well as its open colonnade. On the south side of the square, the corner between Kurfürstendamm and Rankestraße was closed by the rounded façade of the department store Michels & Cie. (rebuilt by Paul Herdich in purified form in 1954). The southeastern flank was dominated by an additional office and shop building from the Wilhelmine period (fig. 2).

A reconstruction of the ideologically contaminated Wilhelminian ensemble was simply unthinkable just after the World War II. Instead, reconstruction was motivated economically, architecturally, technologically and politically in

2 _ Auguste-Viktoria-Platz, 1930s

3 _ Breitscheidplatz, circa 1965

4 _ Paul Schwebes, Hans Schoszberger, Zentrum am Zoo, 1957

the spirit of a new start. Even without an overarching plan, the architects created a significant architectural and urban transformation by taking the prewar architecture as their point of departure, while at the same time pursuing new paths, creating one of the few outstanding public squares from the period in the process (fig. 3). Its northern side along Hardenbergstraße and Budapester Straße was framed by Paul Schwebes and Hans Schoszberger's Zentrum am Zoo (1955–1957), a combination of several building units that on the one hand line the square, but also, as individual components, remain legible as an urban composition in open space. The 16-story slab of the office building on Hardenbergplatz is linked by (now awkwardly altered) buildings to Gerhard Fritsche's recessed Zoo Palast, which continued the glamorous tradition of the site with a spectacular large cinema as the showplace of the Berlinale from 1957 to 1999. The overextended Bikini-Haus, which initially housed the West Berlin fashion industry, owes its name to the 1978 addition of a top floor. At the turn of Budapester Straße, the parallel so-called Kleine Hochhaus (Small High-Rise) and a two-story garage close off the complex (fig. 4).

Stylistically and in terms of urban planning, Zentrum am Zoo, which was illustrated as one of the first model buildings of "Free Berlin" during the Cold War in the *New York Times* in 1957, looked to the recent developments in architecture of the West, primarily in France and England: from Le Corbusier, the architects adopted the use of concrete pilotis that allow the free space to flow into the architecture and keep the ground floor free for pedestrians, and the rhythmific façades, whose rows of windows and loggias were alternated with the use of vibrant colors. From England, they took the concept of the cluster, developed in

5 _ Franz-Heinrich Sobotka, Gustav Müller, Schimmelpfenghaus, 2007

urban planning in the early 1950s by Peter and Alison Smithson. The cluster is a structuring of unique buildings determined not by aesthetics, but functional, social, and technological requirements, linked by connecting buildings and paths on various layers of traffic. This "brutalist" approach, that the Smithsons took to the utmost in their provocative contribution to the Berlin Capital City Competition in 1957/58 (fig. p. 85), also influenced later construction at Breitscheidplatz in the 1960s.[5]

While Paul Schwebes' elegant round Deutsches Familienkaufhaus closed the northeastern flank between Tauentzien and Rankestraße (modernization in 1975, partial demolition in 2012/13), between 1957 and 1960 the Schimmelpfeng-Haus by Franz Heinrich Sobotka and Gustav Müller was built. Demolished in 2009, the building framed the west side of the square. The rigid perforated façade of this cluster building, which bridged across Kantstraße, recalled Müller's Vienna teacher Adolf Loos, while the flat structure placed underneath the main structure with round glass windows was inspired by Sobotka's former boss Erich Mendelsohn (fig. 5). The last of the buildings around the Memorial Church was the Europa-Center, built according the plans of Helmut Hentrich and Hubert Petschnigg from 1963 to 1965. This symbol of West Berlin's economic power crowned with an oversized Mercedes Star, in combination with a shopping mall in a flat building (until 1980 with an ice skating rink in the courtyard) and the highest Berlin office building of its time, explicitly referred to American models like the New York Rockefeller Center (1931–1940) and Lever House by Skidmore, Owings & Merrill (1950–1952) with its curtain-wall aesthetic (fig. 6). The interwoven layers of traffic, like the tunnel in front of Bikini-Haus, demolished in 2006, the four-lane link between Tauentzien and Budapester Straße (demolished in 1978), and the proud steel bridges for pedestrians that spanned the latter and opened the shopping passages of Europa-Center (torn down in 1979), represented the apotheosis of pulsating urban traffic then seen as symbolizing progress and the vitality of the politically threatened island city. The center of Breitscheidplatz was the new Gedächtniskirche (Memorial Church), planned by Egon Eiermann in 1956 and dedicated in 1961,[6] which was

6 _ Helmut Hentrich, Hubert Petschnigg, Europa-Center, postcard, circa 1968

perceived not only as the ideational center, but until just recently was considered the aesthetic highlight of West Berlin. By integrating the tower ruins in the ensemble – a demand of Berlin residents – which consists of the Church octagon, the foyer pavilion, the six story bell tower, and the freestanding chapel, it took on the character of a memorial for peace. This group of buildings surrounded by free space rises above mundane everyday with a shared podium and refer to one another via the variants of their concrete honeycomb façade. The church owes its strong, sacred and emotional impact to the sublime forms of the buildings and their glowing, colorful to deep blue windows. Their impact is in stark contrast to the glittering world of consumerism (fig. 7).

In 1988, Norbert Huse called Breitscheidplatz an ensemble of monuments of "national, indeed European importance that no other German city could offer" and (in vain) warned

7 _ Egon Eiermann, Kaiser Wilhelm Memorial Church, photography of 2010

against destructive interventions.[7] The modernizations, always understood as practical improvements, have increasingly distorted the characteristic urban planning concept and its message. This already began in 1981 - 1983 with the building connecting Europa-Center to the amorphous square and the erection of the Globe Fountain by Joachim Schmettau and the tasteless "furnishing" of the free spaces. The renovation, completion, and "improvement" of the outlying buildings were rarely done tactfully. To prevent the economic and social decline of the City West after the fall of the Wall, the Senate Administration pushed two investor projects for high-rises on the Eastern side of the square that were the follow-up to the new *Planwerk*-doctrine of perimeter block development, thus anticipating the "opening" of Kantstraße. The demolition of the listed Schimmelpfeng-Haus in 2009 de facto led to the destruction of the homogenous square and this unique ensemble of monuments. Urban planning sacrificed the ensemble in the interest of a contemporary city image with a facelift. Christoph Mäckler's Zoofenster (2013) and Christoph Langhof's Upper West opposite (begun in 2013), 120 meters in height, marginalize the former trademark of the Free West with its significant potential for historical memory. A partial success of heritage protection is the maintenance and renovation of the large cinema at Zoo-Palast and the reconstruction of the façades of Bikini Haus and the Kleines Hochhaus (2014), even if extensive additions and reconstructions have significantly changed the proportions and characters of this architectural monument.

Our second example is based on other premises: in 1960, in the dead corner of the sector border amid the empty ruins of the former Tiergartenviertel, the building of the urban landscape Kulturforum, still considered incomplete today (fig. 8), was begun, initially according to plans by Hans Scharoun and his partner of many years, landscape architect Hermann Mattern.[8] Scharoun, who won the competition to design a new Philharmonie in 1956 on Bundesallee in Berlin-Wilmersdorf, hoping for of reunification, pleaded successfully for this location, which was then remote, but until the construction of the wall (and since 1990 once again) opened up to the east. He planned the Philharmonie, built from 1960 to 1963, in the spirit of his philosophy of organic construction, based on the "essence" of the task to make music as a democratic collective experience in a virtually non-hierarchical society optimally audible and experienced for all.[9] The spectacular tent form corpus of the building as a free standing building with its sculptural form powerful from all directions initially dominated the loosely structured greenery that marked the transition to the southern end of Tiergarten. A more radical "contrast" to the round square of the martial north-south axis of the Reichshauptstadt Germania that Albert Speer had planned and already begun building in this terrain is hardly conceivable. Paradoxically, Speer's seizure of property undertaken as part of the persecution of the Jews helped Scharoun's planning, which could be undertaken without regard for private plots.

Although Scharoun had reserved the area in his contribution to the 1957 Capital City Competition in 1957 as a district for diplomats and culture, the concrete plans for Kulturforum only emerged as part of his competition design for the Staatsbibliothek in 1963/64 (realized between 1967 and 1978). The plans live from a relationship of tension between the building conception and materiality the two share and in terms of their architectural form their contrast as stand-alone buildings (Scharoun compared the form of the library to the back of a mountain). Furthermore, the model created at the time (fig. 9) already shows the cubature of

8 _ Kulturforum and Philharmonic Hall under construction, circa 1963

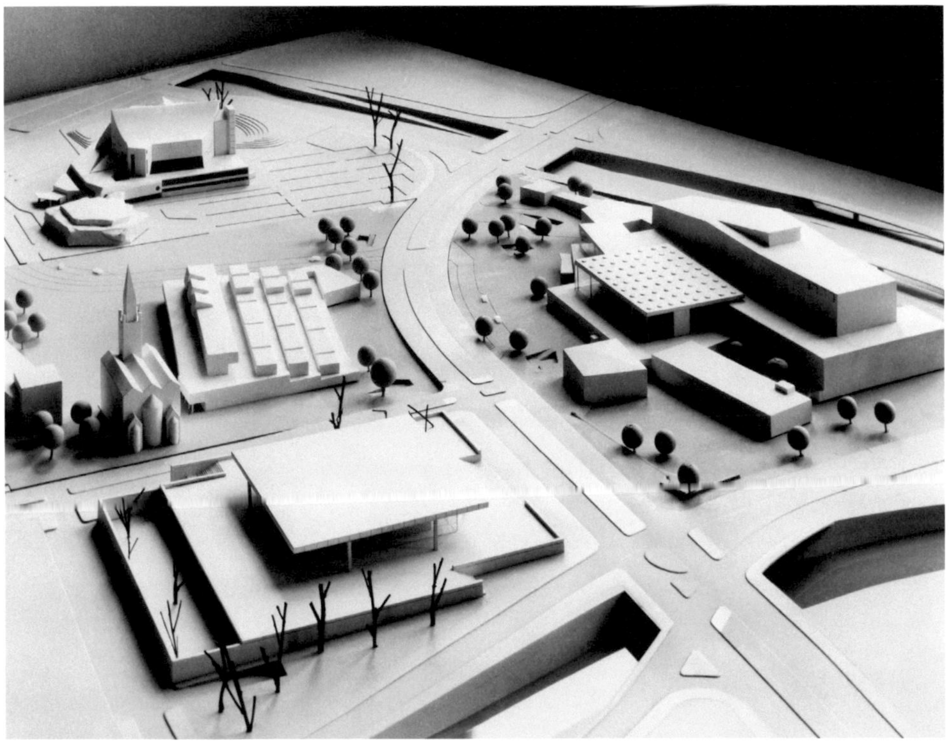

9 _ Hans Scharoun, Kulturforum with Senate guesthouse, 1964

the Kammermusiksaal (Chamber Music Hall, realized from 1984 to 1987 by Edgar Wisniewski) and in the south the Neue Nationalgalerie, designed in 1963 by Ludwig Mies van der Rohe (1965–1968). As Gabi Dolff-Bonekämper has correctly pointed out, with the clear geometric shapes and expansive vanishing lines of his art temple Mies refers explicitly to Friedrich August Stüler's neoclassicist St. Matthäi-Kirche (1843–1846, reconstruction 1956–1960) and its contrary orthogonal spatial arrangement, making him a veritable co-author of this urban landscape.[10] Mediating between the two, Scharoun thus placed his project of a terraced, but cubistically designed guest house for the Berlin Senate in the empty center of this field of tension. As a counterweight to the "mountain" of the Staatsbibliothek, it sought to make Potsdamer Straße into a "valley." And yet it was not just this highway-like traffic axis, but the overly broad Scharounstraße and the Western end of the Stadtautobahn (replaced by the Tiergartentunnel, completed in 2006) which proved a stubborn problem in developing the forum after Scharoun's death in 1972.

The locations of the museums (Gemäldegalerie, Skulpturensammlung, Kupferstichkabinett, Kunstbibliothek, and Kunstgewerbemuseum), already schematically alluded to in Scharoun's model, were finally decided in a competition held by Stiftung Preußischer Kulturbesitz in 1965, which chose the complex cluster design by Rolf Gutbrod. The Kunstgewerbemuseum, erected from 1978 to 1985 as the first part, met with such criticism that the subsequent buildings were awarded in 1987 to the architects Heinz Hilmer and Christoph Sattler. Gutbrod's controversial brutalist building (whose interior was redesigned in 2014 by Kuehn Malvezzi) was contrasted with a postmodern Gemäldegalerie (opened in 1998), whose traditional exhibition hall was based on Leo von Klenze's Munich Pinakothek. After 1984 Heinz Mack had already designed the free space around the museum landscape as a sloping Piazetta that is only impressive from a bird's eye view. While on the one hand offering a spectacular panorama view of the forum and the skyline of Potsdamer Platz, it cannot compensate for the fact that the view of the entrance area to the museums is considered depressing.

10 _ Hans Hollein, Design for the Kulturforum, view of the model from the south, 1983

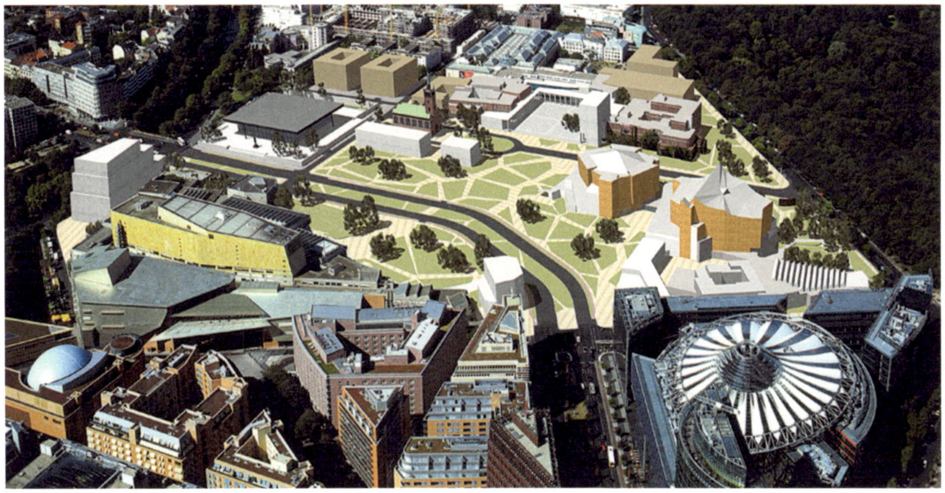

11 _ Master plan for the Kulturforum, simulation model, view from the east, 2005

Also unsatisfactory was the competition held in the run-up to the Internationale Bauausstellung in 1983, that in light of the 750-year celebration of the city in 1987 invited six internationally prominent architects to "complete" the Kulturforum in the spirit of Scharoun. The winning architect, the Viennese architect Hans Hollein, wanted to expand Matthäikirchplatz to Postdamer Straße, shielding it with curved colonnades, and limiting it on the other side with a "city cloister," a "bible tower," and a canal. While he tried to include Nationalgalerie with a rising ramp, the Staatsbibliothek and Philharmonie were moved to the periphery (fig. 10). After reunification, rapid building on Postdamer Platz meant abandoning Hollein's plans, which now have been replaced by the *Planwerk Innenstadt*, proposed by the Senatsverwaltung für Stadtentwicklung since 1996. While the Scharoun employee Wisniewski sought to continue the old Scharoun plan,[11] those who favored the *Planwerk*, in accordance with their philosophy of a return to the pre-modern city space – wanted to link the forum more to Potsdamer Platz and to curtail its character as urban landscape. In the Masterplan Kulturforum, decided by the Senate and Abgeordnetenhaus in 2005/2006 after a controversial public debate[12] (fig. 11) the church is once again placed on a long, architecturally-framed square, whose axial orientation continues along the straightened Herbert-von-Karajan-Straße into Tiergarten. Asymmetrical buildings in a Scharoun-like style condense the entrance situation between the Institut für Musikforschung with the Musikinstrumenten-Museum (1979–1984, by Edgar Wisniewski) and the Staatsbibliothek, and along Landwehrkanal. A colonnade, with its columns reminiscent of the "gau forums" from Nazi neo classicism, along with a "Picture Tower" was planned to replace the piazetta as a monumental entrance to the museums. All open spaces were to be covered with irregular lawns and a decorative net pattern of paved pathways that in the Plan at least, suggest the homogeneity so longed for, but which this urban space resists again and again.

After a change in Berlin's urban planning policy in 2007, this problematic plan was also abandoned and in 2009/10 modified by landscape architects Christoph and Donata Valentien, based on their winning proposal for the landscape architecture from the overall competition in 1998. Taking up the plans of Mies van der Rohe in 1963, they emphasized the orthogonal spatial order of the forum, but refused additional buildings and interventions in the architectural arrangement except for a transparent, loggia in front of the museum (by Hilmer and Sattler). This leaves the visual relationships between the tone-setting solitary buildings undisturbed. In the center of the forum, still misused today as a parking lot, a densely planned quadratic grove of 100 tall pine trees was foreseen, which was to frame St. Matthäi-Kirche spatially and be set off on the eastern side from Postdamer Straße with a lower sculptural wall.[13] The later realization left only a grove planted east of the church, planted much too loosely and reduced to half the surface area with (more affordable) ailanthus trees. This corresponded by no means with the intention, and the trees, except for a few pitiful remains, have all but disappeared. But the recent state of planning shows that the key to the future approach of Kulturforum is not contained in proposals of demolition, a completion of Scharoun's plans or even their destruction by way of dense construction (of which there have not been a few),[14] but in moderate improvements of infrastructure, moderate additions and landscaping accents to the existing square (figs. 12 and 13). Despite its deficits, this existing architecture should be accepted as the historical heritage and should now be better used with cultural management and guided tours: apodictic master plans need to be replaced with a careful process that now includes the construction of a Museum der Moderne on Potsdamer Straße.[15]

From the very beginning, the terrain of Kulturforum represented heterogeneous locations and orders, aesthetic fissures and contradictory historical layers, including the monument for the victims of euthanasia, which was dedicated in September 2014 at Tiergartenstraße 4, once the location of the headquarters where "Aktion T 4" was planned and coordinated. This finding is by no means a contradiction to Scharoun's idea of the urban landscape, which was never intended as an imitation of a beautiful natural landscape, but rather as a structural analogy to nature's very different elements, forces, and structures.

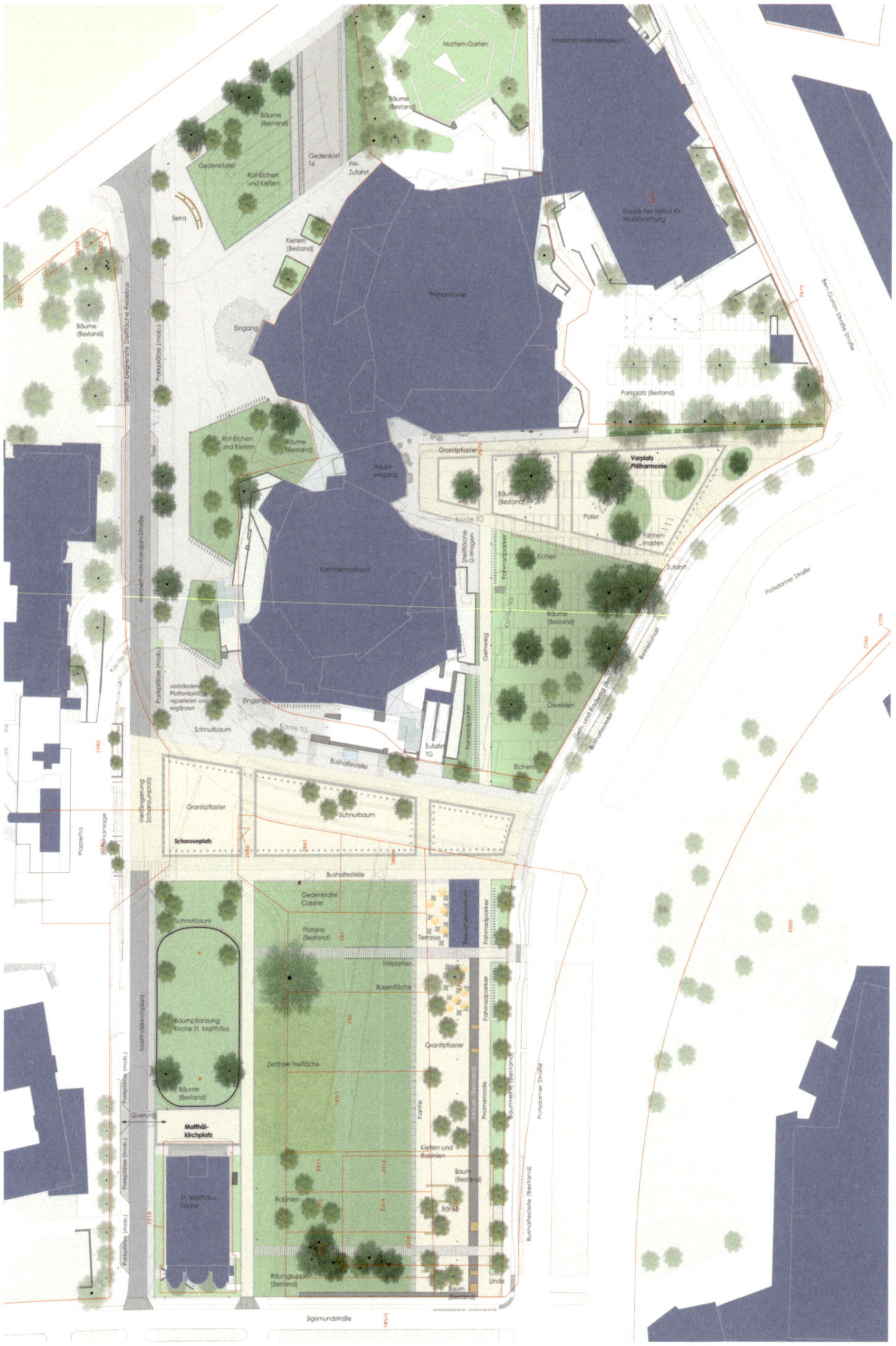

12 _ Donata Valentien, Master plan for the Kulturforum, state of planning 2014

13 _ Kulturforum, circa 2013

NOTES

1 _ Hans Scharoun, lecture for the exhibition *Berlin plant – erster Bericht* (September 5, 1946), *Hans Scharoun: Bauten, Entwürfe, Texte*, ed. Peter Pfankuch (Schriftenreihe der AdK, 10) (Berlin, 1993), p. 158. See Elke Sohn, *Zum Begriff der Natur in Stadtkonzepten anhand der Beiträge von Hans Bernhard Reichow, Walter Schwagenscheidt und Hans Scharoun zum Wiederaufbau nach 1945* (Schriftenreihe der Stipendiatinnen und Stipendiaten der Friedrich-Ebert-Stiftung, 30) (Berlin, 2008).

2 _ Johannes Göderitz, Roland Rainer, and Hubert Hoffmann, *Die gegliederte und aufgelockerte Stadt* (Tübingen, 1957),

3 _ See Senatsverwaltung für Stadtentwicklung und Umwelt (http://www.stadtentwicklung.berlin.de/planen/planwerke/de/planwerk_innere_stadt/index.shtml) and the accompanying publications.

4 _ Christine Hoh-Slodczyk, "Der Berliner City-Betrieb als Herausforderung für den Denkmalschutz," *Architektur und Städtebau der fünfziger Jahre: Ergebnisse der Fachtagung in Hannover 1990*, eds. Werner Durth and Niels Gutschow (Bonn, 1990), pp. 134-143. See the contributions that summarize the literature in Adrian von Buttlar, Kerstin Wittmann-Englert and Gabi Dolff-Bonekämper, eds., *Baukunst der Nachkriegsmoderne: Architekturführer Berlin 1949-1979* (Berlin, 2013).

5 _ See the Smithsons' project for Sheffield University (1953); the term "cluster" was coined at the CIAM congress in Dubrovnik, 1956. *Urban Structuring. Studies of Alison & Peter Smithson* (London/New York, 1967), pp. 33-39; Jürgen Joedicke, *Architektur im Umbruch. Geschichte, Entwicklung, Ausblick* (Stuttgart, 1980), pp. 92-93; Berlinische Galerie, ed., *Hauptstadt Berlin. Internationaler städtebaulicher Ideenwettbewerb 1957/58* (Berlin, 1990), pp. 90-105. A monograph to mark the renovation of Zentrum am Zoo by Peter Lemburg will be published in 2015.

6 _ Most recently: Kai Kappel and Ev. Kaiser-Wilhelm-Gedächtnis-Kirchengemeinde Berlin, eds., *Egon Eiermann – Kaiser-Wilhelm-Gedächtnis-Kirche Berlin 1961-2011* (Lindenberg im Allgäu, 2011); Kerstin Wittmann-Englert, "Kaiser-Wilhelm-Gedächtniskirche," *Baukunst der Nachkriegsmoderne*, eds. von Buttlar et al., see note 4, pp. 15-18. A renovation of the church and its concrete honeycomb walls is planned by the Wüstenrot Stiftung for 2015/16.

7 _ Norbert Huse, ed., *Verloren, gefährdet, geschützt. Baudenkmale in Berlin* (Berlin, 1988), pp. 10-19, here p. 15.

8 _ Anke Fischer, *Das Berliner Kulturforum* (Arbeitshefte des ISR der TU Berlin, 69) (Berlin, 2007); see also Robert Frank, "Das Kulturforum – ein unvollendetes Projekt," *Platz und Monument: Die Kontroverse um das Kulturforum in Berlin 1980-1992* (Berlin, 1992), pp. 73-157 and Hans Stimmann, ed., *Zukunft des Kulturforums. Ein Abgesang auf die Insel der Objekte* (Berlin, 2012).

9 _ Eckehard Janofske, *Architektur-Räume. Idee und Gestalt bei Hans Scharoun* (Braunschweig/Wiesbaden, 1984); Wilfried Wang and Daniel E. Sylvester, eds., *Hans Scharoun: Philharmonie. Berlin 1956-1963* (O'Neil Ford Monograph Series, 5) (Berlin, 2013).

10 _ Von Buttlar et al., eds., *Baukunst der Nachkriegsmoderne*, see note 4, pp. 90ff. See Gabi Dolff-Bonekämper, "Das Berliner Kulturforum. Architektur als Medium politischer Konflikte," *Bauten und Orte als Träger von Erinnerung. Die Erinnerungsdebatte und die Denkmal- pflege* eds. Hans-Rudolf Meier and Marion Wohlleben (Zurich, 2000), pp. 133-143.

11 _ Edgar Wisniewski, "Musik aus der Mitte. Freiheit und Bindung im Konzertsaal der Zukunft," *Berlin baut 4: Der Kammermusiksaal*, ed. Senator für Bau- und Wohnungswesen (Berlin, 1987), pp. 26-43.

12 _ Senatsverwaltung für Stadtentwicklung, ed., *Kulturforum (3). Der Masterplan* (Berlin, 2005).

13 _ Senatsverwaltung für Stadtentwicklung, Umweltschutz und Technologie, ed., *Kulturforum. Hintergrund, Aufgabenstellung, Dokumentation der Wettbewerbsergebnisse und der ersten Realisierungsstufe 1999* (Berlin, 1999).

14 _ See the six Entwürfe für ein neues Stadtquartier by Bernd Albers, Klaus Theo Brenner, Max Dudler, Jan Kleihues, Christoph Sattler and Sergei Tchoban, in: *Zukunft des Kulturforums*, see note 8, pp. 137-185 and Stephan Braunfels' plan published in the fall of 2013.

15 _ Senatsverwaltung für Stadtentwicklung, http://www.stadtentwicklung.berlin.de/planen/staedtebau-projekte/kulturforum/de/masterplan/index.shtml sowie Berlin baut – Kulturforum (June 2014). In November 2014, the Federal Government approved 200 million Euros for a new Museum der Moderne at Kulturforum.

PICTURE CREDITS

Fig. 1 _ Christine Hoh-Slodczyk, Synopsis of Auguste-Viktoria-Platz and post-war building on Breitscheidplatz, 1990, print with drawn annotations © Christine Hoh-Slodczyk

Fig. 2 _ Auguste-Viktoria-Platz, photographer unknown, 1930s, silver gelatin paper, Berlin State Archive F Rep. 290 no. II 10355 © Berlin State Archive

Fig. 3 _ Breitscheidplatz, photograph: Otto Borutta, circa 1965, repro from negative, Berlinische Galerie © Berlinische Galerie

Fig. 4 _ Paul Schwebes, Hans Schoszberger, Zentrum am Zoo, photographer unknown, 1957, silver gelatin paper, Architekturmuseum TU Berlin, inv. no. F 10170 © holder of rights unknown / Architekturmuseum TU Berlin

Fig. 5 _ Franz-Heinrich Sobotka, Gustav Müller, Schimmelpfenghaus, photograph: Alfred Englert, 2007 © Alfred Englert

Fig. 6 _ Helmut Hentrich, Hubert Petschnigg, Europa-Center, postcard, circa 1968 © holder of rights unknown

Fig. 7 _ Egon Eiermann, Kaiser Wilhelm Memorial Church, photograph: Kai Kappel, 2010 © Kai Kappel

Fig. 8 _ Kulturforum and Philharmonic Hall under construction, photograph: Otto Borutta, circa 1963, repro from negative, Berlinische Galerie © Berlinische Galerie

Fig. 9 _ Hans Scharoun, Kulturforum with Senate guesthouse, photographer unknown, 1964, silver gelatin paper, Berlinische Galerie © Berlinische Galerie

Fig. 10 _ Hans Hollein, Design for the Kulturforum, view of the model from the south, 1983, wood, plastic, metal, Berlinische Galerie BG-AS 53/2014 © Berlinische Galerie

Fig. 11 _ Master plan for the Kulturforum, simulation model, view from the east, photographer unknown, 2005 © Senate Offices for Urban Development and the Environment, Dept. Urban Development and Projects

Fig. 12 _ Donata Valentien, Master plan for the Kulturforum, state of planning 2014 © Donata Valentien/ Senate Offices for Urban Development and the Environment, Dept. Urban Development and Projects

Fig. 13 _ Kulturforum, photograph: Alfred Englert, circa 2013 © Alfred Englert

Gerhard Kosel with Hanns Hopp and Hans Mertens, Marx-Engels-Forum with central building, urban-developmental study, out of competition, for the "Competition for ideas for a socialist re-design of the center of the capital of the GDR – Berlin" as further development of a design dated early 1958, 1959 (not built)

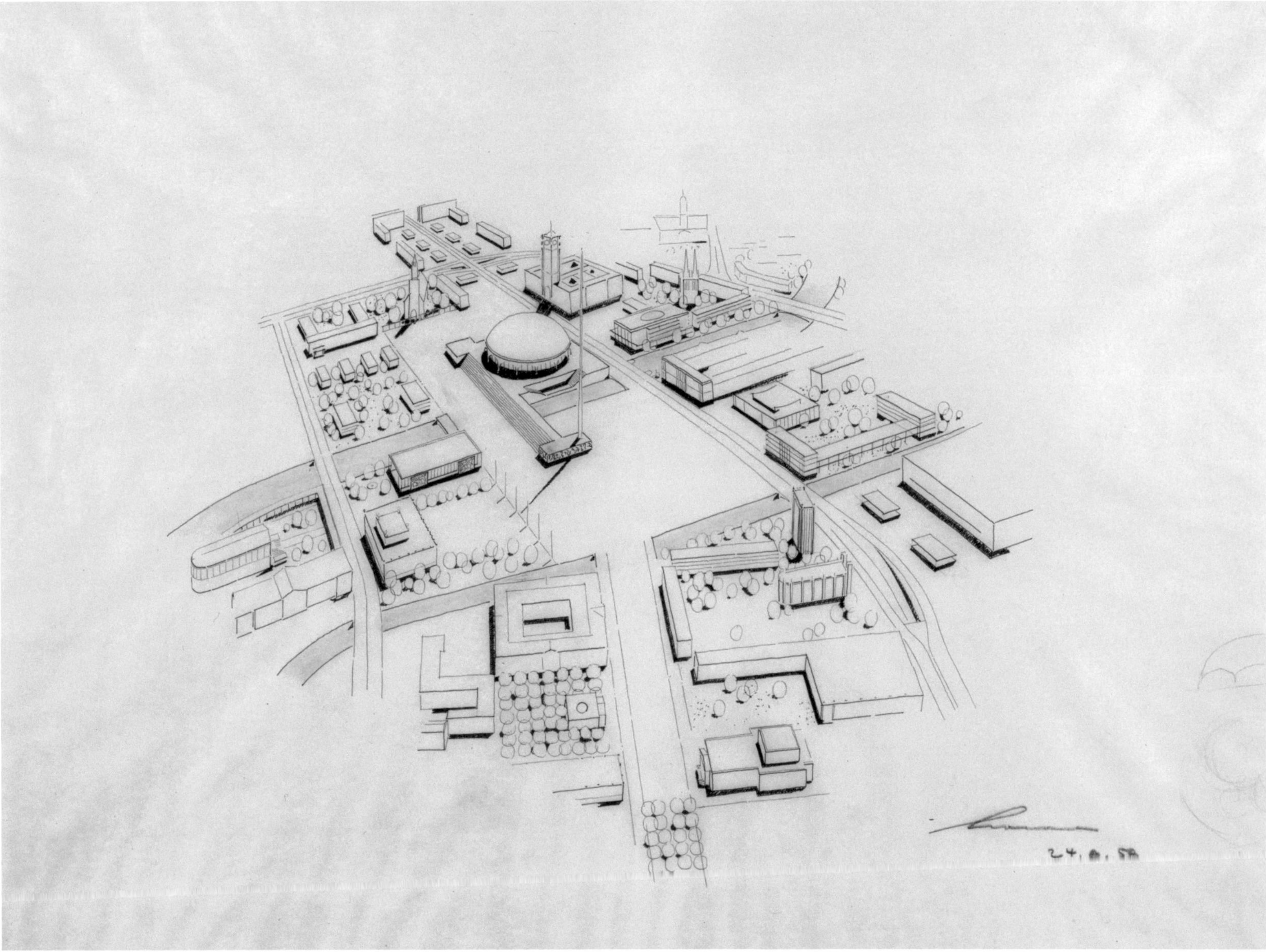

Hermann Henselmann, Design for a “German Pantheon,” counter design to the idea of the governmental high-rise building by the collective Kosel, 1958 (not built)

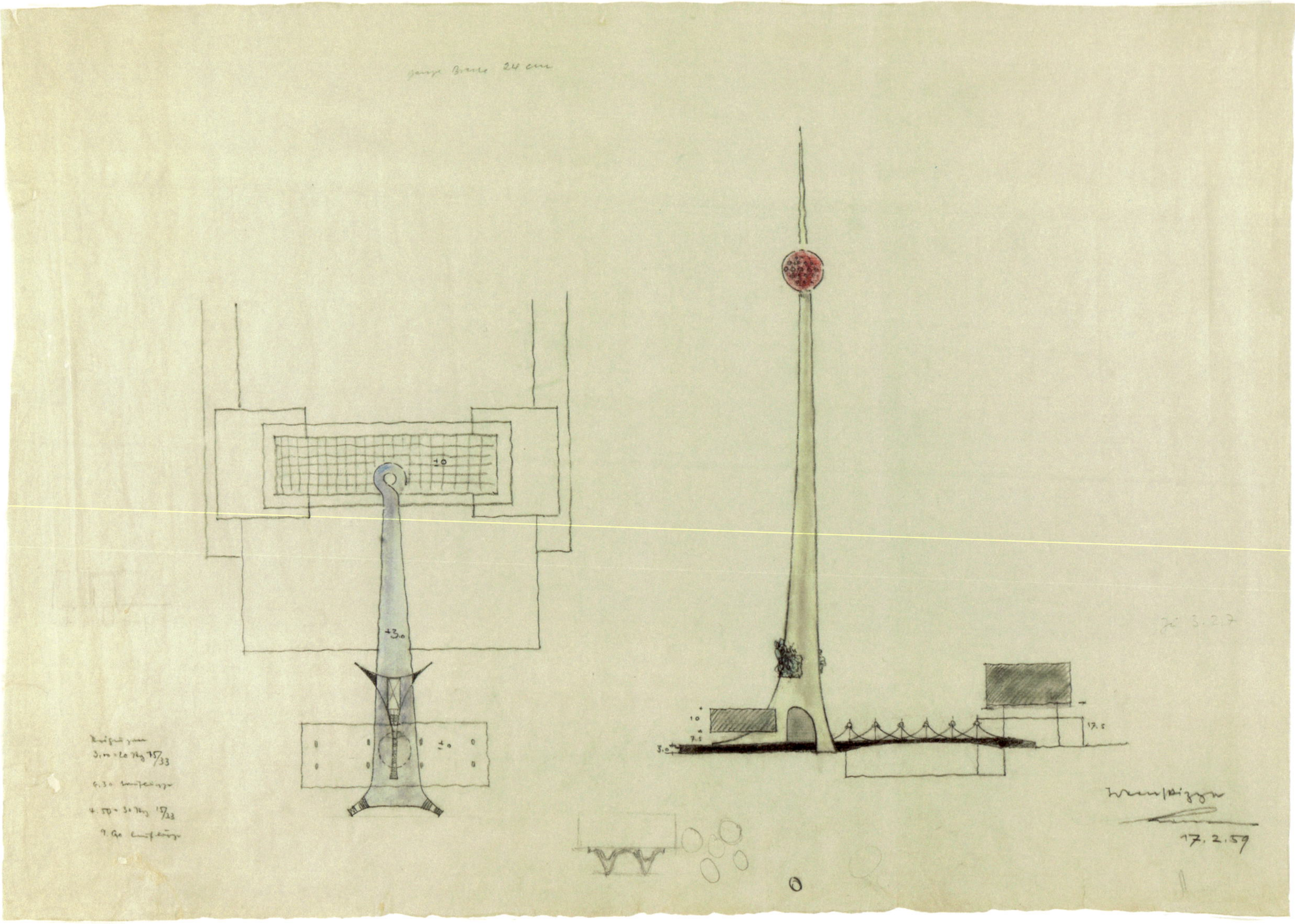

Hermann Henselmann, Sketched ideas with views of the “Tower of Signals,” design out of competition for the “Competition for ideas for a socialist re-design of the center of the capital of the GDR – Berlin,” 1959

Realized television tower in the urban context (1964-69), photograph taken from the high-rise building on the Fischerinsel, 1970

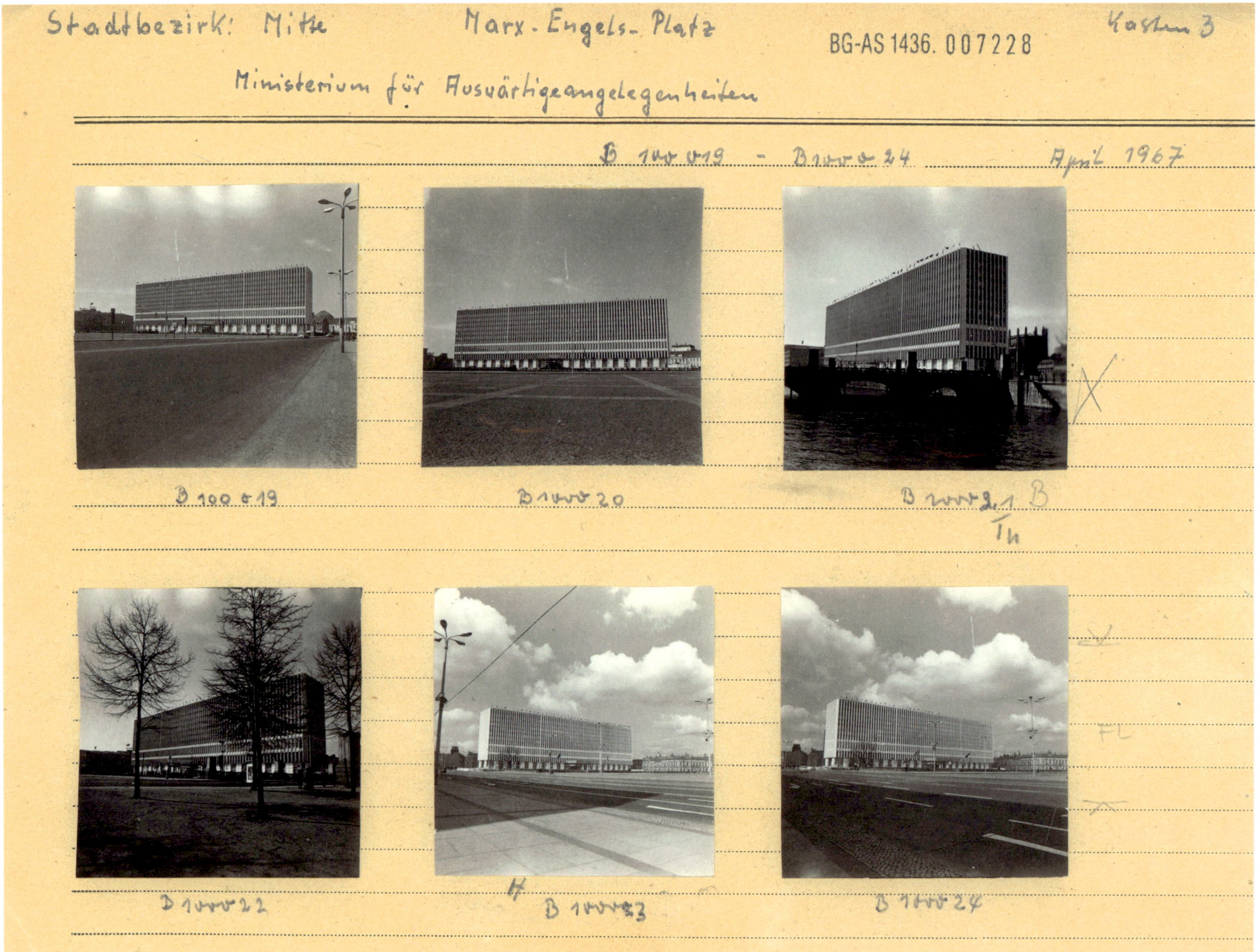
Stadtbezirk: Mitte Marx-Engels-Platz BG-AS 1436. 007228 Kasten 3

Ministerium für Auswärtigeangelegenheiten

B 100 019 – B 100 024 April 1967

B 100 019 B 100 020 B 100 021

B 100 022 B 100 023 B 100 024

Ministry of Foreign Affairs of the GDR (1964–67, demolition 1996), architect: Josef Kaiser, April 1967

The Marx-Engels-Brücke seen from the Altes Museum. In the background is the newly built Ministry of Foreign Affairs of the GDR, circa 1968/negative interpretation 2009

Philharmonic Hall in the urban context, circa 1963

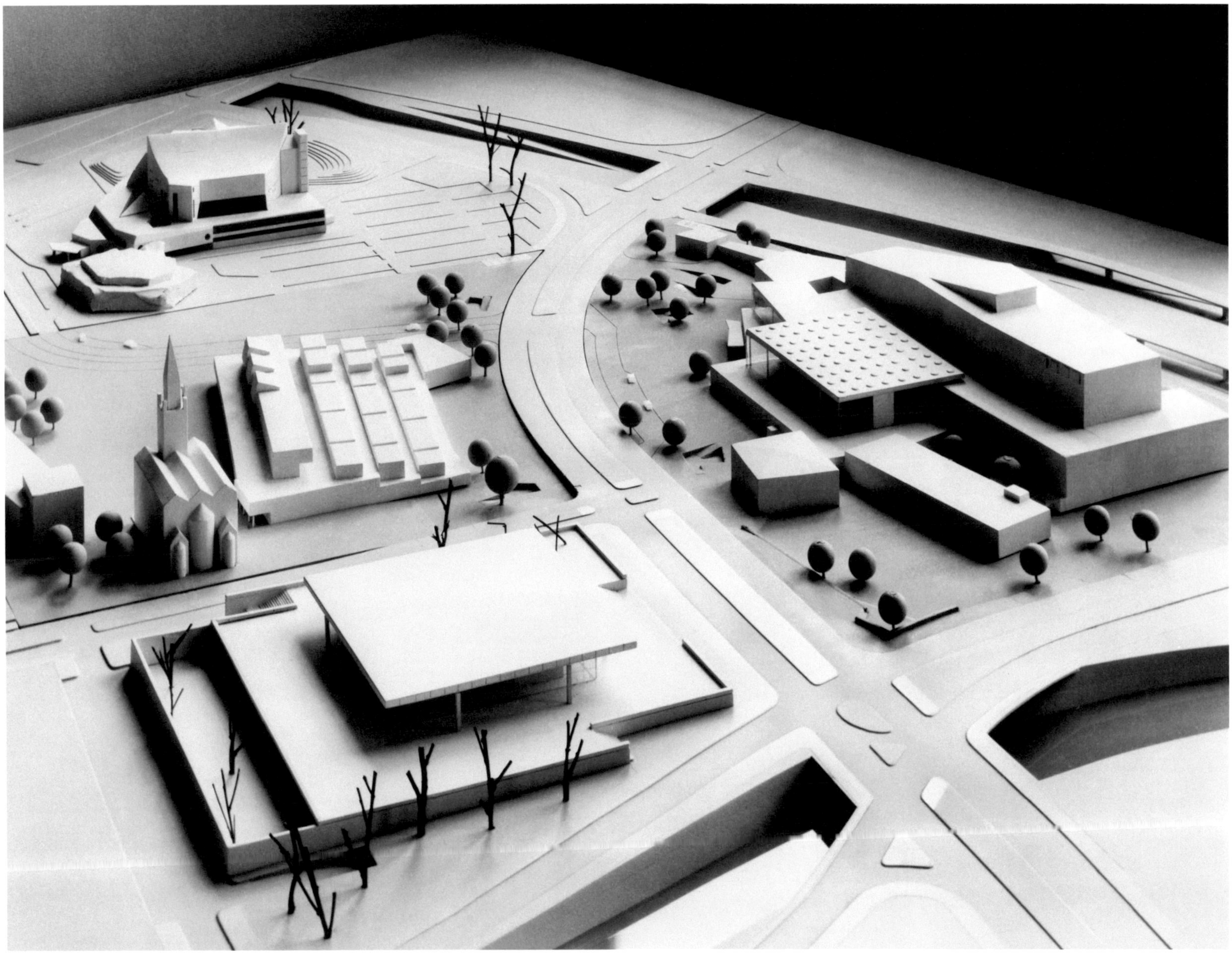

Hans Scharoun, “Kulturforum” with Senate guesthouse and Staatsbibliothek, 1964

Collective Manfred Jäkel, Lothar Kwasnitza, Dieter Urbach, Competition entry housing construction Leninplatz, collaged perspective: Dieter Urbach, 1967

Collective Hermann Henselmann, Heinz Mehlan, Realization of housing construction Leninplatz (since 1992 Platz der Vereinten Nationen) with Lenin monument by Nikolai W. Tomski, 1968–70

Dirk Weilemann

"How Will We Go On Living?" In Search of the City of Tomorrow in East and West

1 _ Hans Räde, Flying house-factory "Autoimme" based on a design by Ull Eisel and Wolfram Siemsen, 1965

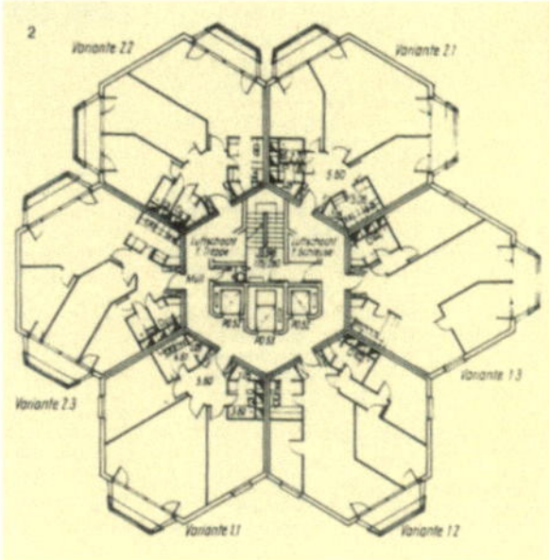

2 _ Collective Ull Eisel, Hexagonal ground plan of a residential building for automated production with the "Autoimme," circa 1969

The 1960s were a time of social transformation in both East and West Germany. Regardless of the system, a "previously unimaginable growth of science and technology"[1] took hold. In East Germany, or the German Democratic Republic, "utopian beliefs in omniscience"[2] and the euphoric sense of a new beginning in the 1950s were gradually replaced by objectivity and a turn towards social reality.[3] In West Germany, policymaking sought to be "rational," with decisions based on scientifically-based analyses.[4] Contemporary prognoses from sociology, political science, and economics made the future seem controllable as an "object of planning."[5] In both German societies, the year 2000 became a "mental vanishing point"[6] for projecting the future. With the successive automation of everyday life – vacuum cleaners, refrigerators, washing machines, telephones, and televisions found in most households by the end of the 1960s – life at the threshold to the 21st century was imagined as highly technological. Together with a faith in unlimited economic growth, a striking sense of "everything's possible" began to spread.

The call to be "scientific" in architecture and urban planning became louder as well. The 1967 interdisciplinary conference of the Bund Deutscher Architekten (German Architects' Association) in Hannover[7] focused on the need of architects to know the future they are building for, while in the GDR East Berlin architect Hermann Henselmann had issued a call to reason a year before: "There needs to be a step back from the Faustian utopia to a scientifically based prognosis."[8] This would provide the foundation for a truly future-oriented architecture.

New Architecture for a Growing Population

The United Nations' predictions of worldwide population growth played a special role. Beginning in the mid-1960s, these studies fomented fears in East and West alike that global demographic change would lead to uncontrolled processes of urbanization and as a result to an increasing scarcity of agricultural surface area. For the GDR, Henselmann assumed that the population would increase by 2 million by the year 2000.[9] Residential buildings would thus rise "up to ten or twenty floors or more."[10] Accordingly, architect Manfred Zumpe developed a 30-story residential high-rise for East Berlin.[11] To supply the strong demand for residential space all across the GDR and to maintain construction, research on the automation of construction was pursued in the spirit of a "scientific-technological revolution." Engineer

3 _ Manfred Kunze, "The City 2000," circa 1968

Ull Eisel, together with her colleague Wolfram Siemsen, developed the technique of *Vorfertigung über dem Standort*, or "above-site prefabrication," in the framework of which the Autoimme (1965–1970) was developed, an automated, flying architectural factory that was supposed to grow with the building (fig. 1).[12] The mobile plant was projected at the start with its own power source; in the last phase of development airships were to be used to transport the building factory to the building site. On site, the "Autoimme" would have created hexagonal room cells of concrete, which could then be installed around a utility and services core, which was also hexagonal (fig. 2). In this way, 168 residential units were to be built in just 14 days, starting in 1973/74.[13] 30 Autoimmes were planned to cover the entire residential construction of the GDR. According to the planners, architectural costs would be decreased dramatically due to the shorter duration of amortization and the elimination of transportation, assembly costs for the heavy segments as well as significant labor costs.[14]

A fictional 1969 reportage from the "City 2000" by Hans-Georg Krumbholz, that developed the model of a Communist city in the twenty-first century also had a lofty vision: loosely grouped "glass, plastic, and concrete high-rises"[15] with up to 80 floors and broad traffic axes with fast roads and "electron express trains" were to be erected around the historical city center and a park landscape intended for cultural activities and recreation (fig. 3).[16] The excessive expansion of the city in terms of surface area would be avoided by the strongly vertical orientation of construction. The ground level was reserved for vehicle transportation, while pedestrians would walk on raised platforms, a model that was already the foundation of Alison and Peter Smithson's contribution to the Capital City Competition Berlin in 1957/58 (fig. 4 and fig. 5).[17] In his report, Krumbholz suggests that courageous urban decisions in the present could lay the foundations for this imaginary future. Similar ideas were developed for East Berlin in 1968 by Josef Kaiser and for the entire city of Berlin by Fritz Haller.[18]

The City as Megastructure

Western Europe had already become aware of the problems of swelling urban centers and increasing traffic around 1960. In his influential 1963 publication *Où vivrons-nous demain?*, the French art and architecture critic Michel Ragon pleaded for a visionary urbanism of a generation of architects who with innovative materials and experimental tech-

4 _ Manfred Kunze, "The City 2000," traffic routing, circa 1968

5 _ Alison and Peter Smithson, Urban-developmental competition "Capital City Berlin," traffic routing, 1957/58

nological constructions, sought to create new settlements – underground, on the water, in the air, or even on the moon.[19] Yona Friedman was a main proponent of these approaches. After moving from Haifa to Paris in 1957, he founded the transnational Groupe d'Études d'Architecture Mobile (GEAM, Mobile Architecture Study Group) in 1958 with likeminded architects.[20] He attributed problems cropping up in urban areas to a poorly understood Charta of Athens and Le Corbusier's principles of the city divided according to functions.[21] With Ville Spatiale (1958–1962), Friedman developed the prototype of a three-dimensional expandable superstructure able to adapt to demographic changes and the needs of its residents (fig. p. 4). In contrast to purely residential settlements, his so-called megastructure was to combine all the functions of a city and bring about a greater mix of work, living, and leisure.[22] Network-like supporting structures were intended to include room cells using cost-effective, industrially-produced construction elements that could be expanded or removed if needed. With the "Spatial City," new surfaces were to be created, for example, over the old city, to achieve a vertical network and to counter suburbanization, or a "bridge city" on water and surfaces placed over traffic, like streets or railways. Friedman's Ville Spatiale was intended as a city for pedestrians. The surfaces under the spatial structure were intended for automobile traffic and in some projects the streets were to be directed through the inner core – a notion that Ralf Schüler and Ursulina Schüler-Witte took up 10 years later in their project Bandstadt Grunewald, developed for West Berlin.[23]

Large-scale Structures in the GDR

In the Soviet Union and the GDR, proposals for "reorganizing the city" were directed at "decreasing residential density combined with an increasing population."[24] After the 22nd Party Congress of the Communist Party in October 1961, the projection of "vertically organized large residential buildings" began,[25] which were also to include cultural and social institutions. In 1962, Bruno Flierl, the editor of the GDR journal *Deutsche Architektur* presented designs of large structures with the theme of collective residential form from Western Europe, Brazil, Japan, and the U.S., to encourage a discussion of previous solutions.[26] Most of the residential projects published served, however, as negative

6 _ Walter Jonas, Intra-houses, circa 1961

examples of "a lack of proportion" and "massification,"[27] for example, the funnel-shaped Intrahaus by Swiss artist Walter Jonas (1961/62), which was intended to combine residential and other urban functions.[28] Flierl accused these architects – not always fairly – of conceiving the task of erecting large residential buildings as a merely "technological-organizational" problem,[29] neglecting the social aspects of living. The idea of the Intrahouse, however, can be found years later with a socialist twist: in a publication on the future of the sciences, for example, the "housing mushroom" integrating numerous social functions was praised as a future possibility for living "in a genuine human community" (figs. 6 and 7).[30]
Hermann Henselmann, who founded the "experimental workshop" of the Institut für Städtebau und Architektur at the GDR's Deutsche Bauakademie in 1969, seemed open to avant-garde technological visions. As early as the mid-1960s, he began departing from the notion that "our generation definitively defines the environment for future generations."[31] Instead, he relied on a "new kind of flexibility and availability, that provides the necessary space for the dynamic of continuous social development."[32] Around 1970 he began to examine the idea of mobile architecture. "The apartments will surely be prefabricated, interchangeable, constructed as spatial cells or room parts, hung in macrostructures in a ferroconcrete or steel skeleton."[33] Henselmann thus absorbed the international developments of room cell construction that the chairman of "Sektion Hochbau" at the Deutsche Bauakademie Richard Paulick discussed in his 1969 contribution *Raumzellen*. Paulick also mentioned the possible construction of a spatial city using plastics, "hung from a steel wire construction," that possesses "rolling sidewalks and escalators" (fig. 8).[34] After several early experiments in the early 1960s, the subject of the spatial cell and the spatial city remained merely theoretical in the GDR.[35] In contrast to this, architects in West Berlin continued to develop their ideas to the building stage.[36]

8 _ Erwin Mühlestein, view into a spacial city, 1963–68

Architecture and the Competition between Political Systems

In the spirit of a competition between systems, the struggle over the city of tomorrow took place not only on paper. In Berlin, which played a special role due to its geopolitical position at the end of the war, architecture and urban planning were used in each of the sectors as a means of communication and propaganda to illustrate their modernity. In both parts of the city, even after the erection of the wall in 1961, the aim was to "build for a capital city."[37] With a socialist reconstruction of the destroyed city center, East Berlin sought to secure its status as capital of the GDR, while West Berlin politicians even in 1963 announced the "unrelenting desire for the fall of the wall, and that Germany must be reunited in freedom with Berlin as its capital."[38] These hopes for the future found their expression in West Berlin

7 _ "Suburb in the future" with "housing mushroom," circa 1970

directly on the inner-German border in the war ruins of the Reichstag (1961–1971). Since the West German parliament was banned from meeting in Berlin under the Four Power Agreement, the redesign remained merely symbolic. The commissioned architect Paul Baumgarten consciously departed from the historicism of the original building with his consciously reticent and transparent formal language. The dome was left out of the reconstruction, the stucco on the façade was removed, the original walls inside covered with simple boards, and the plenary chamber was enlarged and provided with daylight.[39] The design of the inside space with abstract artworks, some by Bernhard Heiliger (fig. p. 25), reveals the new cultural policy of the Federal Republic, which sought to rejoin international modernism and leave the Nazi past permanently behind.

In East Berlin, the still to be rebuilt city center became a projection surface for urban planning in a socialist style. The competition entries to redesign an impressive center with residential construction and a central government building reflect the broad spectrum of debate since Khrushchev's push in 1954 to modernize architecture, after which the monumental historicism of Stalinallee was no longer concerned contemporary. One important example of a visionary project for a city center in East Berlin is the design of a parliament building with a monumental glass dome by East Berlin architect Josef Kaiser.[40]

Although the GDR, in contrast to the Federal Republic, which was the legal successor to the Nazi dictatorship, considered itself the "new democratic Germany" on the side of progress, in the beginning the regime found it difficult to accept a modern formal language. "Modernism seemed like a surface of projection that was too open, and which could represent many different things, depending on the political context."[41] One solution to this dilemma that was often applied was the addition of scenic wall paintings or mosaics to mark the modern architecture as socialist. A special form of political charge was given to the steel-skeleton montage of the Staatsrat, which was built as the first government building at the southeastern end of the former Marx-Engels-Platz (fig. p. 26). Part of its façade was the reconstructed Portal IV of the Berlin Castle, where the socialist republic was declared in 1918. The construction was planned according to the proportions of the portal and thus generates a unique, but not very modern spatial form. On the ideological level, by appropriating the memory of this political event, so important for the GDR's self-conception, a line of German socialist continuity was extrapolated into the present, providing the architectural foundation for the future socialist state.

At the Eighth Party Congress of the Socialist Unity Party in October 1971, the new First Secretary of the Central Committee Erich Honecker called for a "realistic estimation of our powers and possibilities," and declared, clearly referring to exaggerated plans from the past, to not expect "unplanned miracles."[42] In West Germany at the end of the 1960s, despite the call for technology driven urban planning methods, voices began to call for a critical view of "utopias of infinite feasibility."[43] The spatial cities, for example, are for "beings differently conceived than we are,"[44] in the words of architectural historian Julius Posener. When the Club of Rome presented the study *The Limits to Growth* in 1972,[45] which among other things uncovered the "systemic linkages between economic affluence and environmental destruction,"[46] the euphoria in both German states about the future had passed its prime.

NOTES

1 _ Alexander Schmidt-Gernig, "'Futurologie': Zukunftsforschung und ihre Kritiker in der Bundesrepublik der 60er Jahre," *Aufbruch in die Zukunft. Die 1960er Jahre zwischen Planungseuphorie und kulturellem Wandel. DDR, ČSSR und Bundesrepublik Deutschland im Vergleich*, eds. Heinz-Gerhard Haupt and Jörg Requate (Weilerswist, 2004), p. 112.

2 _ Martin Sabrow, "Zukunftspathos als Legitimationsressource: Zu Charakter und Wandel des Fortschrittsparadigmas in der DDR," *Aufbruch in die Zukunft*, eds. Haupt and Requate, see note 1, p. 173.

3 _ Rainer Gries, " 'Und der Zukunft zugewandt' Oder: Wie der DDR das Jahr 2000 abhanden kam," *Der Tag X in der Geschichte: Erwartungen und Enttäuschungen seit tausend Jahren*, eds. Enno Bünz, Rainer Gries, and Frank Möller (Stuttgart, 1997), p. 322.

4 _ Gabriele Metzler, "'Geborgenheit im gesicherten Fortschritt': Das Jahrzehnt von Planbarkeit und Machbarkeit," *Demokratisierung und gesellschaftlicher Aufbruch. Die sechziger Jahre als Wendezeit der Bundesrepublik*, eds. Matthias Frese, Julia Paulus, and Karl Teppe (Paderborn, 2003), pp. 783-784.

5 _ Lucian Hölscher, *Die Entdeckung der Zukunft* (Frankfurt am Main, 1999), p. 224.

6 _ "Todlos glücklich," *Der Spiegel* (1966) 53, p. 80.

7 _ Alfred Simon, ed., *Wie werden wir weiterleben? Dokumentation der Referate und Diskussionen.* (Bundestag/Bund Deutscher Architekten, 42) (Essen, 1967), p. X. Participants included amongst West German architects the social psychologist Otto Walter Haseloff, the futurologist Robert Jungk and guests from Norway, France, and the U.S.

8 _ Hermann Henselmann, "Architektur und Städtebau unter den Bedingungen der wissenschaftlich-technischen Revolution. Bearbeitetes Protokoll, Kulturtheoretische Konferenz des Instituts für Gesellschaftswissenschaften beim ZK der SED, February 24-25, 1966," *Hermann Henselmann: Gedanken, Ideen, Bauten, Projekte*, eds. Wolfgang Heise and Bruno Flierl (East Berlin, 1978), p. 125.

9 _ Hermann Henselmann, "Die Stadt von morgen," *Urania Universum* (1968) 14, p. 482.

10 _ Ibid., p. 483.

11 _ See Anna Maria Heckmann's contribution to this volume, p. 92, fig. p. 133.

12 _ The term "Autoimme" is a compound of the words "auto" for "automat" and "Imme," the old German term for honeybee. The beehive like floor plans of the residential units complete this image. To examine the technique of *Vorfertigung über dem Standort*, Deutsche Bauakademie commissioned Ull Eisel in 1967 to complete a study. After defending the results, under her direction an "innovator collective" of twenty scientists was called into being, awarded the prize MMM (Meister für Morgen) at the 11th Leipzig Fair. The Central Committee cancelled the project after 1970, because it was planned too far in the future (thanks to Ull Eisel for this information, January 21, 2015). See also Ull Eisel and Wolfram Siemsen, "Fliegende Häuserfabriken," *Jugend und Technik* (1966) 1, pp. 50-52; "Bauausstellung Angebotsmesse 70," *Jugend und Technik* (1970) 9, pp. 790-794 and "Die Würfel sind gefallen," *Jugend und Technik* (1969) 1, p. 40.

13 _ See W. Finsterbusch and E. Wolter, "Projektanten gesucht," *Jugend und Technik* (1967) 3, p. 236; and "Bauausstellung Angebotsmesse 70," see note 12, p. 794. There is no reliable information on building height. In the article "Fliegende Häuserfabriken" from 1966, 13 floors were mentioned (Hans Rädes' drawing also shows 13 floors [fig.1]), in the model of a residential building that was depicited in 1970 as a contribution to the construction fair, 27 floors can be counted (including the penthouse floor).

14 _ See Ull Eisel and Wolfram Siemsen, "Lohnt sich die Autoimme?," *Jugend und Technik* (1967) 1, pp. 66-67 and on the Raumzellenbauweise Sara Heinrich, "Wohnungen aus dem Baukasten. Die Raumzellenbauweise," *Entwerfen im System: Der Architekt Wilfried Stallknecht. Ein Kooperationsprojekt des Lehrstuhls Denkmalpflege, des Lehrstuhls Entwerfen/Bauen im Bestand der Brandenburgisch Technischen Universität Cottbus und des Leibniz-Instituts für Regionalentwicklung und Strukturplanung e. V. (IRS)* (Erkner, 2009), p. 19.

15 _ Hans-Georg Krumbholz, "Die Stadt 2000: Eine Reportage, wie sie in 30 Jahren vielleicht geschrieben werden kann!" *Urania Universum* (1969) 15, p. 481.

16 _ Ibid., p. 484.

17 _ See Berlinische Galerie, ed., *Hauptstadt Berlin. Internationaler städtebaulicher Ideenwettbewerb* 1957/58 (Berlin, 1990), pp. 90-105.

18 _ See Anna Maria Heckmann's contribution to this volume, p. 95/96, fig. p. 108 and pp. 160-161.

19 _ See Michel Ragon, *Où vivrons-nous demain?* (Where will we live tomorrow?) (Paris, 1963) and Larry Busbea, *Topologies: The Urban Utopia in France, 1960-1970* (Cambridge, Mass., 2007), pp. 82-90.

20 _ Members of the group included David Georges Emmerich, Paul Maymont, Jerzy Sołtan, Frei Otto, Günter Günschel, and Eckhard Schulze-Fielitz. The founding of GEAM was a reaction to the 10th meeting of the Congrès Internationaux d'Architecture Moderne (CIAM, International Congress of Modern Architecture) in Dubrovnik 1956. Alison and Peter Smithson are reported to have reacted negatively to Friedman's ideas. For him and some of his colleagues, the question of mobility in architecture did not go far enough. Friedman understood "mobile" on the technological level as providing for a flexibility of construction and in social terms the ability to react to personal and social changes of lifestyle (new family members). The 1958 manifesto on Mobile Architecture went far beyond the technological side of architecture, critiquing "eternal" concepts like marriage or property, and in opposition to the idea of the permanence of the built and to the functional city described a model of self-organization of the residents, who are called on to shape their city in a pre-set framework. See Busbea, *Topologies*, see note 19, p. 201 (note 54) and Yona Friedman, *L'architecture mobile* (Paris, 1962, first edition, 1958).

21 _ With Ville Radieuse (Radiant City), Le Corbusier proposed spatially separated spaces for living, working, and recreation that were to be linked via a system of fast roads. In this project, he used approaches based on the Charta of Athens. This charter emerged in 1933 at the fourth CIAM-meeting and criticized both the high residential density and the expansion of the city. See Thilo Hilpert, *Die Funktionelle Stadt. Le Corbusiers Stadtvision – Bedingungen, Motive, Hintergründe* (Braunschweig 1978).

22 _ The term megastructure was coined by Japanese metabolist Fumihiko Maki in 1964 in his study *Investigations*

in Collective Form. Metabolism saw society as a process and sought an architecture that could adapt to growth and change. Around 1959/60, the architects Kishō Kurokawa, Kiyonori Kikutake and Kenzō Tange came together. Later, Fumihiko Maki and Masato Ohtaka joined the group. See Fumihiko Maki and Masato Ohtaka, "Untersuchungen zur kollektiven Form: 'Die Megastruktur,'" *Architekturtheorie 20. Jahrhundert. Positionen, Programme, Manifeste*, ed. Vittorio Magnago Lampugnani (Ostfildern-Ruit, 2004), pp. 222–224; and Vittorio Magnago, *Die Stadt im 20. Jahrhundert. Visionen, Entwürfe, Gebautes*. Vol. 2 (Berlin, 2011), p. 764

23 _ See Anna Maria Heckmann's contribution to this volume, p. 94/95, fig. p. 110–111.

24 _ Bruno Flierl, "Zum Problem der kollektiven Wohnform: Das Großwohnhaus als Wohneinheit und als Strukturelement der Stadt," *Deutsche Architektur* (1962) 6, p. 327.

25 _ Ibid.

26 _ The article discusses Le Corbusier's Unité d'habitation, Brazilian architect Rino Levi's design for a "Super-Block" in Brasília (1956–1957), Intrahaus or Funnel House (1958–1970) by Walter Jonas and Plan Tokyo 1960 for a "city on water" by Kenzō Tange.

27 _ Flierl, *Zum Problem der kollektiven Wohnform*, see note 24, p. 334.

28 _ See Stefan Howald, *Walter Jonas 1910–1979: Künstler, Denker, Urbanist* (Zurich, 2011), pp. 189ff.

29 _ Flierl, *Zum Problem der kollektiven Wohnform*, see note 24, p. 334.

30 _ Werner Müller-Claud, ed., *Wir werden es erleben: An der Schwelle zum dritten Jahrtausend* (Leipzig/Jena/Berlin, 1971), fig. between pages 176 and 177. Beside the illustration of the "residential mushroom," there is an illustration of a "city in the sea," probably inspired by designs like Marine City by Kiyonori Kikutake (1960) or Plan Tokyo 1960 by Kenzō Tange. Flierl reviewed the second design in 1962.

31 _ Henselmann, *Architektur und Städtebau unter den Bedingungen der wissenschaftlich-technischen Revolution*, see note 8, p. 127.

32 _ Ibid.

33 _ Hermann Henselmann, "Menschenbild und Stadtgestalt," *Wir werden es erleben*, ed. Müller-Claud, see note 30, pp. 272–273.

34 _ Quoted in: Richard Paulick, "Raumzellen," *Jugend und Technik* (1969) 1, 65. Paulick traces the plastic spatial city back to the Swiss architect Erwin Mühlestein, and also discusses the experiments in plastic construction of his West-Berlin colleagues Ralf Schüler and Ursulina Schüler-Witte.

35 _ On the room cell building technique, see Heinrich, "Wohnungen aus dem Baukasten," see note 14, p. 19.

36 _ See Anna Maria Heckmann's contribution to this volume.

37 _ Willy Brandt (SPD), Regierender Bürgermeister, *Bericht, 4. Sitzung des Abgeordnetenhauses von Berlin*, March 18, 1963.

38 _ Otto Bach (SPD), president, Abgeordnetenhaus, *Bericht, 4. Sitzung des Abgeordnetenhauses von Berlin*, March 18, 1963.

39 _ http://www.bundestag.de/kulturundgeschichte/architektur/reichstag/architektur/architekten/baumgarten/246948 (January 15, 2015).

40 _ See Anna Maria Heckmann's contribution to this volume, p. 91, fig. p. 91.

41 _ Elmar Kossel, *Hermann Henselmann und die Moderne. Eine Studie zur Modernerezeption in der Architektur der DDR* (Königstein im Taunus, 2013), p. 14.

42 _ Erich Honecker at the VIII. Party Congress of the Socialist Unity Party, 1971, quoted in: Peter Borowsky, "Die DDR in den siebziger Jahren," *Informationen zur politischen Bildung* (2002), p. 258, see also http://www.bpb.de/izpb/10111/die-ddr-in-den-siebziger-jahren?p=all (January 22, 2015).

43 _ Simon, *Wie werden wir weiterleben?*, see note 7, p. VIII.

44 _ Julius Posener, "Aus der Sicht des Baugeschichtlers und Bautheoretikers," *Wie werden wir weiterleben?*, ed. Simon, see note 7, p. 88.

45 _ See Dennis Meadows et al., *The Limits to Growth: A Report for the Club of Rome's Project on the Predicament of Mankind* (New York, 1972).

46 _ Hölscher, *Die Entdeckung der Zukunft*, see note 5, p. 221.

PICTURE CREDITS

Fig. 1 _ Hans Räde, Flying house-factory "Autoimme" based on a design by Ull Eisel and Wolfram Siemsen, 1965, repro from: *Jugend und Technik* (1966) 1, pp. 48-49. © Hans Räde

Fig. 2 _ Collective Ull Eisel, Hexagonal ground plan of a residential building for automated production with the "Autoimme", based on a design by Ull Eisel and Wolfram Siemsen, circa 1969, repro from: *Jugend und Technik* (1970) 9, p. 790.

Fig. 3 _ Manfred Kunze, "The City 2000", circa 1968, repro from: Hans-Georg Krumbholz, "Die Stadt 2000. Eine Reportage, wie sie in 30 Jahren vielleicht geschrieben werden kannt," *Urania-Universum* (1969) 15, pp. 481-486, beginning on p. 480.

Fig. 4 _ Manfred Kunze, "The City 2000", traffic routing, circa 1968, repro from: Hans-Georg Krumbholz, "Die Stadt 2000. Eine Reportage, wie sie in 30 Jahren vielleicht geschrieben werden kannt," *Urania-Universum* (1969) 15, pp. 481-486, on p. 483.

Fig. 5 _ Alison and Peter Smithson, Urban-developmental competition "Capital City Berlin", 1957/58, traffic routing, perspective of the Technical Centre, 1958, 35 x 44.4 cm, ink and watercolors on tracing paper, Deutsches Architekturmuseum, Frankfurt am Main © Frances Loeb Library, Harvard University Graduate School of Design © repro: Deutsches Architekturmuseum, Frankfurt am Main

Fig. 6 _ Walter Jonas, Intra-houses, circa 1961, repro from: Bruno Flierl, "Zum Problem der kollektiven Wohnform: Das Großwohnhaus als Wohneinheit und als Strukturelement der Stadt," *Deutsche Architektur* (1962) 6, pp. 327-339, on p. 334 © Foundation Walter and Rosa Maria Jonas

Fig. 7 _ "Suburb in the future" with "housing mushroom", drawing: unknown author, circa 1970, repro from: Werner Müller-Claud (ed.), *Wir werden es erleben. An der Schwelle zum dritten Jahrtausend* (Leipzig/Jena/Berlin, 1971), colored plate after p. 176.

Fig. 8 _ Erwin Mühlestein, Windowless, variable urban construction module made from plastic and adjustable formed glass parts, 1963-68, section of drawing, repro from: Richard Paulick, "Raumzellen. Eine internationale Umschau zu Problemen der weiteren Rationalisierung im Wohnungsbau," *Jugend und Technik* (1969) 1, pp. 62-68, on p. 67, drawing published in full in: *werk* (1968) 6, p. 369.

Anna Maria Heckmann

Different, Not bashful, Never built: Architectural Visions for Berlin in the 1960s

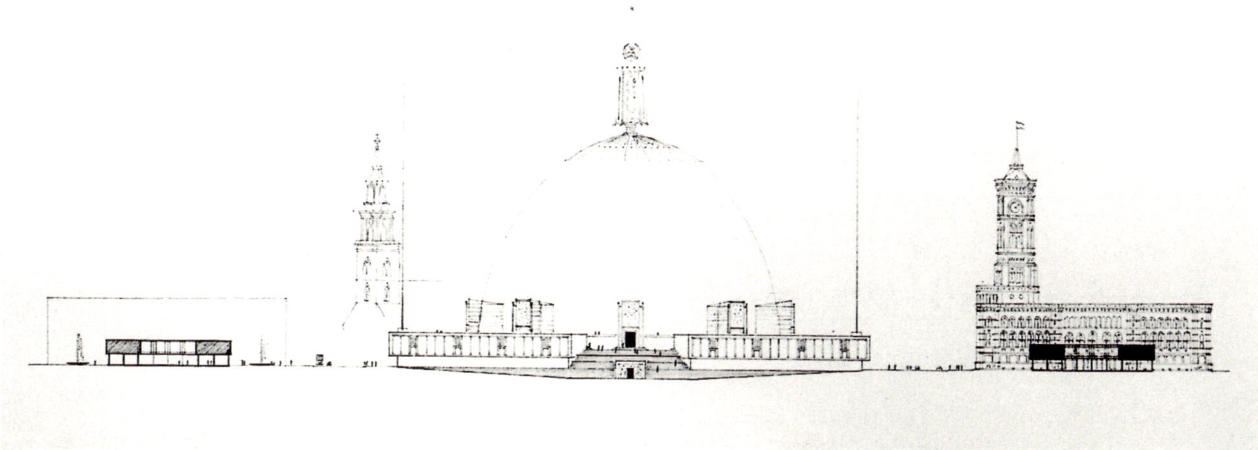

1 _ Josef Kaiser, Hans Gericke, Peter Schweizer, Building development, central square, competition for the center, 1960

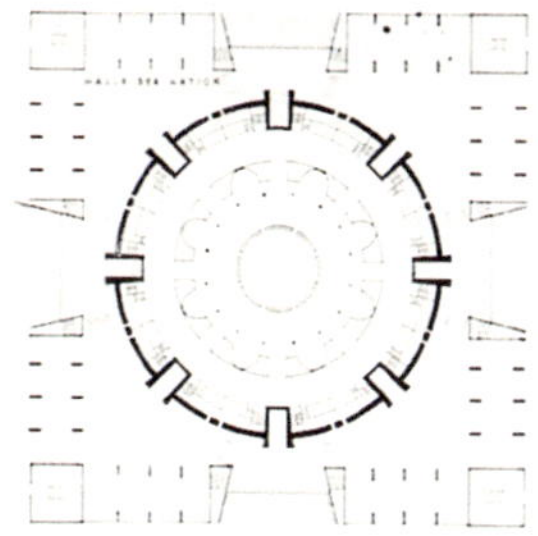

2 _ Josef Kaiser, Hans Gericke, Peter Schweizer, "Central building," ground plan, competition for the center, 1960

A mood of awakening, technological euphoria and a pressing shortage of housing fueled the many architectonic dreams for the future in both parts of Berlin during the 1960s. Such visionary designs were coupled with the desire to develop a better, modern society with the help of this new approach to building. Ideas ranged from the flexibly utilizable module made from plastic and novel variations of prefabricated construction types to architectural megastructures, and even to radical new ideal city layouts, for which any realization was doubtful or even unintended. Most of these dreams for the future were discussed controversially in professional circles and the daily press. For various reasons they remain unbuilt to the present day, so that many plans once put forward with so much conviction have now been forgotten.

Josef Kaiser's Plan for the Center

In the context of reconstruction in the area around Alexanderplatz and Marx-Engels-Platz (today Schlossplatz)[1], which was so significant politically for East-Berlin, in 1960 a "Commission for the reconstruction of Berlin's city center" made up of high-ranking politicians contracted three architectural collectives to outline plans, including the collective around Josef Kaiser, Hans Gericke and Peter Schweizer.[2]
The *Theses on a basic urban-developmental concept for the city center of Berlin* developed by the German Academy of Building (Deutsche Bauakademie) and the municipal authorities gave the architects tight parameters with respect to traffic axes and the functional aspects of buildings in this location.[3] Among others, the demands made included one for a "central structure", which was to comprise a parliament building and an adjacent single high-rise as the seat of the SED government. On the one hand, this correlated to a deliberate demarcation from West-Berlin, whose dominant urban planning features were determined by major commercial interests.[4] On the other hand, the intention of the GDR state leaders was an architectonic staging of political power in Berlin's historic center, as well as accentuating the government as opposed to the parliament.[5]
Deviating from this political accentuation, however, the planning collective around Josef Kaiser designed a ninety-meter-high, double-shell glass dome on a flat, low base structure as the "central building" (fig. 2 on p. 55 and fig. 1). This huge construction was to accommodate a large hall, the people's chamber, visible to Berlin's citizens and directly accessible via four staircases (fig. 2).
In its form and dimensions, this glass dome was reminiscent of Albert Speer's monumental design for a "hall of the people" in the planned "World Capital Germania", which had by no means disappeared from the collective visual memory of the 1960s. But Kaiser's building transformed the National Socialist megalomania into an architectonic symbol of the transparent work carried out by a socialist parliament[6] with the aim to set an urban emphasis to supplement the historical city silhouette without interfering with it.[7]
The technical feasibility of such a bold glass construction's realization was doubtful. In addition, the political signal of the design was unacceptable to Walter Ulbricht. He saw the rejection of the high-rise government building in favor of a people's chamber as indicating a lack of "political ideological clarity" on the part of the architects "regarding the role and perspective of the GDR".[8] None of the three planning collectives commissioned was able to convince the SED leaders, meaning that the second stage of the competition for the center also went unresolved. It was not until 1976, a decade and a half later, that a "central building" was finally erected under different political circumstances – the Palace of the Republic. As a venue for cultural events, its intention was to be accessible to the entire population.

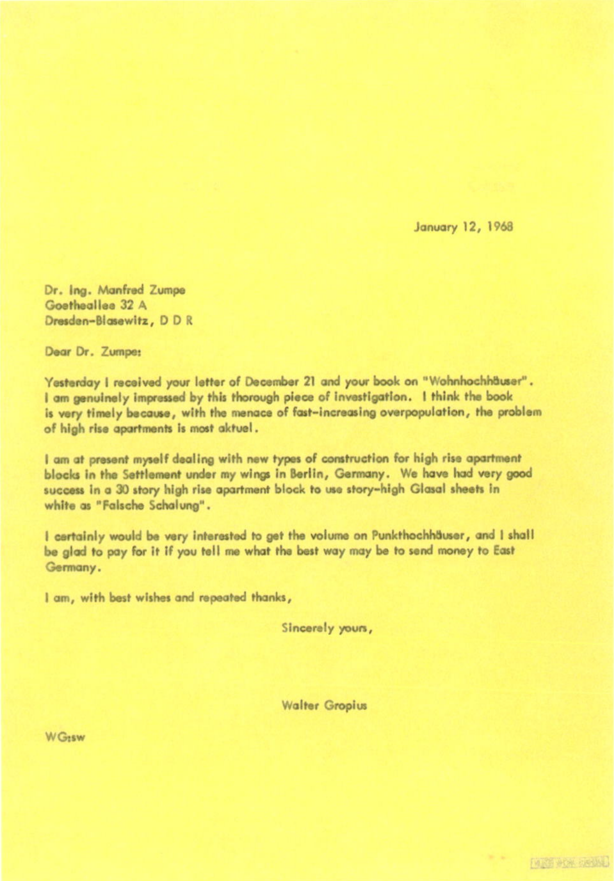
January 12, 1968

Dr. Ing. Manfred Zumpe
Goetheallee 32 A
Dresden-Blasewitz, D D R

Dear Dr. Zumpe:

Yesterday I received your letter of December 21 and your book on "Wohnhochhäuser". I am genuinely impressed by this thorough piece of investigation. I think the book is very timely because, with the menace of fast-increasing overpopulation, the problem of high rise apartments is most aktuel.

I am at present myself dealing with new types of construction for high rise apartment blocks in the Settlement under my wings in Berlin, Germany. We have had very good success in a 30 story high rise apartment block to use story-high Glasal sheets in white as "Falsche Schalung".

I certainly would be very interested to get the volume on Punkthochhäuser, and I shall be glad to pay for it if you tell me what the best way may be to send money to East Germany.

I am, with best wishes and repeated thanks,

Sincerely yours,

Walter Gropius

WG:sw

3 _ Walter Gropius, Letter to Manfred Zumpe, January 12, 1968

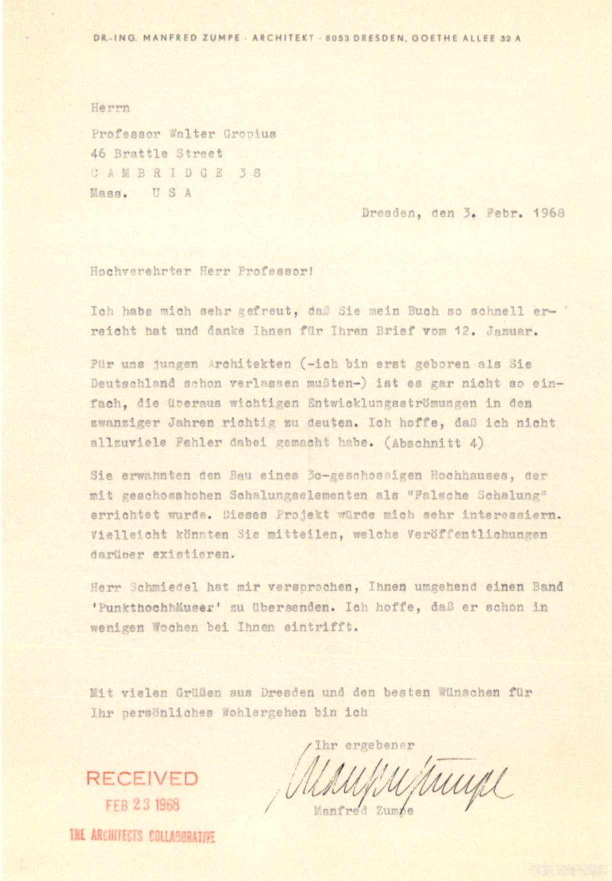
DR.-ING. MANFRED ZUMPE · ARCHITEKT · 8053 DRESDEN, GOETHE ALLEE 32 A

Herrn

Professor Walter Gropius
46 Brattle Street
C A M B R I D G E 38
Mass. U S A

Dresden, den 3. Febr. 1968

Hochverehrter Herr Professor!

Ich habe mich sehr gefreut, daß Sie mein Buch so schnell erreicht hat und danke Ihnen für Ihren Brief vom 12. Januar.

Für uns jungen Architekten (-ich bin erst geboren als Sie Deutschland schon verlassen mußten-) ist es gar nicht so einfach, die überaus wichtigen Entwicklungsströmungen in den zwanziger Jahren richtig zu deuten. Ich hoffe, daß ich nicht allzuviele Fehler dabei gemacht habe. (Abschnitt 4)

Sie erwähnten den Bau eines 3o-geschossigen Hochhauses, der mit geschosshohen Schalungselementen als "Falsche Schalung" errichtet wurde. Dieses Projekt würde mich sehr interessiern. Vielleicht könnten Sie mitteilen, welche Veröffentlichungen darüber existieren.

Herr Schmiedel hat mir versprochen, Ihnen umgehend einen Band 'Punkthochhäuser' zu übersenden. Ich hoffe, daß er schon in wenigen Wochen bei Ihnen eintrifft.

Mit vielen Grüßen aus Dresden und den besten Wünschen für Ihr persönliches Wohlergehen bin ich

Ihr ergebener

Manfred Zumpe

RECEIVED
FEB 23 1968
THE ARCHITECTS COLLABORATIVE

4 _ Manfred Zumpe, Letter to Walter Gropius, February 3, 1968

Manfred Zumpe's 30-storey High-rise

Besides the planning of the city center, rapid construction of housing for a quickly growing population in East-Berlin was another urgent task. After Khrushchev's stipulation in 1954 that housing should be constructed "more cheaply, more quickly, and better", the housing construction collective in East-Berlin (VE WBK) concentrated on building large numbers of less economized, prefabricated building series.[9] Architect Manfred Zumpe, head of a design department at the VE WBK in Berlin from 1963 to 1971, sought to counter the threat of architectural monotony by developing new ideas. In collaboration with his colleague Hans-Peter Schmiedel he supplemented the established series with alternative design types, such as the "windmill"[10] and the arrow house. These variations in housing construction were supposed to be more attractive aesthetically and offer greater diversification than the few previously customary types, while remaining reasonably priced in production and quick to build.[11]

Zumpe's planning ideas were based on his many years of scientific investigation into international developments in the field of prefabricated housing construction. During his research, in January 1968, he contacted one of the best-known forerunners of mass prefabricated housing construction in the world, Walter Gropius. In the subsequent exchange of letters, Gropius directed the attention of his young colleague from the GDR to his own 31-storey residential high-rise building Ideal in Britz-Buckow-Rudow (today's Gropiusstadt) (figs. 3 and 4). At a height of 90.85 meters, this was still the tallest in Germany in 1968, although the construction of multi-storey, high-rise apartment blocks had already been viewed as a political issue in both parts of the country at the beginning of the 1960s[12] (fig. 5). Manfred Zumpe indicated his interest in his reply to Gropius and requested further information material about the project.[13]

In 1971, albeit without a commission, he finally submitted the design for a type of 30-storey, twelve-cornered house[14] to the East-Berlin housing construction collective, a type characterized by the great plasticity of the building volume[15] (fig. p. 133). According to Zumpe's argument, his new type of building had been adapted optimally into a construction system already being realized by the Berlin WBK[16] since 1967, so that if it was realized, it would even be possible to achieve a reduction in construction costs by comparison to previous prefabricated structures with a comparable number of housing units.[17] Zumpe was so convinced by his own design that he had all the financial calculations and statics necessary for the realization of the project carried out at his own expense. Due to the "complacency" and lack of willingness to take risks on the part of those responsible in the housing construction collective, however, the 30-storey high-rise – like many of Zumpe's other type variations – remained unrealized.[18]

5 _ Horst Siegmann, Topping out ceremony, with mayor Willy Brandt, for the high-rise building on Alexandrinen-/ Franz-Künstler-Straße; on the left the numbering of the storeys, 1960

6 _ Ionel Schein, Mobile hotel cabin, 1957

Georg Kohlmaier's "Rucksack-WC"

In West-Berlin the Berlin Senate's Building Office planned the large-scale demolition of old buildings to make space for new industrially made apartments.[19] Besides the desire for a strict new urban-developmental order, the complete restoration of existing old buildings appeared too expensive and time-consuming, among other things because of their inadequate sanitary facilities. For example, in the mid-1960s only very few of West-Berlin's apartments in old buildings had inside toilets and bathrooms.[20]

By contrast, Georg Kohlmaier and Barna von Sartory regarded the preservation of existent historical buildings and cheap rents in old buildings as a social necessity. In 1969, therefore, they had their idea of the "Rucksack-WC", a brightly-colored sanitary module made from pressed plastic with foam thermal insulation, which was made for mounting onto the outside façades of old buildings in need of restoration (fig. p. 167). Inside the suspended plumbing unit, set out to save as much space as possible, the plan envisaged a bath, WC and wash basin, as well as various heating and extraction equipment. Drainage would be organized through down pipes which could be heated on the outside wall. Depending on requirements, the aim was for the "Rucksack-WC" either to be built into the apartment interiors permanently during subsequent restoration or removed and re-used elsewhere in the case of demolition. Georg Kohlmaier submitted the design for approval by the Senate Department of Building and Housing. Ultimately, the idea failed due to the Berlin Building Regulations.[21]

The idea of a separate, mobile element that can be mounted onto an architectural carrying structure had already been developed by French architect Ionel Schein with his mobile hotel cabin in 1956 (fig. 6).[22] Interest in the flexibly utilizable module, the plug-in or clip-on, was aroused by the world-wide debate on so-called megastructures.[23]

7 _ Ralf Schüler, Ursulina Schüler-Witte, Ribbon development Grunewald, site plan, 1973

Schüler/Schüler-Witte's Bandstadt (Ribbon Development) Grunewald

The plan was to create a megastructure under the direction of Ralf Schüler and Ursulina Schüler-Witte in 1971. Their design – commissioned by the BASF in order to promote the use of new plastics by the building industry – envisaged the construction of a 9.5 kilometer-long ribbon development over the motorway lanes of the AVUS in Berlin-Grunewald (fig. 7).[24]

The planned housing structure was terraced, thirty meters high and one hundred meters wide, using a solid steel-skeleton carrying system and in-filling single elements made from plastic reinforced with glass fiber. AVUS, railway and local public transport were to run beneath the housing block (fig. p. 110–111). Cable car transport within the ribbon development of almost ten kilometers was envisioned to convey residents to their neighbors and to shared car parking areas at each end of the housing structure.

The planning of the housing units derived from numerous preliminary studies and designs relating to houses made with synthetic materials completed by Schüler and Schüler-Witte in the years 1967 to 1969.[25] In particular, their Indapt-System[26] developed in 1969 would have been realized for the first time. With the help of this construction system, the housing units of the ribbon development Grunewald were to be adapted optimally to the individual needs of the residents by means of easily altered ground plans. Interestingly, the entire design process took place in close collaboration with social scientist Dr. Otto Walter Haseloff and several psychologists. Their jointly developed housing concept was

8 _ Walter Gropius, "Housing Mountain," 1928

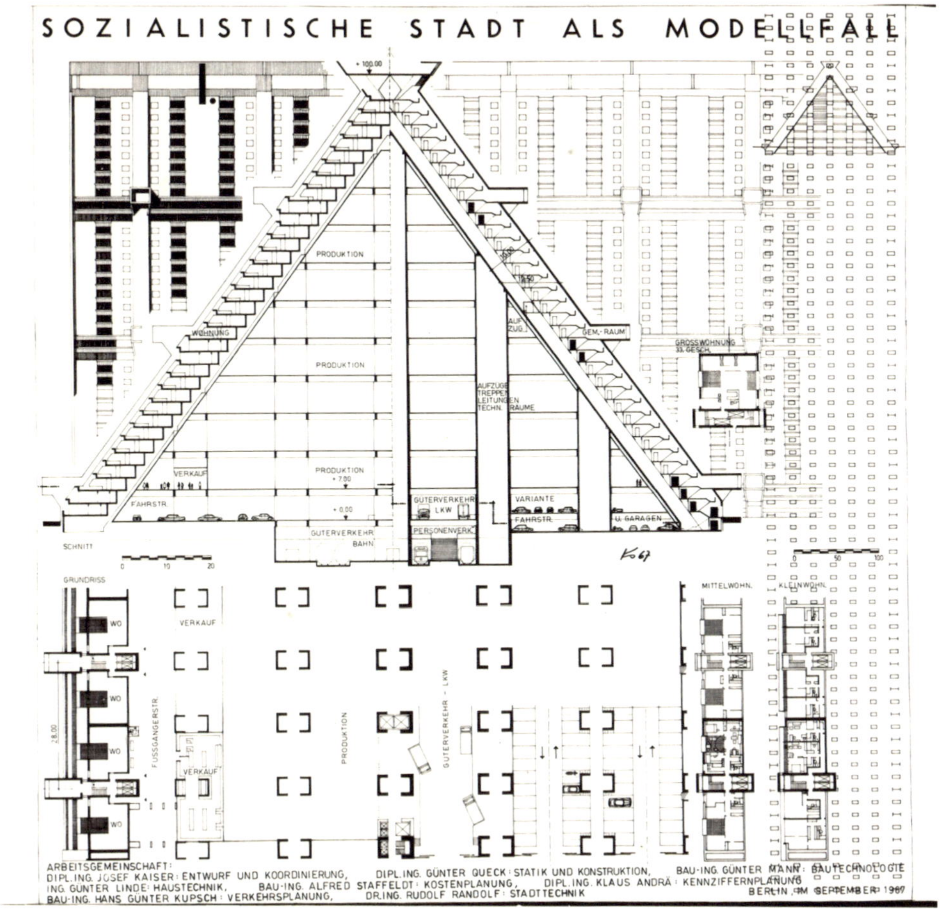

9 _ Socialist city as a model case, cross-section of a "large hill house," 1967

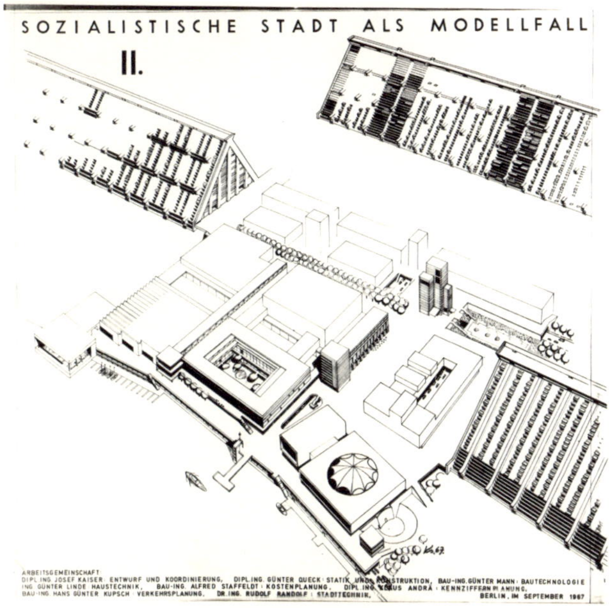

10 _ Josef Kaiser, Socialist city as a model case, entire planned urban development, 1967

based on prognoses for the future as well as studies on *Wohnen im Jahr 2000* (Living in the Year 2000)[27] and envisaged numerous communal spaces for adults and youths. The identification of different user groups with specific demands defined the arrangement and allocation of the housing units. Before moving in, the future residents would have been allocated to these different groups, patterns of interaction, and social roles by means of tests, and would have been prepared for living together through subsequent training in communication and conflict control.

The ribbon development Grunewald was developed to the point of construction, but the onset of the oil crisis in 1973 drove up the price for plastics and ultimately prevented the realization of the project.

Josef Kaiser's Großhügelhäuser

Despite the sector borders and construction of the Wall, as one of the GDR's most high-profiled architects Josef Kaiser was always very well informed about the current state of international architectural discussion and planning utopias.[28] When he began his study on the socialist city as a model instance on his own initiative in 1968, he was probably already aware of the concept of the "Wohnberg" (housing mountain, 1928) (fig. 8) attributed to Walter Gropius, as well as the "housing hills" realized in Marl by Stuttgart-based architects Hermann Schröder and Roland Frey between 1965 and 1967.[29]

Kaiser's idea was a model city with short paths, whereby the structure would be "opened out" but with "dense housing".[30] The intention was to offer space to a growing population, to make sense economically, and at the same time to counter the urban developmental monotony of prefabricated construction. At intervals of around 250 meters, Kaiser grouped several pyramid-shaped terraced structures, so-called "large hill houses", around a central core, in which he envisaged a mix of functions by contrast to Schüler/Schüler-Witte's purely residential structure. He arranged the apartments in the outer part of the building, so that they would benefit from natural daylight. The plan was to locate less staff-intensive production units in the artificially lit, air-conditioned heart of the building – separated acoustically and constructively from the residential area (fig. 9). At a length of one kilometer and a height of one hundred meters, each building would have offered space for up to 22,000 residents, as well as accommodating production sites with 10,000 jobs and an office area of 64,000 m².[31] Despite its gigantic dimensions, Kaiser described his megastructure as "a friendly hill with hanging gardens, open and accentuated

11 _ Dieter Urbach, Image collage "large hill house," design: Josef Kaiser, 1971

by a scattering of communal facilities such as gymnastic rooms, play areas or a snack bar, each on the various floors, easily reached via lift"[32] (fig. p. 108).
At the center of the socialist model city there were low terraced buildings for all institutions and services of public interest such as stores, boulevards, and leisure and cultural facilities. There were to be representative administration and government buildings in a prominent position, as well (fig. 10).
The infrastructure would be protected and air pollution prevented by means of strict division into various traffic levels: with the exception of the green areas, Kaiser planned the footpaths on a raised plateau, about seven meters above ground. Steps and moving staircases would have connected the pedestrian city to the various transport levels for cars and rail tracks at ground level and below ground[33] (fig. 11).
Kaiser assumed that his "large hill houses" would show significantly higher cost-effectiveness in terms of construction, operation and maintenance in comparison to "traditional development" and therefore reckoned with good prospects for their realization.[34] He published his model of the "socialist city" in the January issue of *Deutsche Architektur* in 1968 but met with divided opinion in the GDR professional world.[35] While Kaiser's visionary initiative was praised basically as productive and inspiring, the Institute of Urban Development and Architecture of the Association of German Architects expressed substantial criticism of several points. In a statement dated February 12, 1968, with reference to current sociological studies it was noted that in face of the increasing differentiation of people's housing needs, such a gigantic housing project was absurd.[36] Doubt was also cast on the asserted cost-effectiveness of the building.
Although further planning was prohibited by the district office for building the municipality of Greater-Berlin, Kaiser held fast to his idea and as late as 1970, he transferred the model into a study on the prognosis for urban development in the year 2000.[37] However, his "large hill houses" were never realized.

Fritz Haller's *total city*

At almost the same time as Kaiser, architect Fritz Haller conceived a similarly systematic and elemental urban model with his *total city* (1968). However, Haller did not start out from the feasibility of his conceptual experiment: "no one will build a city according to this model," he wrote in *totale stadt. ein modell*.[38] The system of order he had developed as a prototype was too abstract, too radical, too totalitarian. In order to counteract the feared collapse of the urban infrastructure, he designed the vision of a "total settlement" on a completely new scale; a settlement that would be capable of coping with even billions of inhabitants.
Haller concretized his model for the city of the future using, among others, the example of Berlin. First of all, it envisaged a strict geometric lay out, which was to straddle the entire existing city regardless of special geographical features such as hills or the course of rivers or lakes (fig. p. 160–161). He wished to replace the old existing structures gradually but completely with high-rise slab blocks, and to designate the latter, grouped in settlements, to a central unit and two ribbon-shaped peripheries in the north and south.[39] Haller planned a system of clearly structured settlement units, which in the case of Berlin would offer space for six million inhabitants and would be accessed via a strict, grid-shaped transport network. By means of an ideal systemizing of urban functions such as administration, leisure time, housing and working, he hoped to counter the feared urban chaos, rising energy consumption, air pollution and overburdening of transport routes and water and sewerage facilities.
These conceptual designs by Haller echo models from the 1920s like Ludwig Hilberseimer's *high-rise city* (1924) or Le Corbusier's *Ville contemporaine de trois millions d'habitants* (1922), which also forced a completely new beginning in urban development.[40] Considering the expectation of a future with entirely changed conditions and the simultaneously associated fears, such radical ideas were becoming more attractive again in the atmosphere of upheaval during the 1960s.

NOTES

1 _ On this, cf. the interview with Bruno Flierl, pp. 54-61.

2 _ Regarding the course of the competition, see Werner Durth, Jörn Düwel, and Niels Gutschow, *Architektur und Städtebau der DDR*,.Vol. 2: *Aufbau. Städte, Themen, Dokumente* (Frankfurt am Main, 1998), pp. 248-277.

3 _ On these theses, see ibid., pp. 273-274.

4 _ Ibid., p. 277.

5 _ Bruno Flierl, "Der Zentrale Ort in Berlin – zur räumlichen Inszenierung sozialistischer Zentralität," *Kunstdokumentation SBZ/DDR 1945-1990. Aufsätze, Berichte, Materialien*, eds. Günter Feist, Eckhart Gillen, and Beatrice Vierneisel (Cologne, 1996), p. 322.

6 _ Ibid., p. 339.

7 _ Dorothea Tscheschner, "Sechzehn Grundsätze des Städtebaus und die Charta von Athen?", *Stadt der Architektur, Architektur der Stadt. Berlin 1900-2000*, eds. Thorsten Scheer, Josef P. Kleihues, and Paul Kahlfeldt (Berlin, 2000), p. 268.

8 _ Durth/Düwel/Gutschow, *Architektur und Städtebau der DDR*. Vol. 2 (see note 2), p. 277.

9 _ Harald Engler, *Wilfried Stallknecht und das industrielle Bauen. Ein Architektenleben in der DDR* (Berlin, 2014), pp. 107-109.

10 _ The name came from the ground plan of the building, which was similar to a windmill.

11 _ Interview held with Manfred Zumpe by Ursula Müller in Dresden on October 1, 2013.

12 _ Even higher residential buildings were not erected until 1970: for example, the Colonia high-rise in Cologne, the Wintergarten high-rise in Leipzig, and Mannheim's Collini-Center.

13 _ Exchange of letters between Walter Gropius and Manfred Zumpe from January 12/February 3, 1968, Bauhaus Archive, BHA_GS19_Mp778.

14 _ The name came from the shape of the building's ground plan.

15 _ *Erläuterungsbericht 30-geschossiger Wohnturm*, Berlinische Galerie, BG-AS 17/2013,341, no pag.

16 _ This construction system was implemented, for example, in the housing blocks on the Fischerinsel and in the residential and commercial buildings on Karl-Liebknecht-Straße.

17 _ *Erläuterungsbericht 30-geschossiger Wohnturm*, Berlinische Galerie, BG-AS 17/2013,341, no pag.

18 _ Conversation with Manfred Zumpe on January 11, 2015.

19 _ The basis was Willy Brandt's first Berlin Program for Urban Renewal: Willy Brandt (SPD), Governing Mayor, *Bericht der 4. Sitzung des Abgeordnetenhauses von Berlin*, March 18, 1963. cf.: http://www.stadtentwicklung.berlin.de/staedtebau/foerderprogramme/stadterneuerung/de/einleitung.shtml.

20 _ In the area of concentrated restoration in Neukölln, for example, only 20 % of apartments in old buildings had an inside WC, and only 15 % had their own bathrooms. Cf. Georg Kohlmaier and Barna von Sartory, *Projektbeschreibung Rucksack-WC. Dossier Georg Kohlmaier*, Berlinische Galerie.

21 _ Expert report by the Senate Department for Construction and Housing, Dept. IV dated June 25, 1969 in response to the documentation submitted by Kohlmaier and von Sartory, *Dossier Georg Kohlmaier*, Berlinische Galerie.

22 _ Christoph Düesberg, *Megastrukturen. Architekturutopien zwischen 1955 und 1975* (Berlin, 2013), p. 40.

23 _ See Dirk Weilemann's contribution to this volume, pp. 84-85.

24 _ Ursula Müller, "1971. Ralf Schüler und Ursulina Schüler-Witte. Grunewald-Bandstadt," *Das ungebaute Berlin. Stadtkonzepte im 20. Jahrhundert*, ed. Carsten Krohn (Berlin, 2010), p. 199.

25 _ Ursulina Schüler-Witte, *Bausysteme aus Kunststoff* (1967-1974), p. 136. Unpublished manuscript, *Dossier Ralf Schüler*, Berlinische Galerie.

26 _ The abbreviation stands for "individual adaptation to family circumstances". Ralf Schüler and Ursulina Schüler-Witte, "Die Indapt-Systeme," *Bauwelt* (1971) 30, p. 1224.

27 _ Unpublished manuscript of Ralf Schüler's autobiography, *Eine Deutsche Vita durch vier Staaten*, p. 23. *Dossier Ralf Schüler*, Berlinische Galerie.

28 _ Notes and bibliographies from his estate show that Kaiser was well informed about the international scene. Besides the seminal literature, he was also aware of designs for megastructures such as Kenzō Tange's building over Tokyo Bay, the funnel building by Walter Jonas, or Yona Friedman's Space City. Undated manuscript, estate of Josef Kaiser.

29 _ In a reader's letter to the magazine *Deutsche Architektur* Roland Frey complained, among other things, that his direct precursor building remained unmentioned in the publication of Kaiser's design. Correspondence, April 2, 1968, estate of Josef Kaiser.

30 _ Josef Kaiser, "In der Stadt der Zukunft," Kultur im Heim (1969) 3, p. 4.

31 _ Josef Kaiser, "Sozialistische Stadt als Modellfall. Ein Vorschlag zur Erneuerung des Städtebaus," *Deutsche Architektur* (1968) 1, p. 48.

32 _ Josef Kaiser, "In der Stadt der Zukunft," see note 30, p. 23.

33 _ Josef Kaiser, "Sozialistische Stadt als Modellfall," see note 31, p. 48.

34 _ Ibid., p. 49.

35 _ Detailed statements made by two departments of the BDA and the municipal authorities of Greater Berlin, readers' letters to *Deutsche Architektur*. Correspondence January to April 1968, estate of Josef Kaiser.

36 _ Unpublished statement by the BDA, February 12, 1968, estate of Josef Kaiser.

37 _ *Studie über die Grundrichtung der langfristigen Prognose des Industrie- und Landwirtschaftsbaues bis zum Jahre 2000*, made for the Institute of Further Education of the College of Architecture and Construction Weimar, date of delivery October 15, 1970.

38 _ Fritz Haller, *totale stadt. ein modell / integral urban. a model. Studie 1* (Olten, 1968), p. 9.

39 _ Fritz Haller, Therese Beyeler, and Roberto Medici, eds., *Fritz Haller – bauen und forschen. Dokumentation der Ausstellung*. Exhib. cat. Kunstmuseum Solothurn 1988 (Solothurn, 1988), p. 3.4.1.

40 _ Christian Gänshirt, "1968. Fritz Haller. Totale Stadt," Krohn, *Das ungebaute Berlin*, see note 24, p. 193.

PICTURE CREDITS

Fig. 1 _ Josef Kaiser, Hans Gericke, Peter Schweizer, Building development, central square, competition for the center, stage 2, photograph: Gisela Dutschmann, 1960, repro from negative, Berlinische Galerie BG-AS 1436.001769 © Gisela Dutschmann/Berlinische Galerie

Fig. 2 _ Josef Kaiser, Hans Gericke, Peter Schweizer, "Central building", ground plan, competition for the center, stage 2, photograph: Gisela Dutschmann, 1960, repro from negative, Berlinische Galerie BG-AS 1436. 001769 © Gisela Dutschmann/Berlinische Galerie

Fig. 3 _ Walter Gropius, Letter to Manfred Zumpe, January 12, 1968, Bauhaus Archive Berlin, folder BHA_GS19_Mp778_01 © Bauhaus Archive Berlin

Fig. 4 _ Manfred Zumpe, Letter to Walter Gropius, February 3, 1968, Bauhaus Archive Berlin, folder BHA_GS19_Mp778_01 © Bauhaus Archive Berlin

Fig. 5 _ Horst Siegmann, Topping out ceremony, with mayor Willy Brandt, for the high-rise building on Alexandrinen-/Franz-Künstler-Straße; on the left the numbering of the storeys, on September 20, 1960, Berlin State Archive F Rep 290-01, 0071464 © Horst Siegmann/Berlin State Archive

Fig. 6 _ Ionel Schein, Mobile hotel cabin, 1957, 25.5 x 34.5 x 25 cm, plastic model, Collection FRAC Centre, Orléans, inv. no. 997 01 41 © Philippe Magnon/FRAC Centre, Orléans

Fig. 7 _ Ralf Schüler, Ursulina Schüler-Witte, Ribbon development Grunewald, site plan, 1973, Berlinische Galerie Schüler/Schüler-Witte Archive © Ursulina Schüler-Witte/Berlinische Galerie

Fig. 8 _ Walter Gropius, "Housing Mountain", 1928, repro from: Winfried Nerdinger, *Der Architekt Walter Gropius. Zeichnungen, Pläne und Fotos aus dem Busch-Reisinger-Museum der Harvard University Art Museums*, Cambridge/Mass. and Bauhaus Archive, Berlin; with a critical catalogue of works (Berlin, 1996), p. 247.

Fig. 9 _ Josef Kaiser, Socialist city as a model case, cross-section of a "large hill house", 1967, ink on transparent paper, estate of Josef Kaiser © Michael Kaiser

Fig. 10 _ Josef Kaiser, Socialist city as a model case, entire planned urban development, 1967, ink on transparent paper, estate of Josef Kaiser © Michael Kaiser

Fig. 11 _ Dieter Urbach, Image collage "large hill house", design: Josef Kaiser, 1971, repro from negative, Berlinische Galerie BG-AS 44/2013,100a © Dieter Urbach/Berlinische Galerie

Techno-
Geometries

Josef Kaiser, Elevated road at Alexanderplatz, junction Liebknechtstraße, with roadside development, perspective drawing, 1957 (not built)

Georg Kohlmaier, Barna von Sartory, Autobahn planning Oranienplatz, photomontage, 1969 (not built)

Karl-Heinz Kraemer, On-site assembly simulation, TV tower, April to November 1967

Karl-Heinz Kraemer, TV tower under construction, montage of façade segments, 1968

Josef Kaiser, Design for the entrance building of the TV tower, collage of images: Dieter Urbach, 1964 (not built)

Dieter Urbach, Collaged interior perspective of the entrance building of the TV tower according to a design by Josef Kaiser, 1964

Ralf Schüler, Ursulina Schüler-Witte, Design of the Tower Restaurant Steglitz, photo-collage, 1968/69 (not built)

Ralf Schüler, Ursulina Schüler-Witte, Tower Restaurant Steglitz with underground station Schloßstraße, 1972

Meinhard von Gerkan, Volkwin Marg, Tegel Airport (1965–75), aerial view, circa 1975

Tunnel Grunerstraße and Haus des Lehrers, 1969

Junction Halensee with Rathenauplatz, postcard, 1960

Dieter Urbach, Collaged perspective of the Großhügelhaus ("large hill house") with residents according to a design by Josef Kaiser, 1971 (not built)

Ulrich Müther with Gerhard Lehmann, Rüdiger Plaethe, Helmut Stingl, Large pub-restaurant “Ahornblatt” (1971–73, demolition 2000), 1977

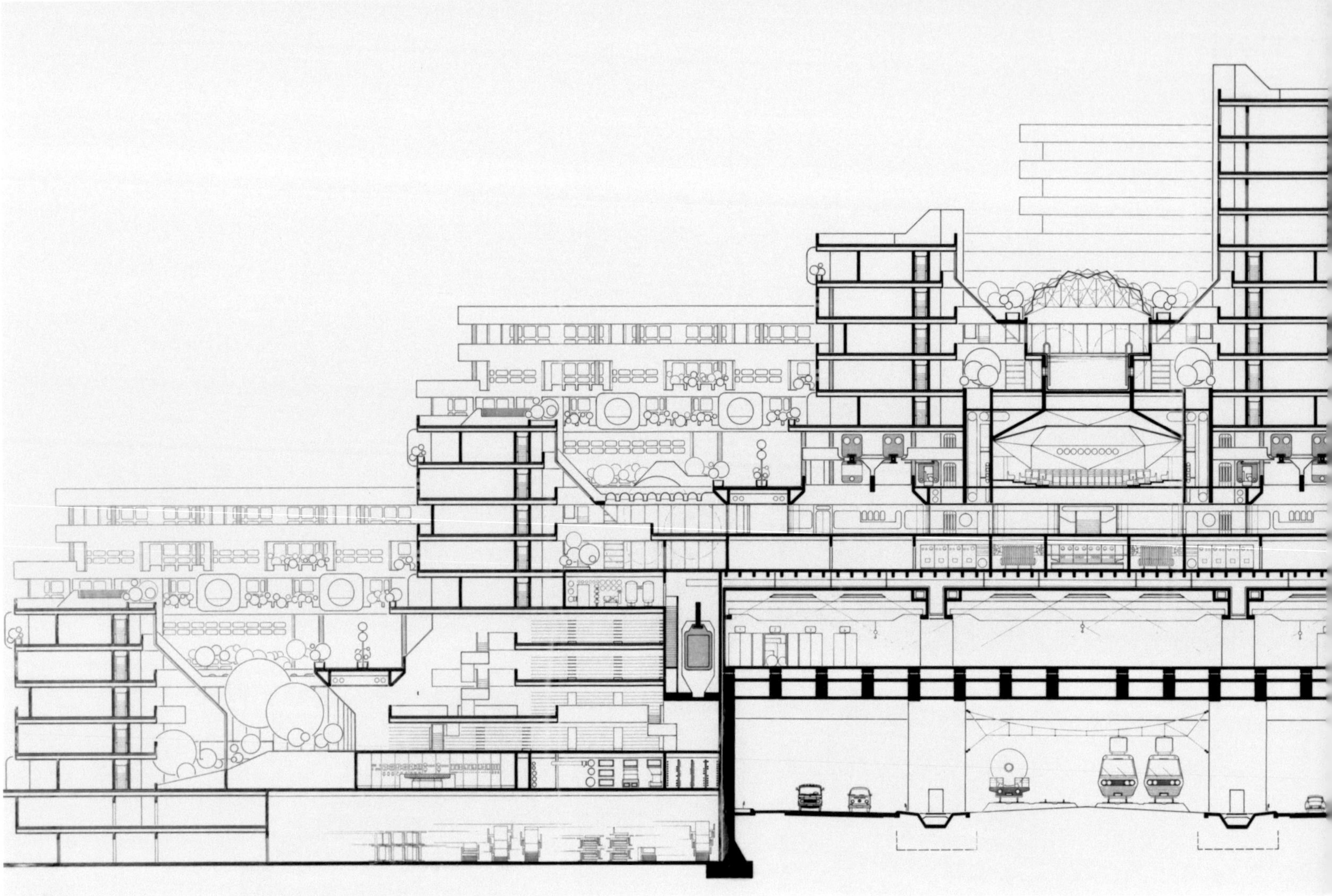

Ralf Schüler, Ursulina Schüler-Witte, Ribbon development Grunewald, 1973 (not built)

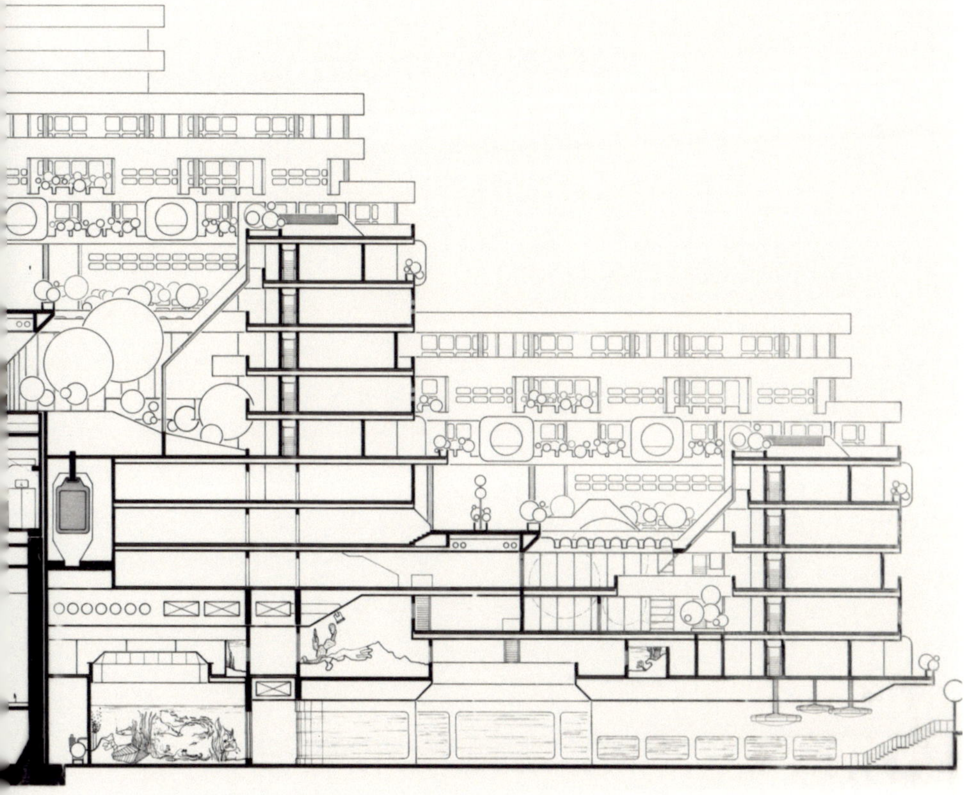

Bernhard Boës, Ribbon development Grunewald, perspective drawing based on a design by Schüler/Schüler-Witte, 1973 (not built)

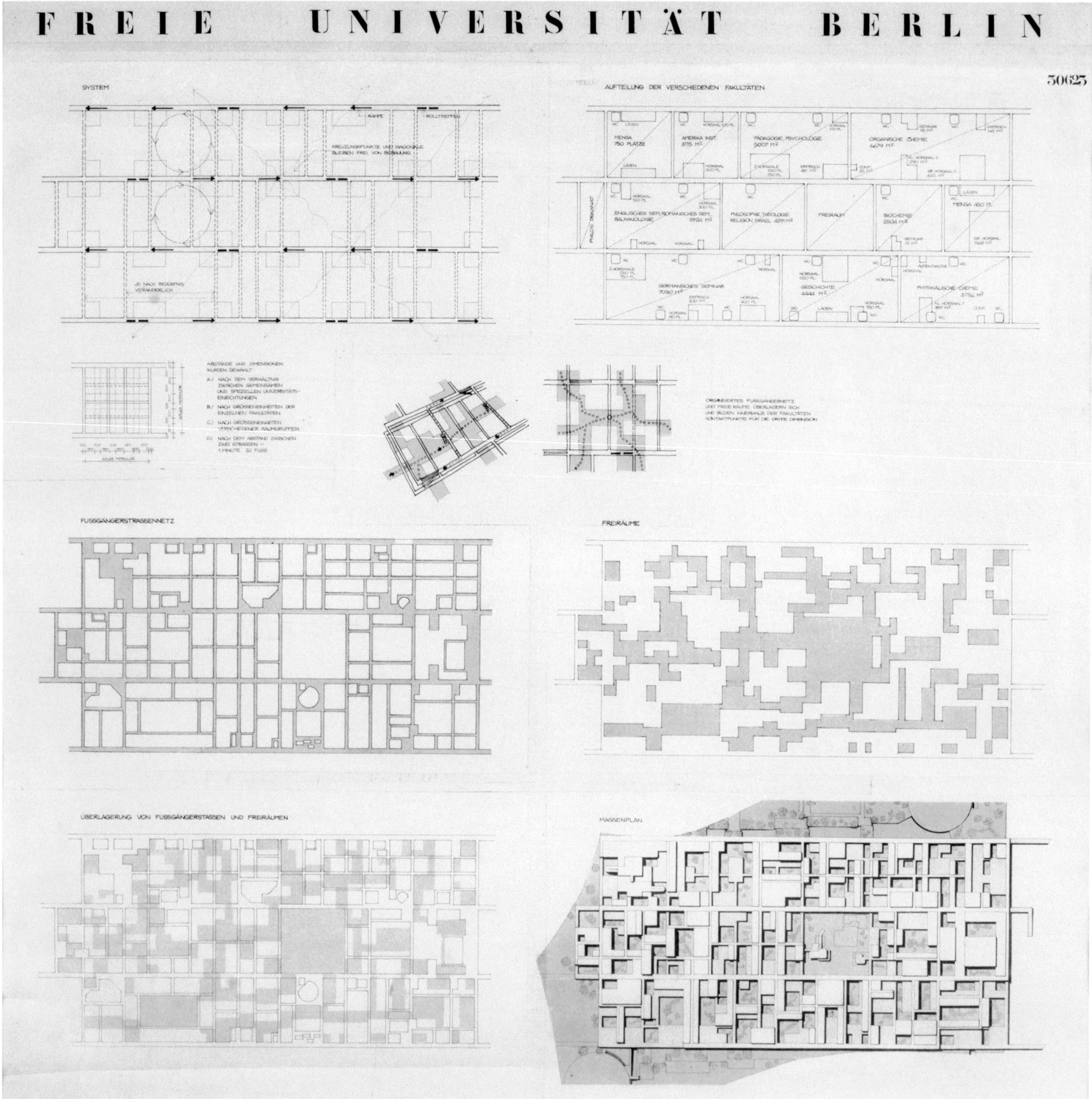

Georges Candilis, Alexis Josic, Shadrach Woods with Manfred Schiedhelm, Presentation plan for the competition "Development of the fruit-growing site of the Freie Universität Berlin," 1963

Georg Kohlmaier, Barna von Sartory, Moving pavements on the Kurfürstendamm, 1969 (not built)

Frank Seehausen

The Swing in the Future: Staging the Flow of Traffic in 1960s Berlin

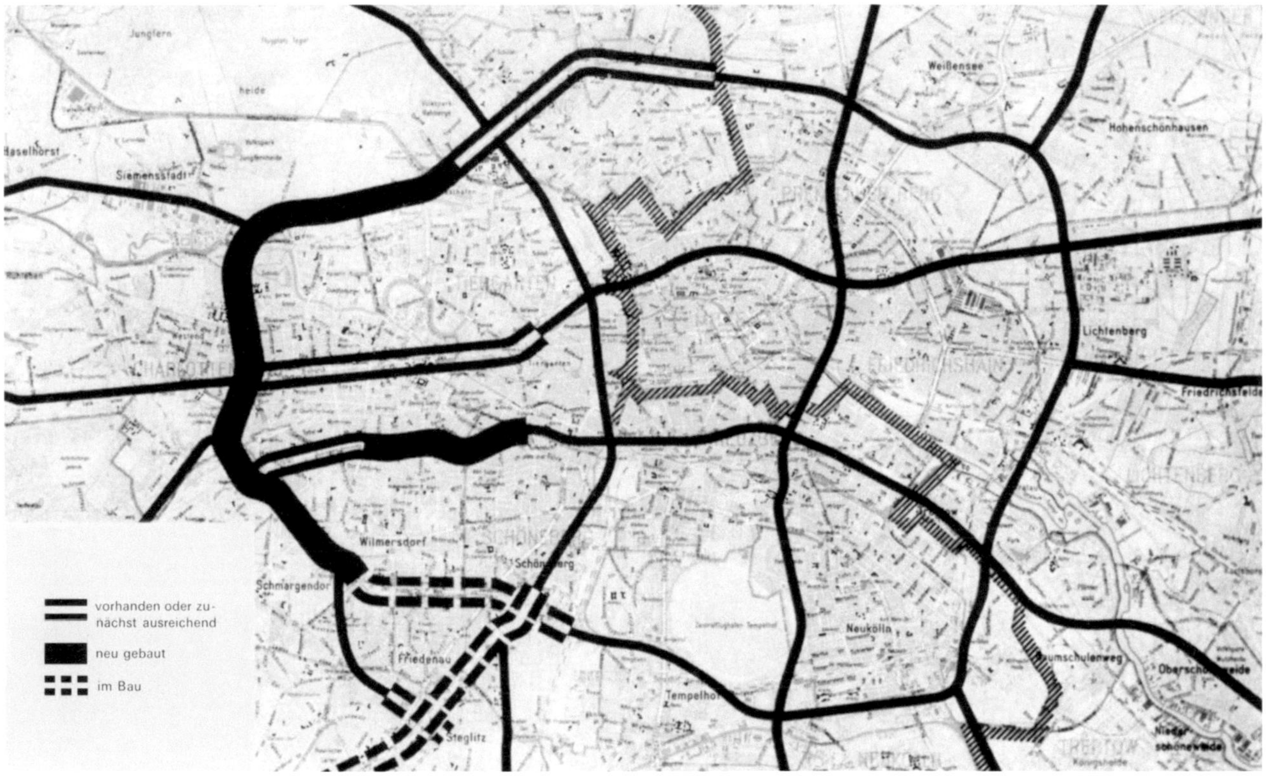

1 _ Schematic depiction of the system of highways in Berlin with stages of development, circa 1968

2 _ Junction city motorway – AVUS, circa 1968

While the political division became spatially manifest in 1961, in traffic planning, surprisingly, there was a great deal of similarity between the systems. Already in the 1950s, similar conceptions of flowing, primarily automotive traffic facilitated the professional exchange among experts and made it possible to expand the network of streets on a large scale in the divided city and anchor it in the respective plans for surface area use and traffic.[1] In both systems, this was linked not only to the practical task of managing traffic, but also the aesthetic vision of a dynamic mise en scène of the city as a promise for a better future, cast in concrete and fueled by gasoline.[2]
Parallel to the re-planning of the southern part of Hansaviertel, construction of the city highway in West Berlin began, and already during the 1957 Internationale Bauaustellug in 1957 the Halensee entrance ramp could be viewed at the western end of Kurfürstendamm.[3] Large-scale urban planning was explicitly staged here: although the term *Stadtautobahn* was initially avoided for political reasons – until the early 1960s the term *Schnellstraße* was used.[4] The senate decision on July 4, 1955 to build the Western ring highway connected to the AVUS foresaw a highway parallel to the city's rail ring that would frame a network of grade-separated highways with four major interchanges (figs. 1 and 2).[5] Since groundbreaking on April 1, 1956, the Western segments were completed at an amazing speed: in November 1958, the section from Halenseestraße to Hohenzollerndamm, in 1960 the section from Hohenzollerndamm to Mecklenburgische Straße, in 1962 and 1964 the section connecting Halenseestraße and Jakob-Kaiser-Platz. In no small way the financing with federal moneys made clear that there was more at stake here than just solving a traffic problem: West Berlin was to

3 _ Junction Halensee with Rathenauplatz, postcard, 1960

be made more attractive for companies and young people and the benefits and achievements of modern Western urban and traffic planning were to be demonstrated in the "shop window of the west." The foundation for the plan was to meet the traffic needs of a prognosticated 250,000 employed residents in the city center and, in case of reunification, five million residents.[6]

Whenever possible, the new highways were visually emphasized in the cityscape. Iconic importance here was achieved by the already mentioned Halensee interchange in connection with Rathenauplatz, which opened in 1958 (fig. 3). While on the southern side of Rathenauplatz a glass gallery linked the BVG bus station to the highway, offering pedestrians a weather-protected panorama view of the road, on the northern side exits and tunnels were distributed very generously on the grounds of Luna Park, demolished in 1935. The composition of broad highway ramps leading together in an arch framing the tunnel, best seen from the perspective of a driver, was impressively elegant. Together with the clean lines of the apartment high-rise by Felix Hinssen, erected from 1956 to 1958, drivers coming from the north saw the emblematic image of a modern and dynamic city, condensing a vision of Berlin's future. It is striking how often this same motif was reproduced in photographs and postcards from the 1960s. The climax was surely its inclusion in the stamp series *Das neue Berlin*, with which Deutsche Bundespost presented a series of iconic new buildings in West Berlin, including Deutsche Oper, Europa-Center, and Ernst-Reuter-Platz.[7]

The intention of urban planners to design city highways as a visual experience is evident in the presentation drawings of the Senate administration created between 1955 and 1959. These show striking views of the highway primarily from a bird's-eye perspective or from the perspective of the driver. The planned gallery appears as an evening urban scenario on Rognitzstraße in Charlottenburg from the slightly elevated point of view of a Mercedes driver looking over the front hood (fig. 4). Overall, the artists were clearly seeking to depict a certain atmosphere. The composition and details evoke memories of American highways that in those years had an increased presence in Germany

4 _ Planned elevated stretch of road on Rognitzstraße/Knobelsdorffbrücke, circa 1955

have learned that their civil rights are not infringed when they are not allowed direct access to the parkway, but that it is use-

306. "The Pretzel," intersection of Grand Central Parkway, Grand Central Parkway Extension, Union Turnpike, Interboro Parkway, and Queens Boulevard, New York City, 1936–37. *One of the most elaborate and highly organized of all recent solutions of the problem of division and crossing of arterial traffic.*

5 _ Junction "The Pretzel," New York City, circa 1937

primarily due to photography and film.[8] The representation of the intersection of a southern and a western tangent with their long radii and the raised roads organized on three levels seem to be inspired by the aesthetic canon of suburban highways in the U.S.[9]

Individual stretches of the Berlin city highway can even be identified with certain models, for example the AVUS interchange, which is strikingly similar to the interchange on New York's Grand Central Parkway that Sigfrid Giedion called "The Pretzel" (fig. 5).[10] The complex lines, with their gentle curves and the overlapping layers of traffic, were intended to offer a special experience not only for drivers. Its actual design could only be seen from the viewing or restaurant platform of the neighboring Radio Tower.

In light of the immense advantage held by the U.S. in terms of motorization, it seems only natural that their roadway constructions were considered to be model in character. After the Senate construction director and later Senator building commissioner Rolf Schwedler had already visited the United States in preparation for highway construction in 1953 and 1954, in the Winter of 1957 those responsible for highway construction at the Berlin Building Authority travelled the U.S. for several weeks. Under the direction of Friedrich Fürlinger, then building commissioner in Berlin-Wilmersdorf, the team systematically examined technical and planning aspects of American city highways in Boston, Detroit, and Los Angeles, and returned to Berlin not only with extensive material, but also with a palpable enthusiasm for the roadways experienced there.[11]

The View of the Street

Traffic was architecturally organized ten years after the construction of the AVUS knot with the Schildhornstraße hub, an original construction of traffic experience first published by the architects Ursulina Schüler-Witte and Ralf Schüler in a first draft in 1969.[12] Compact and yet spatially well-conceived, the highway exit Steglitz, with its city bus stops, subway station, and the ground level street intersection, featur-

6 _ Gerhard Murza, View from the visitors' platform of the TV tower to Alexanderplatz and the second constructed section of Karl-Marx-Allee, circa 1973

ing a striking tower restaurant with "UFO-like" visitor levels, was to be anchored in the cityscape of the most important Steglitz shopping district.[13] The ensemble of traffic, especially the gaze on car traffic, was declared an attraction, and, just as in the 1920s, architecture and traffic fused to form an image of the rejuvenated city (fig. p. 105).

The collective plan developed under the direction of Hans Scharoun in 1945/46 already planned to anchor traffic in a network-like structure in a new, green cityscape.[14] The road as a vision of the future ultimately won out in subsequent decades, despite individual voices of critique, and with car-oriented decisions in the surface-use plan from 1965, several-story street intersections were a standard feature in West Berlin planning. The position of the Posthochhaus by Prosper Lemoine on Hallesches Ufer, completed in 1971, and the rear sides of the high-rises designed by Werner Düttmann for Kreuzberg's Mehringplatz still mark the course of the planned "southern tangent," for which an oversized turbine intersection was foreseen in the area of Oranienplatz. A complete urban redesign of Kreuzberg would have been the consequence, as was made clear by the only slightly exaggerated montage of Georg Kohlmaier and Barna von Sartory (fig. p. 101). In addition, another raised road shaping the cityscape was planned: an s-shaped raised road at An der Urania and Lietzenburger Straße, where the large format and rhythmically shaped marginal architecture was built with the course of the roads and the visual experience of urban space with the journey by car in mind.

During the second half of the 1950s a large-scale system of highways was also planned In East Berlin that broke with the historical city layout. However, elaborate bridge constructions and intersections with grade separation were not realized in the city center and in fact traffic construction initially seemed hardly to be emphasized. All the more radical was the planning for the new city center with the television tower erected from 1965 to 1969 that replaced the party skyscraper that had once been planned as an iconic center for Marx-Engels-Forum. From a rotating panorama restaurant 200 meters high, the modernized city center in the spirit of socialism lay at the feet of the visitors, like an architectural model (fig. 6). The spectacular view, spatially and

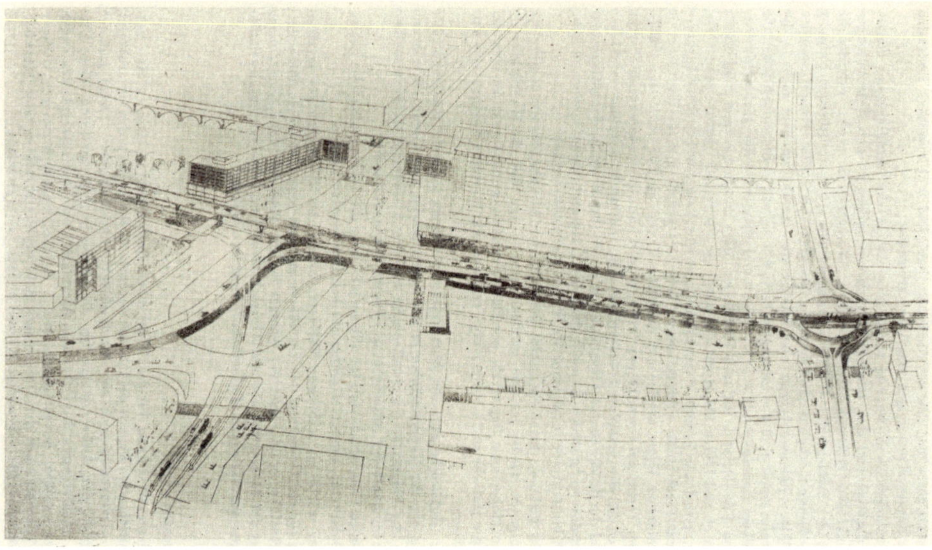

7 _ Eberhard Radicke et al., Elevated street at Alexanderplatz with depiction of the buildings along the edge, based on sketches by Josef Kaiser, 1958

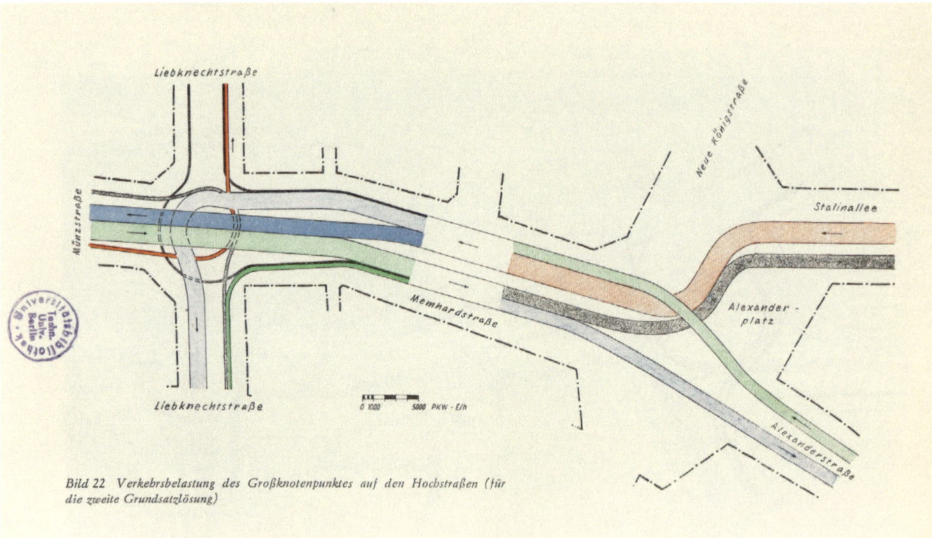

8 _ Eberhard Radicke et al., Traffic inquiry regarding intersection Alexanderplatz, 1958

9 _ Josef Kaiser, Elevated road at Alexanderplatz, junction Liebknechtstraße, with building along edge, 1957 (not built)

mechanically distanced by the elevator and the rotating platform, made the modern center of the capital of the GDR legible as the model for a new social order. Broad streets with orderly flowing traffic became a synonym of a prosperous future.[15]

In fact, the explicit display of flowing car traffic in the cityscape of East Berlin only became an important issue in the late 1950s and early 1960s. In 1958, Eberhard Radicke, the traffic planner at Deutsche Bauakademie, presented a study for building a raised roadway over Alexanderplatz: today's Karl-Marx-Allee and Alexaderstraße were to be continued in a huge overpass six to eleven meters high and continued toward Memhardstraße and Karl-Liebknecht-Straße (figs. 7 and 8) as part of a planned east-west road along the Spree.[16] According to designs by Josef Kaiser the perspective drawings were complemented with a fleetingly drawn sketch of buildings along the sidelines which took its dimensions and orientation entirely from the speed of automobile traffic.[17] There were strong proponents of this idea within the Bauakademie. A perspective drawing of the junction Liebknechtstraße shows, that they continued working on the project and designed impressive elevated roads on a large scale (fig. 9). In 1963, when there was traffic chaos in East Berlin resulting from the building of the wall, Edmund Collein presented a new version of a raised roadway that due to its clothoid curve would have been very comfortable to drive around Alexanderplatz.[18] The city government was only able to block these plans with some difficulty.[19] Particularly in the 1958 version, the projected roadway, influenced by the American raised highway, would have offered car drivers a visual choreography like the one implemented a short time later in Halle an der Saale.[20] Here, the overpass towards the modern new city floated past the old city, which was now reduced to a silhouette – the beginning of a new society was staged as a driving experience and the road became a metaphor of a new start. It is thus not surprising that with the broad median of Karl-Marx-Allee and along the northern flank of Alexanderplatz enough room was left to later insert the raised roadway. Until then, cars could be parked there. The lack of covered garages made it possible to ostentatiously stage the supposed progress of motorization.[21]

The Moving Gaze

With the increase and acceleration of automotive traffic, and the expansion of the road network to manage the flowing traffic, a new understanding of urban conglomerates and a new perception of the city developed increasingly in the 1960s. The influence of the car was already described by Peter Behrens[22] and Erich Mendelsohn[23] as the "moving gaze." Beginning in the 1940s, writers like Sigfried Giedion explored the perception of architecture and urban areas under the influence of automobile traffic.[24] In the GDR, aspects of urban and visual experience were intensely discussed. Hans Schmidt, head architect at the Institut für Städtebau und Architektur (Institute for Urban Planning and Architecture) at the Deutsche Bauakademie wrote in 1963 on attempts to derive a new aesthetic conception of architecture from the "appearance of rapid movement of traffic through space."[25] Referring to a basic spatial experience of modernism, he formulated as follows: "The new highways over long distances, divorced from construction, add decisively to the structure of the city in space, physically as a silhouette, if they are not seen merely as conduits for traffic, but also as a spatial element."[26] With the turn to modern forms of architecture in the GDR the rhythmic framing of the second phase of Karl-Marx-Allee (formerly Stalinallee) and the construction at Alexanderplatz with its accentuating high-rises ornamented with monumental art work, were not only directed at the marching masses, but more importantly the driver. The newly created urban space with buildings framing the roads and special structures intended to mark "changes in direction" or to serve to "close off the space" were consistent with the "theory of visual signs" that was developed to create effective urban spaces.[27] The belief was that a counter-model had been founded to the supposedly dense, vertical towering city centers of capitalist countries: in socialist city centers, as shown by the gaze down from the Television Tower, the experience was to be one of expanse and order.

The concept of monumental artworks, since the 1960s usually linked directly to the architecture, was adjusted to con-

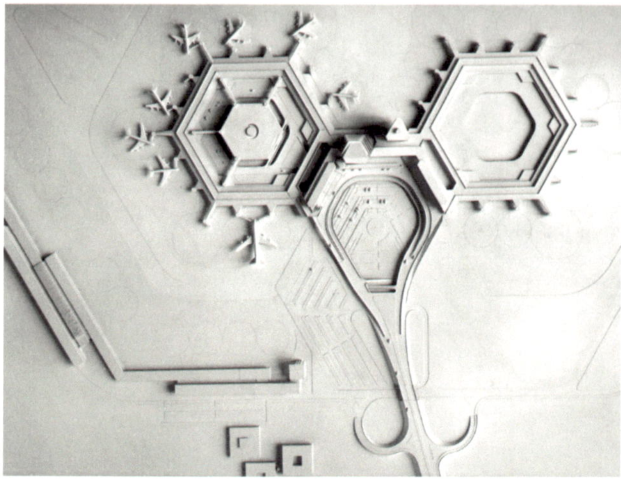

10 _ Meinhard von Gerkan, Volkwin Marg, Tegel Airport, model with both rings of gates, circa 1968

form to the new dimensions of urban space and perception moving in flowing traffic. The images were visible from a distance and gave the modern high-rises the desired political marking.[28] Walter Womacka's frieze on Haus des Lehrers (Building of the Teacher) and his copper relief on Haus des Reisens (Building of Travel) are exemplary here. They were placed on the high-rises intentionally in a way that corresponds to the angles of the movement of car drivers and/or political marches. Accordingly, Haus des Lehrers and Haus des Reisens framed Interhotel, which was then the highest building in the socialist countries and marked the turn of traffic down Karl-Liebknecht-Straße. These murals also referred to a frieze by Willi Neubert on the Presse-Café at Berliner Verlag, placed at the end of this axis as a large-scale artwork.[29] In light of such decidedly urban-visual strategies, it seems clear that perception under the conditions of accelerated movement and the building of appropriate spaces was also an important matter in the GDR. In the center of East Berlin it might have been the central issue.

The gaze onto the silhouette and the landscaped space of Berlin was to become an object of visual mis-en-scene, as shown by the 950 meter long Nordbogenbrücke (Rudolf-Wissell-Brücke) in West Berlin. Opened to traffic in 1961, the raised road resting on only twelve supports enabled its users an unhindered 16-meter-high, nearly cinematic perception of the Berlin glacial valley that was already the basis of Hans Scharoun's plans.

A particularly ambitious example of the flowing traffic mise-en-scène can be found at Berlin-Tegel Airport, a design that was the result of an architectural competition held in 1965.[30] Linked to the city highway near Rudolf-Wissell-Brücke, Germany's first drive-in airport was realized (fig. 10). Here, the architects Meinhard von Gerkan, Volkwin Marg and Klaus Nickel in addition to complying with Lufthansa's request for a car-based link between road and air traffic, they also created an unprecedented elegant monument to flowing traffic.[31] The particularly impressive thing about Berlin-Tegel is its artful spatial staging of the change in mobility as a series of architectural and dynamizing images. An emblematic image already emerged during the approach to the airport, by a slight gradient of the road, just before the access tunnel, the reception hall seems to be located directly on the runway. With its cut off ends, rounded façades, and recessed ground floor, the building from here looks like a passenger airplane (fig. 11). The effect intended here is also illustrated in visual material from the 1978 monograph on the architectural firm, where precisely this perspectival overlapping of terminal and airplane was shown.[32] The sunken road beneath the runway contrasts with the upward, swinging movement of the entrance. Inside the terminal the motifs of mobility continue: alongside the dynamizing angles and balustrade motifs, a shopping arcade, as a genuine urban motif of a "covered street," links the two rings of departure gates. Finally, the access to the gangway picks up as a theme the flowing, intermodal shift with its bright red façade elements. The close intervals of the softline windows refer to the airplanes standing directly beyond, and the 750 meter long "belly façade" clearly stands out from the rest of the concrete structure.[33]

Summary

The idea of flowing traffic and the city built for traffic equally shaped urban planning in the post-war period in East and West Berlin. Especially in the 1960s, when motorization in the West became a mass phenomenon and in the east had long become a consumerist promise, streets were expanded on a large scale even in the city center. Increasing motorization was considered an indication of economic growth and was staged in space. Even if demonstrations and mass assemblies still played an important role in urban planning and design decisions in East Berlin during the late 1950s, the automobile – as is clearly shown by the planned raised roadway – had already taken on great importance at the turn of the 1960s.[34] The principles of East Berlin center planning corresponded to the ideas of a visual city, to be kept in motion – virtually like a monumentalized festival architecture. This intention, as formulated in the "16 basic principles of urban planning" in 1950 by Lothar Bolz, minister of reconstruction, was reinterpreted in the 1960s in the spirit of modernism and based on solutions for the automo-

11 _ Tegel Airport, View from the access road to the terminal building, circa 1975

bile.[35] Decisive in the competition between the systems, in East Berlin the relatively free access to real estate made such generous planning possible – unthinkable in such dimensions in the West.

In West Berlin, traffic planning played a decisive role in modernizing the city since the post World War II reconstruction began. Contemporary publications emphasized that road and residential construction needed to be implemented as a rejuvenation that was seen as urgently necessary to strengthen economic power. New squares, including Innsbrucker Platz and Ernst-Reuter-Platz, new neighborhoods, like the Opernviertel or Märkisches Viertel, or central streets, like the "city-ribbon" at the Urania with the planned raised roadbed, were spacious streetscapes framed by rhythmically arranged high-rises, that explicitly need to be seen in relation to the perception from the automobile. Unusual architecture from the late 1960s, such as the Bierpinsel (Beer Brush) or the pop-art architecture of Raststätte Dreilinden, presented flowing traffic as an image of modernity and prosperity.

West Berlin's city highway took on a central importance, and it is no accident that since the 1960s explicitly automobile-linked and extremely prestigious large building complexes were arranged in relation to it, including the two *Gesamtkunstwerke* Tegel Airport and Internationales Congress Centrum ICC, and not least the highway crossing at Schlangenbader Straße, built in 1972 and still unique today. Already with Rudolf-Wissell-Brücke and the Halensee interchange, in addition to realizing technical solutions, street artworks were created in the form of consciously designed engineering structures that organize an aesthetic experience of driving and thus a relation to the city. But most importantly, West Berlin's city highway took on a compensatory importance after 1961. As Werner Düttmann summed it up in 1967: "Today, the city is surrounded by a wall, as in the Middle Ages, and has to try to make possible the happiness of its citizens within narrow confines. And the residents are pleased that Mies van der Rohe has built his museum on Kemperplatz, are proud of the Philharmonie, they curse the new housing developments, and those that live there enjoy living there. They race down their city highway, because it gives them a sense of distance and a feeling of expanse, the expanse that had always characterized this city."[36] The promise of liberty and the emotional experience of the fast road with its link to flowing lines, unlimited driving, and unusual, modern architecture would form a large-scale conception of West Berlin as a location of progress.

In the early 1970s, Berlin photographer Wolf Lücking began to explore this visual experience in his photography. He mounted a camera on the roof of his car, and used a remote release to photograph West Berlin from the perspective of drivers. The series of black and white panorama pictures that he published in 1973 are unique documents of modern urban photography.[37] Lücking moved his camera-car systematically through the parts of the city that were redesigned in the 1960s, recording the city highway, Bundesallee, Schloßstraße in Steglitz, Ernst-Reuter-Platz, but also Märkisches Viertel and Gropiusstadt. With his unadorned photographs that scarcely show any depth Lücking shows the limits of the "automobile perception" of the city, that functions less as an architectural single image and more as a deliberately composed flow of images: for his contemporaries this was somewhat alienating, leading them to reject the pictures.[38]

NOTES

1 _ See Barbara Schmucki, *Der Traum vom Verkehrsfluss: Städtische Verkehrsplanung seit 1945 im deutsch-deutschen Vergleich* (Frankfurt am Main, 2001).

2 _ Frank Seehausen, "Rhetorik einer mobilen Moderne: Visuelle Inszenierungen von Stadt durch Autobahnen und Hochstraßen in der Nachkriegsmoderne," *Die Metaphorik der Autobahn: Literatur, Kunst, Film und Architektur nach 1945*, ed. Jan Röhnert (Vienna, 2014), pp. 35-76.

3 _ See the maps on Interbau 1957 in *Bauwelt* (1957) 24, p. 593.

4 _ Ural Kalender, *Die Geschichte der Verkehrsplanung Berlins* (Cologne, 2012), pp. 354 and 374.

5 _ Senatsbeschluss No. 715/55 on the building of the city ring highway.

6 _ Hanns Tockuss, "Ein städtisches Schnellstraßennetz am Beispiel Berlin," *Planen und Bauen im neuen Deutschland*, ed. Bund Deutscher Architekten (Cologne, 1960), pp. 90-91.

7 _ The motif of the stamp showed the ensemble from a driver's perspective. The first day covers and sheets in several variants also added a bird's eye view over the square looking towards the Radio Tower and a perspective from behind the steering wheel of a Mercedes.

8 _ On the reception of American photography, see Jutta von Zitzewitz, *Die Stadt, der Highway und die Kamera: Fotografie und Urbanisierung in New York zwischen 1945 und 1965* (Berlin, 2014). In Germany, numerous books were published that were intended for a general audience. For example: Hermann Schreiber, *Sinfonie der Straße: Der Mensch und seine Wege von den Karawanenpfaden zum Super-Highway* (Berlin, 1956). This volume was published in several editions until 1965. Urban and traffic planners also systematically collected photographs of American highways. See Museum Folkwang, ed., *Urbanität gestalten: Stadtbaukultur in Essen und im Ruhrgebiet 1900 bis 2000* (Essen, 2011), pp. 186-187.

9 _ See the intersection of Harbor and Hollywood Freeways in Los Angeles.

10 _ The structure called the "Pretzel" links Grand Central Parkway, die Grand Central Parkway Extension, then Union Turnpike, the Interboro Parkway and Queens Boulevard with one another. See Sigfried Giedion, *Space, Time and Architecture* (Cambridge, Mass., 1946), p. 557.

11 _ Directly after his strip, Rolf Schwedler commissioned the planning of a graded network of Berlin highways that was based largely on the surface use plan from 1950s and was to include a ring with four interior tangents. See Kalender, *Die Geschichte der Verkehrsplanung Berlins*, see note 4, p. 368. The results of Fürlinger's team, that travelled around the US in Winter 1957, were presented in 1961 in a research report: Rationalisierungs-Kuratorium der deutschen Wirtschaft, ed., *Stadtautobahnen. Erfahrungen deutscher Fachleute in den USA* (Wiesbaden, 1961). For more on the trip, see "Dreispurig durch Berlin," *Der Spiegel* (1959) 3, pp. 46-47.

12 _ *Bauwelt* (1969) 15, pp. 491-492.

13 _ The realization was completed in altered form: the building is popularly referred to as the "Bierpinsel", or "beer brush."

14 _ In 1947 the planning collective under the direction of Hans Scharoun presented a complete redesign of Berlin on the basis of a network of highways using grade separation. See Johann Friedrich Geist and Klaus Kürvers, *Das Berliner Mietshaus 1945-1989* (Munich, 1989), pp. 180-181.

15 _ The decision to building the Television Tower was made in September 1964 and corresponded to the idea of creating a characteristic city silhouette. This was based on a suggestion of the French architect Jean Faugeron to build a tower on at the end of Friedrichstraße that he presented in 1957/58 as a variant in the framework of the capital competition. He sought to create an unmistakable capital legible from an airplane with outstanding architectural-political monuments. See Berlinische Galerie, ed., *Hauptstadt Berlin: Internationaler städtebaulicher Ideenwettbewerb 1957/58* (Berlin, 1990), pp. 105-106, 114-115.

16 _ Eberhard Radicke, "Untersuchungsgrundlagen für die Neugestaltung schwer belasteter städtischer Straßenknotenpunkte," *Verkehr und Stadtplanung*, ed. Deutsche Bauakademie (Berlin, 1958), p. 12. Eberhard Radicke was a member of the Forschungsinstitut für Gebiets-, Stadt-, und Dorfplanung, Deutsche Bauakademie. Members of the engineering collective also included: Erwin Schulz (head architect of the Institute), Kurt Thiele, Paul Preßke.

17 _ Ibid., p. 56.

18 _ See Dorothea Tscheschner, "Der Alexanderplatz: Seine Entwicklung nach 1945," *Alexanderplatz. Städtebaulicher Ideenwettbewerb*, ed. Kristin Feireiss (Berlin, 1994), p. 51. Clothoids, which were especially easy to drive due to their curvature which always slowly increased proportionally to the length of the arch, were first used in highway construction in 1934, and during the second half of the 1950s became a fundamental element in highway planning after the publication of *Die Klothoide als Trassierungselement* by Hugo Kasper, Walter Schürba and Hans Lorenz (Bonn, 1954).

19 _ LAB 100-05/1279, April 23, 1964, signed by N. Ullas, I. Bordulow, W. Chodatajew. See Kalender, *Die Geschichte der Verkehrsplanung Berlins*, p. 433 (note 27).

20 _ See Manuel Sanchez-Arcas, *Stadt und Verkehr: Verkehrs- und Stadtplanung in den USA und in Westeuropa* (Berlin, 1968), p. 16.

21 _ On garages in East Berlin, see René Hartmann, *Architektur für Automobile. Hochgaragen und Parkhäuser in Deutschland. Eine Auto[mobil]-Vision im 20. Jahrhundert.* (Thesis, TU Berlin, Institut für Kunstwissenschaft und Historische Urbanistik, Fachbereich Kunstgeschichte) (Berlin 2014).

22 _ Peter Behrens, "Einfluß von Zeit- und Raumausnutzung auf moderne Formentwicklung," *Jahrbuch des deutschen Werkbundes 3. Der Verkehr*, ed. Deutscher Werkbund (Jena, 1914), pp. 7-10.

23 _ Erich Mendelsohn, "Die internationale Übereinstimmung des neuen Baugedankens oder Dynamik und Funktion" (1923), *Das Gesamtschaffen des Architekten* (1930) (Braunschweig/ Wiesbaden, 1988), p. 28.

24 _ On the mutual relationship of the automobile and architecture, see Frank Seehausen, *Das Auto als Architekt*, lecture at the TU Berlin, January 2014; Giedion, *Space, Time and Architecture*, see note 10; Kevin Lynch, Donald Appleyard, and John R. Myer, *The View from the Road* (Cambridge, Mass., 1964).

25 _ Hans Schmidt, "Stadt und Raum," *Deutsche Architektur* (1963) 11, pp. 666-671.

26 _ Ibid., pp. 669-670.

27 _ On the image-sign theory, see Thomas Topfstedt, *Städtebau in der DDR 1955-1971* (Leipzig, 1988), pp. 48, 59, 168-169 and Bruno Flierl, *Zur sozialistischen Architekturentwicklung in der DDR: Theoretische Probleme und Analysen in der Praxis* (Berlin, 1979), pp. 132-133. Quoted in: Gerd Wessel and Gerd Zeuchner, "Räumliche

Gliederung und Raumwirkung," *Deutsche Architektur* (1974) 4, pp. 214–215.

28 _ See Bruno Flierl, "Synthese von Architektur und bildender Kunst im Wandel," *Architektur und Kunst* (Dresden, 1984), p. 30. On the political marking using art in architecture, see Elmar Kossel, *Hermann Henselmann und die Moderne. Eine Studie zur Moderne-rezeption in der Architektur der DDR* (Königstein im Taunus, 2013).

29 _ Today, the former press café is used as a steakhouse. The frieze still exists, but is covered.

30 _ The open competition for architects from West Germany, West Berlin, and countries in the EEC and EFTA was announced in May 1965. 68 proposals were submitted by November 15. The international jury under the direction of Senate Building Commissioner Werner Düttmann met in March 1966 and awarded the design to the young office of Gerkan, Marg und Partner. See Flughafen-Gesellschaft mbH/Berlin Airport Company, eds., *The New Terminal Area of the Berlin-Tegel Airport: Result of a Competition* (Berlin, 1967).

31 _ See Günther Kühne, "Einen Flughafen planen," *Bauwelt* (1964) 23, 649; Hans Süssenguth, "Das Drive-in-Flughafen-Projekt der Lufthansa," *Bauwelt* (1964) 23, p. 658. Although Lufthansa was not allowed to serve Tegel, the VO were internationally standard. The plan expressly included a refusal of a subway link. Instead, 45 percent of the guests were to arrive by bus, 25 percent by taxi, and 30 percent in their own cars. See *Bauwelt* (1966) 22, p. 659.

32 _ Meinhard von Gerkan, Volkwin Marg, *Architektur 1966–78 von Gerkan, Marg und Partner* (Stuttgart, 1978), p. 35.

33 _ Ibid., pp. 52–53.

34 _ Gerhard Kosel, "Aufbau des Zentrums der Hauptstadt des demokratischen Deutschlands Berlin," *Deutsche Architektur* (1958) 4, pp. 182-183.

35 _ Siehe Lothar Bolz, *Von deutschem Bauen: Reden und Aufsätze* (Berlin, 1951), pp. 44–45.

36 _ Werner Düttmann, "...Was wir hier und in unserer Stadt tun: Vortrag zu den Berliner Bauwochen," *Berlin ist viele Städte* (Berlin, 1984), p. 38.

37 _ Horst Cornelsen (Fotos Wolf Lücking), *Gebaut in 25 Jahren: Berlin (West)* (Hamburg, 1973). My thanks go to Ursula Müller for this reference.

38 _ An interview between Ursula Müller and Wolf Lücking at Berlinische Galerie on March 16, 2012.

PICTURE CREDITS

Fig. 1 _ Schematic depiction of the system of highways in Berlin with stages of development, circa 1968, Senate for Building and Housing Berlin © Senate for Building and Housing Berlin

Fig. 2 _ Junction city motorway – AVUS taken from the radio tower towards Halensee, aerial photograph: Otto Borutta, circa 1968, Berlinische Galerie © Berlinische Galerie

Fig. 3 _ Junction Halensee with Rathenauplatz, June 3, 1960, postcard, Archive Frank Seehausen © holder of rights unknown

Fig. 4 _ Planned elevated stretch of road on Rognitzstraße/Knobelsdorff-brücke, perspective drawing: unknown author, circa 1955, Berlin State Archive, File B Rep. 009, no. 88 © holder of rights unknown/Berlin State Archive

Fig. 5 _ Junction "The Pretzel", New York City, aerial photograph, circa 1937, repro from: Sigfried Giedion, *Space, Time and Architecture. The Growth of a New Tradition* (Harvard, 1946), p. 557.

Fig. 6 _ Gerhard Murza, View from the visitors' platform of the TV tower to Alexanderplatz and the second constructed section of Karl-Marx-Allee, circa 1973, repro from: Hans Joachim Kaddatz and Gerhard Murza, *Berlin – Architektur in der Hauptstadt der DDR* (Leipzig, 1973), p. 42.

Fig. 7 _ Collective Eberhard Radicke, Elevated street at Alexanderplatz with depiction of the buildings along the edge, based on sketches by Josef Kaiser, 1958, repro from: Deutsche Bauakademie, ed., *Verkehr und Stadt-planung* (Berlin, 1958), p. 55, fig. 27.

Fig. 8 _ Eberhard Radicke, Traffic inquiry regarding intersection Alexanderplatz, basis for a new design of heavily used urban intersections, repro from: Deutsche Bauakademie, ed., Verkehr und Stadtplanung (Berlin, 1958), fig. 22.

Fig. 9 _ Josef Kaiser with Günter Jannikoy, Elevated road at Alexander-platz, junction Liebknechtstraße, with building along edge, perspective drawing, 1957, photograph: Gisela Dutschmann, 1960, repro from 13 x 18 cm negative, Berlinische Galerie BG-AS 1436.003349 © Michael Kaiser, repro © Gisela Dutschmann/ Berlinische Galerie

Fig. 10 _ Meinhard von Gerkan, Volkwin Marg, Tegel Airport, model with both rings of gates, scale 1:1000, photo-grapher unknown, circa 1968, Archive of gmp Architekten von Gerkan, Marg und Partner © Archiv gmp Architekten von Gerkan, Marg und Partner

Fig. 11 _ Tegel Airport, View from the access road to the terminal building, photographer unknown, circa 1975, Archive of gmp Architekten von Gerkan, Marg und Partner © Archiv gmp Architekten von Gerkan, Marg und Partner

Serial Diversity

Sollmannweg

Storkower Straße

Schillingstraße

Kandeler Weg

Fritz-Erler-Allee

Treuenbrietzener Straße

Erich-Kuttner-Straße

Leipziger Straße

Bismarckstraße

Grüntaler Straße

Alte Jakobstraße

Storkower Straße

Alexandrinenstraße

Alte Jakobstraße

Fischerinsel

Imbuschweg

Rathausstraße

Glinkastraße

Ritterstraße

Schillingstraße

Klausingring

Berlin

Fritz-Erler-Allee

Bismarckstraße

Wilhelmsruher Damm

Theodor-Loos-Weg

Wilhelmsruher Damm

Unter den Linden

Storkower Straße

Krowelstraße

Unter den Linden

Fritz-Erler-Allee

Maulbeerallee

Schillingstraße

Unter den Linden

Maulbeerallee

Neuköllner Straße

Neuköllner Straße

Wallstraße

Johannisthaler Chaussee

Unter den Linden

Falkenhagener Feld

Berlin

Franz Heinrich Sobotka, Gustav Müller, Pepper-House, circa 1964

Collective Peter Senf, Office building of the GDR's foreign trade company Wiratex, 1964

Josef Kaiser, Ministry for Foreign Affairs, view of the model, circa 1964

Roland Korn, Heinz Scharlipp, Hans-Erich Bogatzky, Interhotel Stadt Berlin, 1971

Helmut Hentrich, Hubert Petschnigg, Europa-Center, circa 1964

Hans Wolff-Grohmann, High-rise building Handjeryplatz, 1962

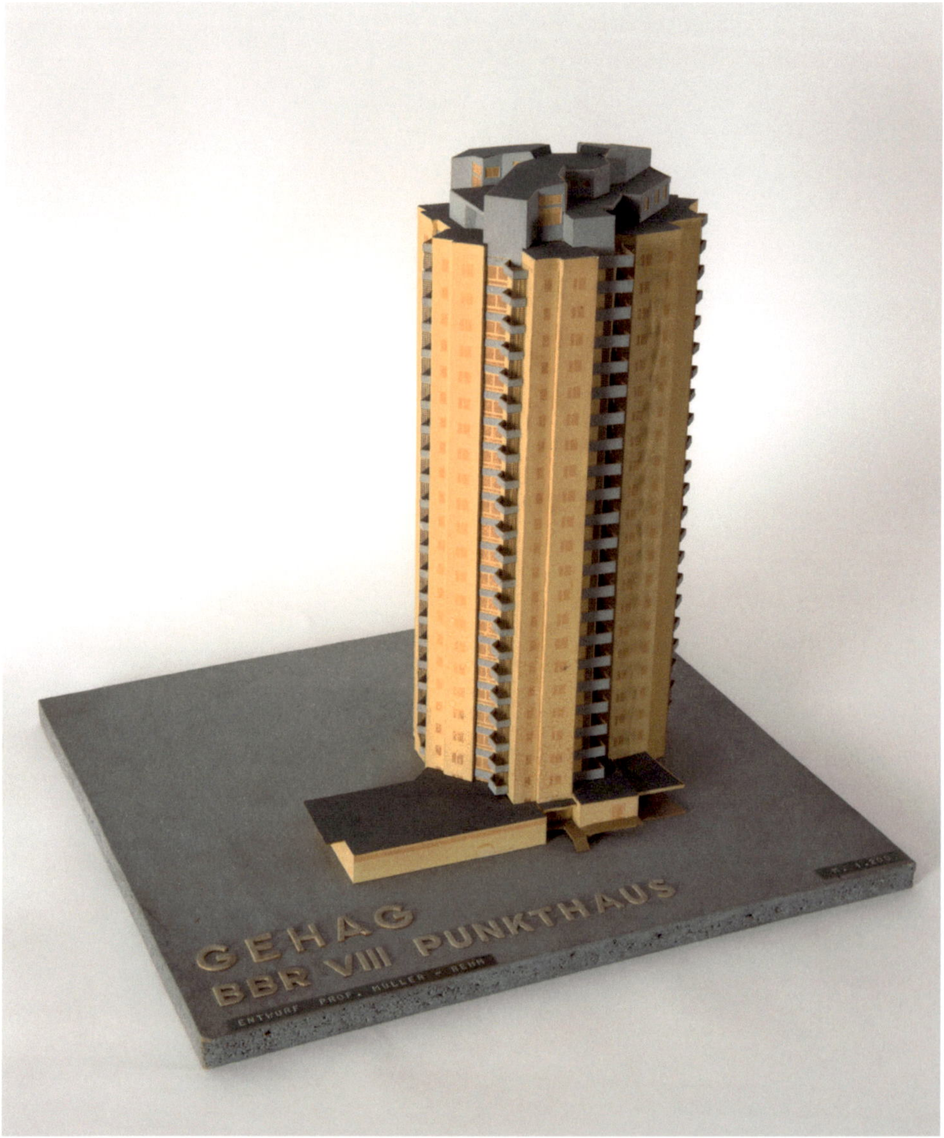

Klaus Müller-Rehm, Spindel-House, Sollmannweg, large-scale housing estate Britz-Buckow-Rudow (BBR), circa 1970

Walter Gropius, Alexander Svianovic, Residential high-rise building “Ideal,” large-scale housing estate Britz-Buckow-Rudow (BBR), photograph of the model, circa 1966

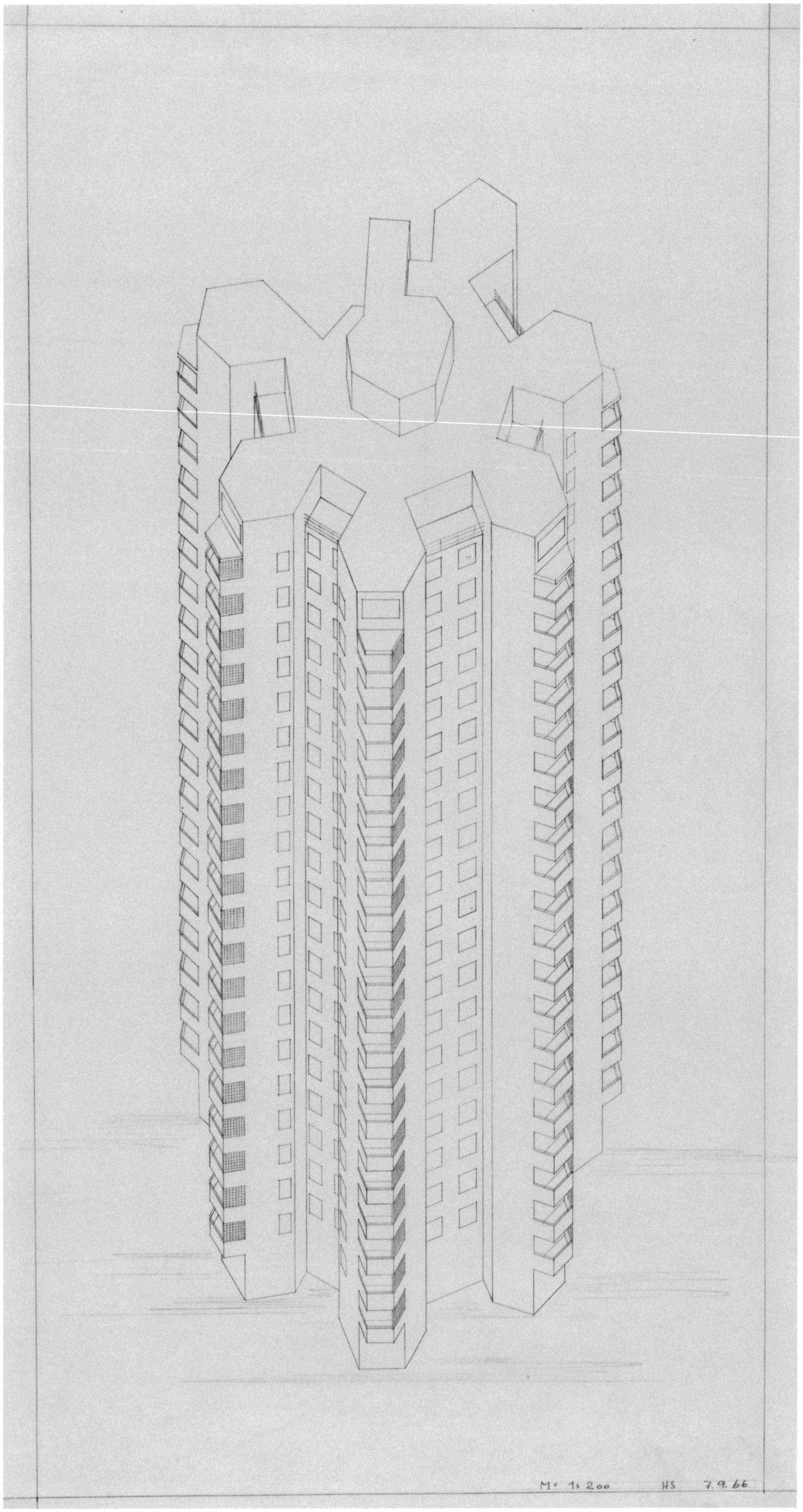

Klaus Müller-Rehm, “Sternhaus,” Residential area Heerstraße Nord, 1966

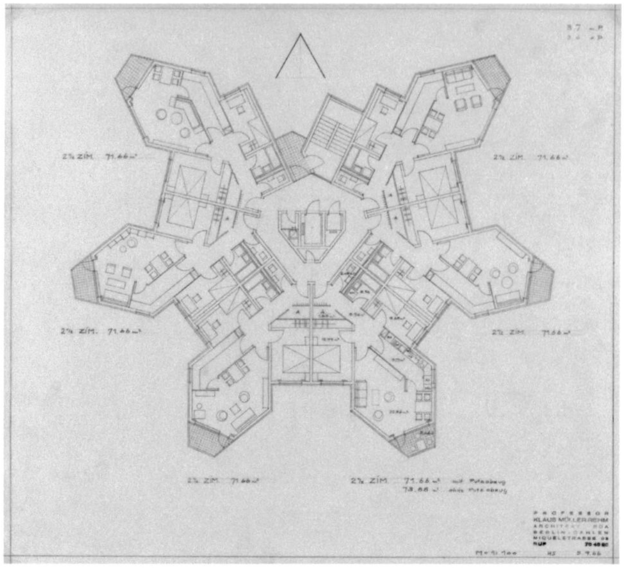

Klaus Müller-Rehm, ”Sternhaus,” Residential area Heerstraße Nord, 1966

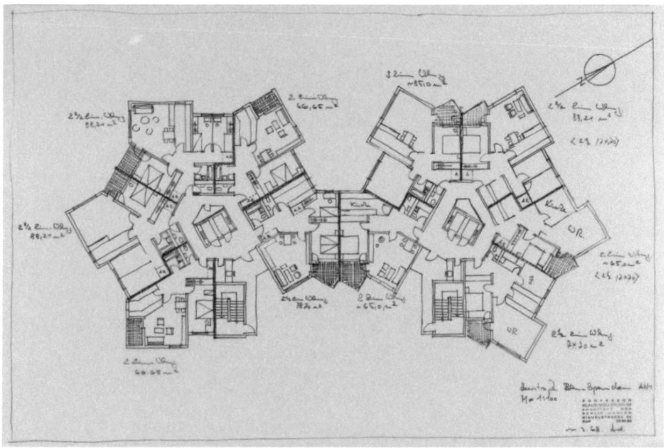

Klaus Müller Rehm, Residential buildings Heerstraße Nord, normal floor type C, 1968

Manfred Zumpe, 30-storey residential tower block using large panel construction method 6.3 MP, 1971 (not built)

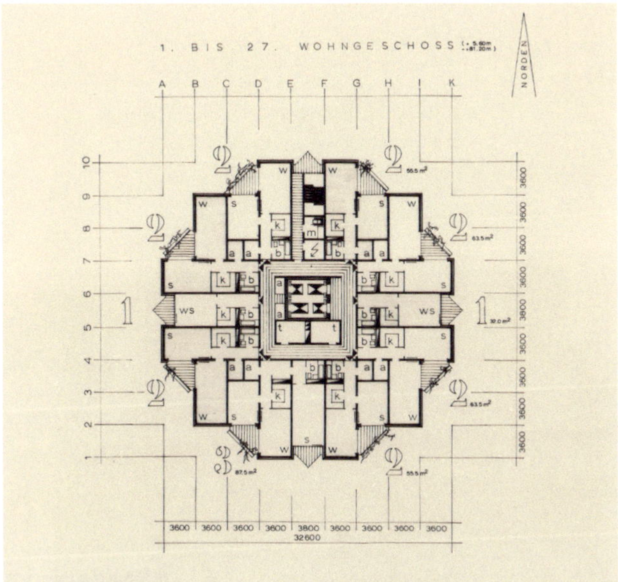

Manfred Zumpe, Ground plan of 30-storey residential tower block, 1971

Josef Kaiser, Design for a monolithic industrial building, residential high-rise blocks using sliding panel and tunnel sheeting methods, circa 1969 (not built)

Manfred Zumpe, Hans-Peter Schmiedel, Design for residential tower block type, circa 1968 (not built)

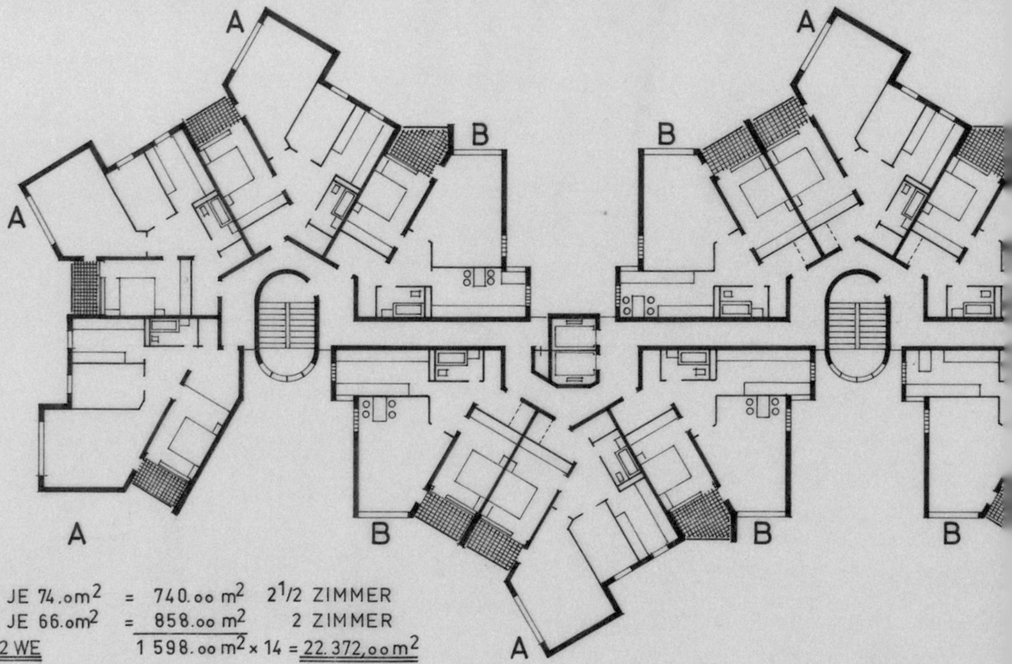

10 WE TYP A JE 74.om² = 740.oo m² 2 1/2 ZIMMER
13 WE TYP B JE 66.om² = 858.oo m² 2 ZIMMER
23 WE ×14 = 322 WE 1 598.oo m² × 14 = 22.372,oo m²

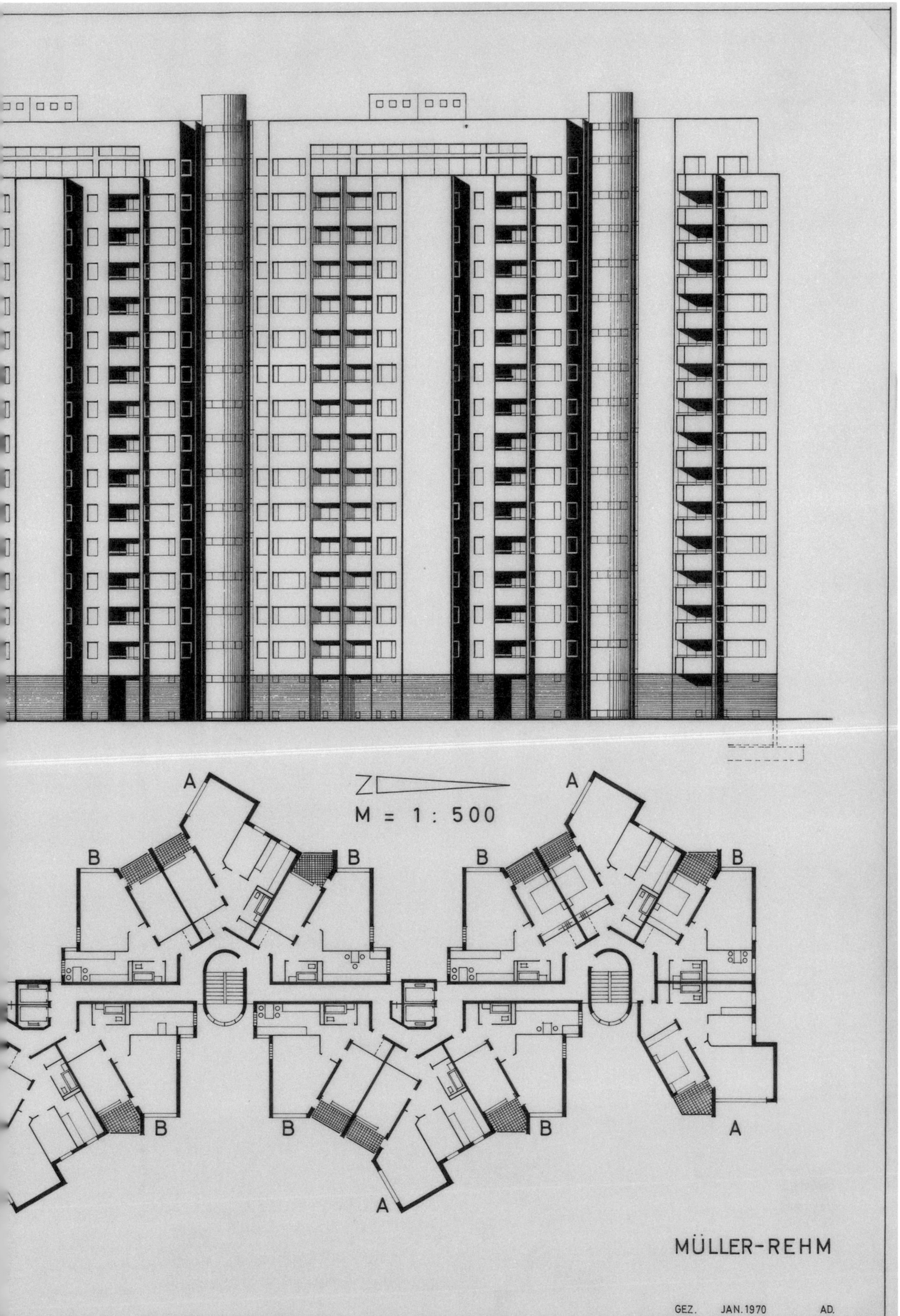

Klaus Müller-Rehm, Residential area Heerstraße Nord, façade and ground plan forms, 1970

Stanislaus von Moos

"No Fear of Monotony" On Hans Schmidt and Edmund N. Bacon

1 _ Arkadi Mordwinow, Residential buildings along Kalugaer Avenue, after 1934

2 _ Paul Artaria, Hans Schmidt, Schorenmatten Estate, Basel-Eglisee, 1929

In 1952, when Kurt Liebknecht presented the magnificent volume *Dreißig Jahre sowjetische Architektur* to his Swiss colleague Hans Schmidt at the end of the latter's visit to Berlin, it would have been difficult to imagine that the architecture praised in the book was about to be discarded just two years later (fig. 1).[1] We do not know whether Liebknecht, then president of the Deutsche Bauakademie, already entertained the possibility of bringing Schmidt to Berlin at that time. Schmidt, who had moved to the Soviet Union in 1930 and who later played a major role in planning and building the city of Orsk, among other things, before hastily returning to Basel in 1937, held several lectures in Switzerland during the war to foster understanding among his colleagues for the architectural culture of socialist realism.[2] Though that must have made a positive impression in Berlin, it was not what four years later, in 1956, was valued most by his German comrades: i.e. his historical role as a key ideologue of industrialization in building and his solid expertise in this field (fig. 2). On January 1, 1956, Schmidt began working as chief architect at the Institut für Typung (Institute for Typification) at East Berlin's Deutsche Bauakademie.

"No Fear of Monotony"

"No fear of monotony!" This is what, at the very beginning of his career in Berlin, Schmidt had to say in response to the then widespread lamentations regarding the danger of anonymization in the environment.[3] "One should not use the term 'boring' schematically!", Schmidt wrote somewhat later. "The uniform can, just like its opposite, the multifarious, be seen as justified, meaningful, even beautiful in certain circumstances, while it may be seen as meaningless or ugly in others."[4] "Monotony," Schmidt insists, is not inherent to things themselves, rather it results in the beholder from a "negative reaction" to the effect of uniformity and the "massive repetition of identical elements."[5] Thus, the phenomenon existed "long before the emergence of industrial mass production." And furthermore: "If it is posited that the sensation of monotony has its cause in the unlimited repetition

3 _ "Industrial building in Germany during the 1920s," from: Hans Schmidt, *Beiträge zur Architektur*, 1965

of identical elements, the key to its abolition lies on the one hand in limiting their number and on the other in creating an overarching whole that represents an irrepeatable entity."[6] For example, the "endless series of identical windows on Prague's Hradčany, the façades of Venice's Piazza S. Marco or the Rue de Rivoli, one kilometer long [...] are not considered monotonous because they are subject to the overall form of the given situation, to the dominant façade of a square, or of a long city street" (fig. 4).[7] Schmidt found, for example, that the "modern" Western expansion of Karl-Marx-Allee (formerly Stalinallee) seems "unnecessarily divided into small sections," since the length of the blocks had been limited to 80 meters. To ameliorate the situation, he suggested combining the residential blocks to extremely long rows, for the "large form" in urban design allows us to overlook "repetition that could be conceived as monotonous", provided that our attention be directed towards the whole (fig. 5).[8]

The Pros and Cons of the Nineteenth Century

Schmidt was of course aware that with his pleas in favor of the traditional form of the closed urban street he was contradicting the dogma of "open planning", and especially Le Corbusier's assertion that the *rue corridor* has no place in modern urbanism. In fact, it was this very position that Schmidt now considered outdated. Even though its role as a means of circulation has changed, the street has "not lost its importance as a space and location of urban life," Schmidt writes. In French urban planning, he continues, the current task thus is seen as the *recherche de la rue*, the "search for the street."[9] What he probably had in mind was the reconstruction of Le Havre by Auguste Perret, an architect he admired (fig. 6).[10]

In the "official" architectural schools of Western Europe and the United States, the 19th century city was no longer current as a model after 1945. And yet, traditional urbanism had not simply disappeared from the radar of urbanistic thinking. The modernization of Paris under Napoleon III was still the standard against which later attempts at bringing the entire city under a unifying plan were measured. But regardless of the grandiose monotony of the seemingly endless Rue de Rivoli (built long before Haussmann's interven-

4 _ Hans Schmidt, Studies on the problem of repetition in urban development, from: Hans Schmidt, *Beiträge zur Architektur*, 1965

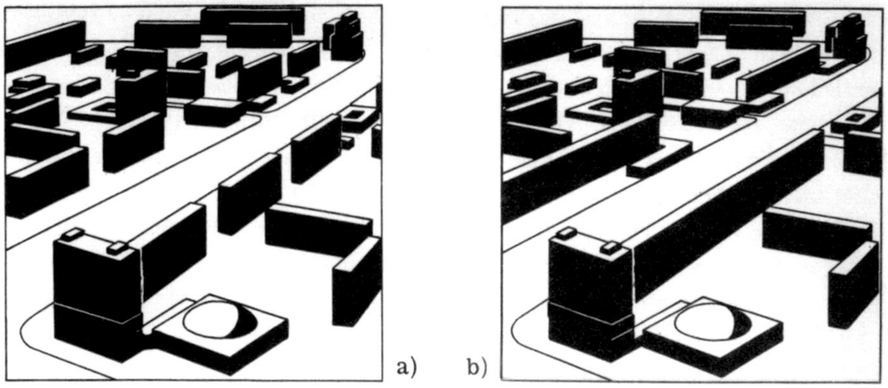

5 _ Hans Schmidt, Karl Marx-Allee with the Haus des Lehrers as realized (a), and with standardized building along the edge of the street (b), from: Hans Schmidt, Rolf Linke, Gerd Wessel, *Gestaltung und Umgestaltung der Stadt. Beiträge zum sozialistischen Städtebau*, 1969

6 _ Auguste Perret, Reconstruction of Le Havre, France, 1945–64, axonometric view of Place Gambetta with Bassin du Commerce, circa 1950

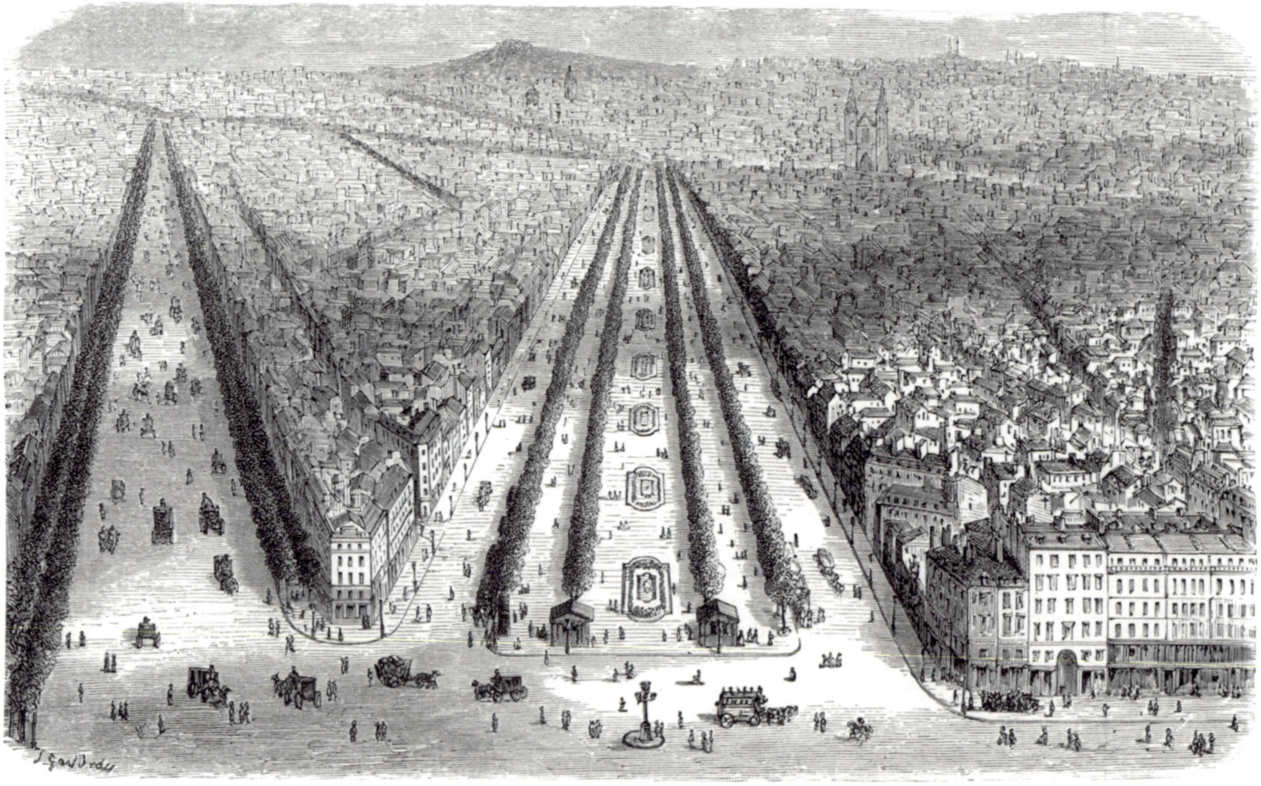

7 _ View from the Colonne de la Bastille to Boulevard Richard Lenoir, Paris, probably around 1870, from: Sigfried Giedion, *Space, Time and Architecture*, 1967

tions) and the perspectival draw of the Boulevards Beaumarchais and Richard Lenoir that organize the labyrinth of Central Paris as if with a magic wand towards the vanishing point of the Place de la Bastille, this form of city was now considered historical (fig. 7).[11] Le Corbusier's verdict against the *rue corridor* had cancelled it from the agenda pf progressive urbanism, tacitly yielding to the more recent, American, model of organizing transportation by ways of urban freeways – this "pyramid building with a vengeance", as Lewis Mumford put it at an early date: "a tomb of concrete roads and ramps covering the dead corpse of the city."[12]

Edmund N. Bacon and Philadelphia

For Hans Schmidt, *longue durée* in urban design was inconceivable without considering Munich's Ludwigstraße, Haussmann's Parisian boulevards, and not least Moscow's avenues of the 1930s (see figs. 1 and 4).[13] Even though socialist realism was no longer in power as state doctrine, the classical tradition continued to be seen as the one principle capable of organizing the visuals of the technical era over the long term. What was at stake was in fact nothing less than the survival of the architect as an authority in the production of the environment, if not, actually, to bring about a "renaissance of the architect."[14] Granted the obvious differences in the way urbanism was practiced here and there, Edmund N. Bacon (1910–2005), Schmidt's somewhat younger American colleague who became chairman of the Philadelphia City Planning Commission in 1949, argued no differently.

It was Bacon who made Philadelphia into the widely known laboratory of a comparatively "reasonable", even "soft" form of urban renewal (fig. 9).[15] While New York's Robert Moses had entire neighborhoods torn down to create new

8 _ Edmund N. Bacon, *Stadtplanung von Athen bis Brasilia*, Zurich 1968

9 _ The so-called "Triangle Area" between Market Street West and Benjamin Franklin Parkway with the already partly realized Penn Center, Philadelphia, aerial view, circa 1960

housing, Bacon was able to move from the "bird's-eye viewpoint of most planning" to a more cautious "renewal on the house-to-house scale."[16] His work met with interest around the world.[17] In his *opus magnum Design of Cities: From Athens to Brasilia* (fig. 8), written to anchor his work as an urban planner in Philadelphia in a universal context, Bacon even tried to present "his" Philadelphia as a synthesis of 16th century Rome and 20th century Brasília, casting himself as a reincarnation of Sixtus V (fig. 11).[18] Just as Hans Schmidt, Gerd Wessel, and Rolf Linke will do somewhat later in their book *Gestaltung und Umgestaltung der Stadt,* Bacon based his argument on insights drawn from the psychology of perception.[19] Using an ink drawing by Francesco Guardi, he sums up what is most important about urban space: the creation of a varied skyline, the animation of the depth of space by ways of differences in height and layerings, the rhythmic placement of accents, the tension between convex and concave forms, etc. In Guardi, this all served the purpose of creating a dynamic relationship among the figures in the image, Bacon argued. To further highlight the priority of the pedestrian in urban design, Bacon uses a plate from G. B. Vignola's *Le due regole della prospettiva pratica to close the chapter* (fig. 10).

"Monotony" is not an explicit concern for Bacon. Standardization and modular order in architecture are not at stake. Indeed the book altogether avoids discussing the aesthetics of current architecture, an issue with which he was confronted daily as the director of the Office of Urban Planning. Instead, he argues for the splendor and variety of the European cityscape, while also dedicating considerable space to Brasília, a "lively expression of city as totality", as he put it (fig. 12). Note that, Philadelphia ultimately proved rather resistant to Bacon's dream of a synthesis between Baroque absolutism and industrialization – but that is another story.[20]

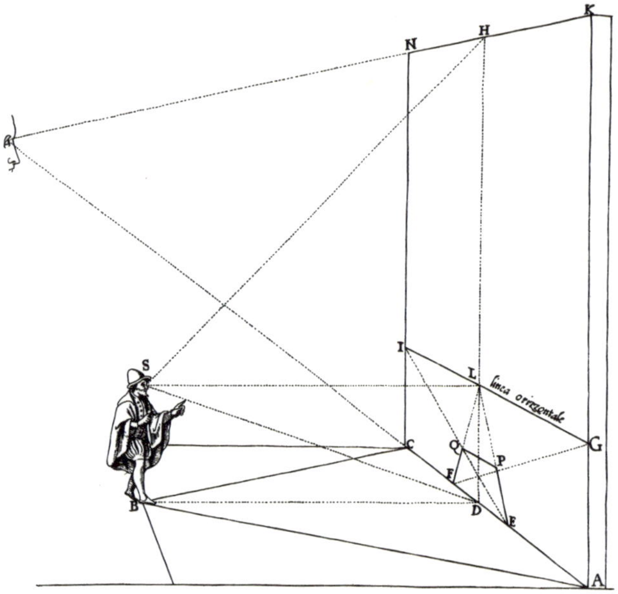

10 _ Giacomo Barozzi da Vignola, Study on the perspective construction of space, 16th century, from: Edmund N. Bacon, *Design of Cities. From Athens to Brasilia*, 1968

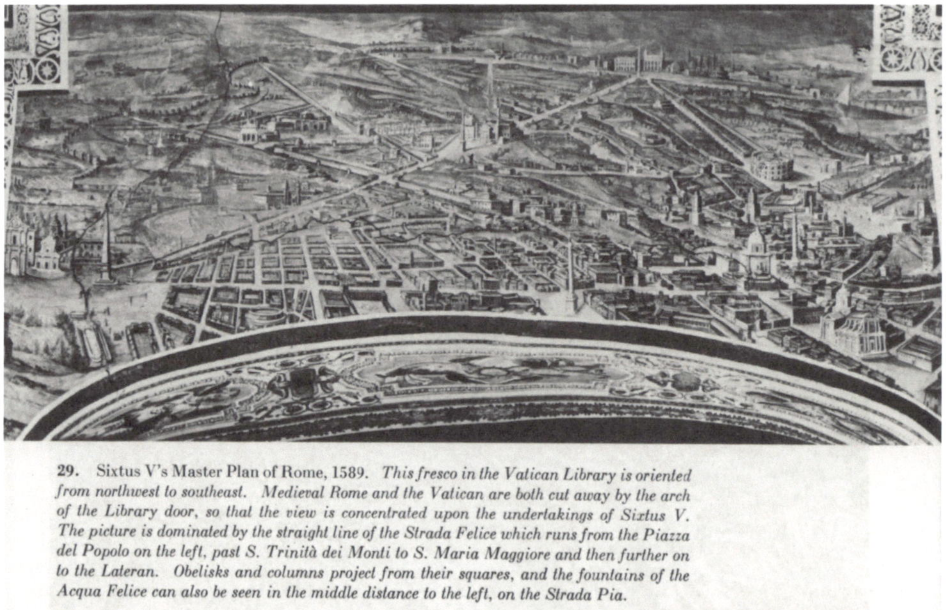

29. Sixtus V's Master Plan of Rome, 1589. *This fresco in the Vatican Library is oriented from northwest to southeast. Medieval Rome and the Vatican are both cut away by the arch of the Library door, so that the view is concentrated upon the undertakings of Sixtus V. The picture is dominated by the straight line of the Strada Felice which runs from the Piazza del Popolo on the left, past S. Trinità dei Monti to S. Maria Maggiore and then further on to the Lateran. Obelisks and columns project from their squares, and the fountains of the Acqua Felice can also be seen in the middle distance to the left, on the Strada Pia.*

11 _ Fresco in the Vatican Library, "Sixtus V's Master Plan of Rome 1589," 16th century, from: Sigfried Giedion, *Space, Time and Architecture*, 1967

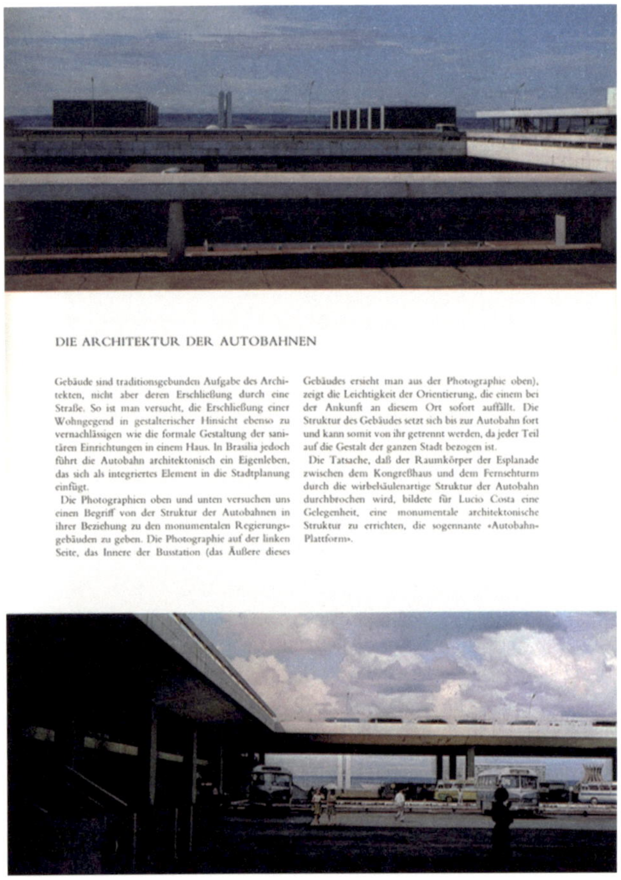

DIE ARCHITEKTUR DER AUTOBAHNEN

Gebäude sind traditionsgebunden Aufgabe des Architekten, nicht aber deren Erschließung durch eine Straße. So ist man versucht, die Erschließung einer Wohngegend in gestalterischer Hinsicht ebenso zu vernachlässigen wie die formale Gestaltung der sanitären Einrichtungen in einem Haus. In Brasilia jedoch führt die Autobahn architektonisch ein Eigenleben, das sich als integriertes Element in die Stadtplanung einfügt.

Die Photographien oben und unten versuchen uns einen Begriff von der Struktur der Autobahnen in ihrer Beziehung zu den monumentalen Regierungsgebäuden zu geben. Die Photographie auf der linken Seite, das Innere der Busstation (das Äußere dieses Gebäudes ersicht man aus der Photographie oben), zeigt die Leichtigkeit der Orientierung, die einem bei der Ankunft an diesem Ort sofort auffällt. Die Struktur des Gebäudes setzt sich bis zur Autobahn fort und kann somit von ihr getrennt werden, da jeder Teil auf die Gestalt der ganzen Stadt bezogen ist.

Die Tatsache, daß der Raumkörper der Esplanade zwischen dem Kongreßhaus und dem Fernsehturm durch die wirbelsäulenartige Struktur der Autobahn durchbrochen wird, bildete für Lucio Costa eine Gelegenheit, eine monumentale architektonische Struktur zu errichten, die sogenannte «Autobahn-Plattform».

12 _ "The architecture of motorways" taking Brasília as an example, from: Edmund N. Bacon, *Design of Cities. From Athens to Brasilia*, 1968

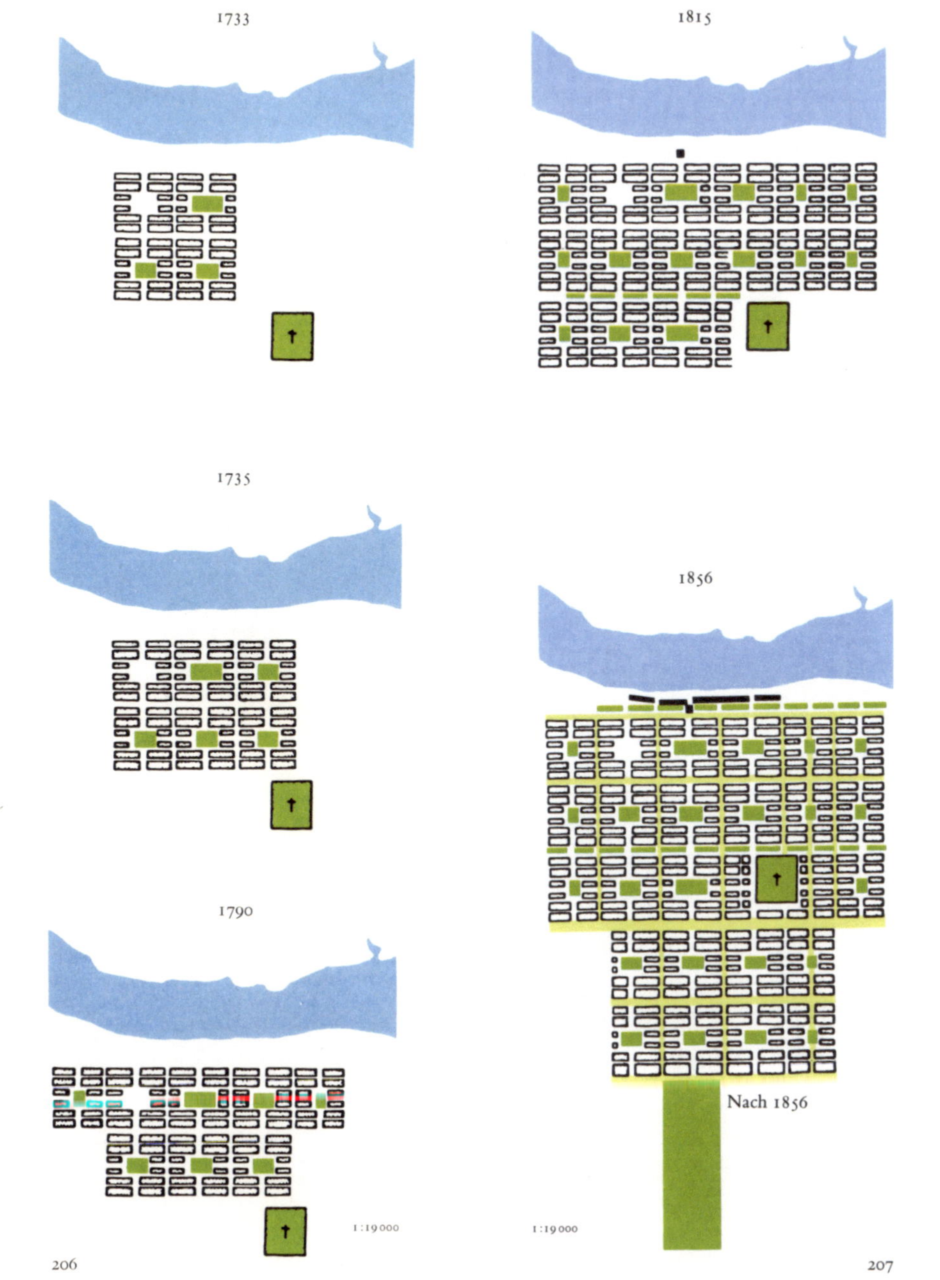

13 _ City maps of Savannah, GA, USA, 1733, 1735, 1790, 1815, 1856, and after 1856, from: Edmund N. Bacon, *Design of Cities. From Athens to Brasilia*, 1968

Vitruvius in America

For Bacon, just as for Schmidt, urbanism is the "linkage of experience along an axis of movement in space."[21] The key tool in this context is "scientific perspective." And, according to Bacon, the triumphs of European urbanism all belong to the Baroque and the Classical eras. Thus, with its countless reproductions of prints from the 18th and 19th centuries, *Design of Cities* turns out to be a veritable compendium of architectural representation in the era of absolutism. And yet, rather than large-scale urban form as such, it is the ways by which a chosen strategy can be adapted to varying needs of the moment that interests Bacon most, an aspect that naturally did not take precedence for the socialist Schmidt. If "uniformity" is of any interest at all to Bacon, then at best in the American adaptations of Renaissance concepts of the ideal city (figs. 13).[22] Since the rigorous grid underlying the American founding cities of the 17th and 18th centuries and the processes of addition and multiplication by which units are linked to one another, i.e. the mechanics of city growth, are primarily revealed in the blueprint, the respective section of the book lacks renderings from the user perspective, otherwise so favored by Bacon. On the other hand, these "monotonous" plan geometries are expressly attributed to "Vitruvius".[23]

In contrast to Bacon's lavishly illustrated book, ostentatiously linking Athens to Brasilia, i.e. the humanist past to the future of the city, if not of mankind, Schmidt's ideas about urban design appeared in the modest format of a small paperback. Compiled in teamwork and subjected to grievous censorship, the book takes on the character of a dry textbook.[24] But when reading, it becomes clear that Schmidt was actually better informed about recent American trends in urban planning than Bacon himself. Rather than following the picturesque tradition as practiced in the "Townscape" movement, Schmidt's considerations on the "image of the city" refer directly to research in communication and information theory undertaken at MIT and elsewhere in the US since the 1950s.[25] Unfortunately, perhaps, the functionalist graphics of the small volume somewhat stand in the way of its humanist agenda, evoking more the writing on the wall of police acumen and control than the humanist ideal of the "perspectival" city, given its logo that rather recalls the 1970s television credits from the still running crime show "Tatort" (fig. 14; see also fig. 10).

If Bruno Flierl is right, Schmidt's role in the GDR ended up being hardly more than that of a "committed consultant and critic."[26] What a contrast to Edmund N. Bacon's comparatively spectacular career in Philadelphia![27] Though it seemed plausible that Schmidt finally became director of the Institut für Theorie und Geschichte at Berlin's Deutsche Bauakademie, considering his ambition to create a "Vitruvius" that would guide architects and planners towards an appropriate handling of the socialist city, it soon became clear that his office increasingly stood in the way of his determination to practice theory as an integral part of his day to day work as an architect in charge of buildings.[28] Being relegated to the realm of theory was all the more difficult for him.

It is futile to speculate to what degree the architect Schmidt might have lived up to his own standards of quality, were he given a chance to practice architecture in his later years. Perhaps his position takes on all the more importance precisely because we cannot automatically identify it with any particular project. At least this was Aldo Rossi's view: Schmidt's characteristic "despise" of modern architecture's pietist belief in the necessity to create a specific form for every individualist desire allowed Schmidt, according to Rossi, "to absorb the entire development of modern architecture on a sure foundation and to live and practice the transition of Soviet architecture from modernism to socialist realism without abjuration, but also without scandal."[29]

One essential key to this non-sectarian understanding of architecture lies in the classical training that Schmidt had enjoyed with his teachers Karl Moser and Hans Bernoulli, and whose message still resonates in the aesthetic rules that he sought to impose upon the "new city" of socialism in the 1960s.

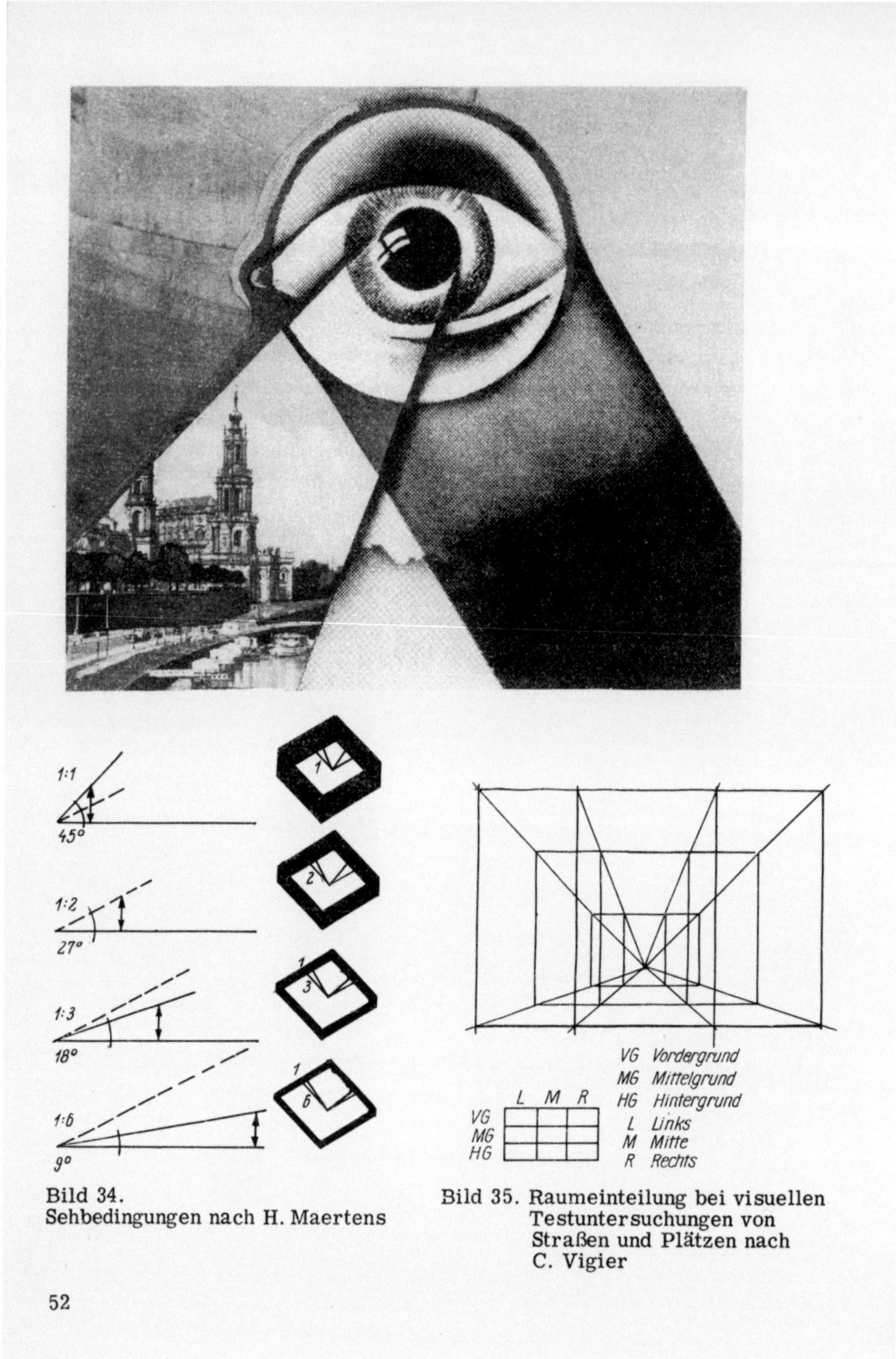

17 _ "Conditions of seeing according to H. Maertens," from: Hans Schmidt, Rolf Linke, Gerd Wessel, *Gestaltung und Umgestaltung der Stadt. Beiträge zum sozialistischen Städtebau*, 1969

NOTES

1 _ For more on Hans Schmidt, see Ursula Suter, ed., *Hans Schmidt 1893–1972: Architekt in Basel, Moskau, Berlin-Ost* (Zurich, 1993). The volume *Dreissig Jahre sowjetische Architektur* can be found in the Hans Schmidt Estate, gta Archiv, ETH Zürich. On the "big turn" in GDR architecture, see "Die große Wende im Bauwesen," *Deutsche Architektur* 5 (1956) 1, pp. 1–3. On the impact of the architectural turn in the Soviet Union, see Andrej V. Ikonnikov, *L'architecture russe de la période soviétique* (Paris, 1990), pp. 283–343.

2 _ See for example Hans Schmidt, "L'architecture en URSS," *Habitation* (1947) 4, pp. 5–11. See also the essay from ten years prior, "Aufgaben der Sowjetarchitekten," *Deutsche Zentralzeitung* (May 18, 1937), somewhat 'purified' by Schmidt for reprinting in the 1960s: see Schmidt, *Beiträge zur Architektur 1924–1964* (Basel, 1965), pp. 108–109.

3 _ Hans Schmidt, "Keine Furcht vor Monotonie," *Deutsche Architektur* (1956) 8, p. 389. Later, the buzzword "monotony" became highly charged in the West as well. For more on this, see Alexander Wilde, *Das Märkische Viertel* (Berlin, 1989), p. 128 and passim, and especially Florian Urban, *Tower and Slab: Histories of Global Mass Housing* (Abingdon, 2012), pp. 64–68.

4 _ Hans Schmidt, "Muss industrielles Bauen langweilig sein?," *Beiträge zur Architektur 1924–1964* (Zurich, 1993), pp. 163–167. As revealed by Schmidt's notebooks, for example, the "question of monotony" was once again the subject of controversy in 1965 and 1966, most importantly in a contribution by Hermann Henselmann to a BDA colloquium on August 24, 1966. Schmidt and his assistants later responded in Hans Schmidt, Rolf Link, and Gerd Wessel, *Gestaltung und Umgestaltung der Stadt* (Berlin, 1969), pp. 111–116.

5 _ Schmidt et al., *Gestaltung und Umgestaltung der Stadt,* see note 4, p. 112.

6 _ Ibid., p. 114.

7 _ Ibid.

8 _ Ibid. A few years prior, in light of the building undertaken in Hoyerswerda, Schmidt had pointed to the advantages of "over 100 m long blocks" vis-à-vis the originally planned blocks only 60 meters long. "Due to the long blocks, large dimensions are achieved, fitting for the landscape." (Note, August 20, 1958, after a meeting of BDA, notebook March–November 1958, Estate of Hans Schmidt, gta Archiv, ETH Zürich). In the meantime, the overall form has been obliterated, according to Schmidt, "by way of adding completely random loggias" that ruin the overall effect. See Schmidt et al., *Gestaltung und Umgestaltung der Stadt,* see note 4.

9 _ Hans Schmidt, "Einführung," *Straßen und Plätze: Beispiele zur Gestaltung städtebaulicher Räume*, eds. Konrad Lässig, Rolf Linke, Gerd Wessel et al. (East Berlin, 1968), p. 15.

10 _ The "foreign examples" of closed streetscapes mentioned are Gorky Street and Novy Arbat (formerly Kalinin-Propect, both in Moscow) and Avenue Foch in Le Havre. As an example of striking disregard for streetscape he shows a recent student project from the ETH Zurich.

11 _ Sigfried Giedion, *Space, Time and Architecture: The Growth of a New Tradition* (Cambridge, Mass., 1967), pp. 707–775.

12 _ Lewis Mumford, *The Highway and the City* (London, 1953), p. 180.

13 _ See Schmidt et al., *Gestaltung und Umgestaltung der Stadt*, see note 4, pp. 115–116 (fig. 80) and especially: Simone Hain, "Hans Schmidt in der DDR. Annäherung aus historischer Sicht," *Hans Schmidt 1893–1972*, ed. Suter, see note 1, pp. 83–108.

14 _ See Simone Hain, "Gestalten der Arbeit. Renaissance des Architekten im Zeichen der Industrialisierung. Die wirtschaftlich begründete Ästhetik von Hans Schmidt – ein modernes Konzept," *Werk: Bauen + Wohnen* (2000) 11, pp. 40–46.

15 _ For more on Edmund N. Bacon, see Gregory L. Heller, *Ed Bacon: Planning, Politics, and the Building of Modern Philadelphia* (Philadelphia, 2013). I discuss these matters in more detail in: "Monument? Forum? Fair? Louis Kahn, Edmund Bacon, and Philadelphia," *Louis Kahn: The Power of Architecture*, eds. Mateo Kries, Jochen Eisenbrand, and Stanislaus von Moos (Weil am Rhein, 2012), pp. 29–49.

16 _ Christopher Klemek, *The Transatlantic Collapse of Urban Renewal: Postwar Urbanism from New York to Berlin* (Chicago, 2011), pp. 79–80; on Bacon's career, see ibid., pp. 70–77. On the beginnings of "urban renewal" in the United States and its political dimensions, see Thomas J. Sugrue, *The Origins of the Urban Crisis: Race and Inequality in Postwar Detroit* (Princeton, 1996). On Robert Moses, see Robert Caro, *The Power Broker: Robert Moses and the Fall of New York* (New York, 1975).

17 _ See for example Werner Rietdorf, "Über die Umgestaltung des Stadtzentrums von Philadelphia," *Deutsche Architektur* (1965) 11, pp. 694–699; this study was preceded by publications in magazines such as *Werk*, *Casabella*, and others.

18 _ Edmund N. Bacon, *Design of Cities: From Athens to Brasilia* (New York, 1967), pp. 116–147. Bacon's discussion of Pope Sixtus V is based on Giedion, *Space, Time and Architecture*, see note 11, pp. 75–106 ("Sixtus V., 1585–1590, and the Planning of Baroque Rome").

19 _ While Schmidt, Wessel, and Linke tried to back up their arguments scientifically, Bacon relied on the power of conviction of poetry and modern art (in this case Walt Whitman and Paul Klee, see Bacon, *Design of Cities*, see note 8, pp. 14–21).

20 _ On Brasília see Bacon, *Design of Cities*, see note 8, pp. 220–227.

21 _ Ibid., p. 109.

22 _ Ibid., pp. 202–207.

23 _ Ibid., p. 203.

24 _ Schmidt et al., *Gestaltung und Umgestaltung der Stadt,* see note 4. The "true" title of the book, *Ästhetik der Stadt*, was rejected by the publisher. (Letter from Hans Schmidt to the urban planner Hans Blumenfeld, August 31, 1971; Estate of Hans Schmidt, gta Archiv, ETH Zürich).

25 _ A few months before the book appeared, and in response to Schmidt's question about new research in the perception of urban form, Hans Blumenfeld, Philadelphia, had suggested the work of Kevin Lynch and James Marston Fitch (letter from Blumenfeld to Schmidt, February 28, 1968; Estate of Hans Schmidt, gta Archiv, ETH Zürich). The bibliography of *Gestaltung und Umgestaltung der Stadt* includes the German version of Lynch's book *The Image of the City.* Research on the perception of urban form continued to play an important role in the period after Schmidt as well, see Bruno Flierl, *Zur Wahrnehmung der Stadtgestalt. Beispieluntersuchung im Stadtzentrum von Berlin* (Berlin, 1979) and Olaf Weber and Gerd Zimmermann, "Orientierungen in der Stadt," *Form und Zweck* (1980), pp. 21ff.

26 _ Bruno Flierl, "Hans Schmidt in der DDR: Reflexionen eines Mitarbeiters," *Hans Schmidt 1893–1972*, ed. Suter, see note 1, p. 65.

27 _ See Heller, *Ed Bacon,* see note 15, and Alexander Garvin, *The Planning Game: Lessons from Great Cities* (New York/London, 2013), pp. 165–195.

28 _ This effectively was Schmidt's demotion, according to Kathrin Siebert in "Hans Schmidt (1893–1972). Seine Zeit als Architekt und Theoretiker in der DDR zwischen 1956 und 1969" (unpublished thesis, ETH Zurich, 2009), p. 37.

29 _ Aldo Rossi, "Hans Schmidt und das Problem der Monotonie," *Werk – Archithese* (1978) 12, pp. 17–18. On Hans Schmidt's impact upon Aldo Rossi's architectural thinking see now Angelika Schnell, „Die sozialistische Perspektive der XV. Triennale di Milano", *Candide. Journal of Architectural Knowledge* (2010) 2, pp. 33–72.

PICTURE CREDITS

Fig. 1 _ Arkadi Mordwinow, Residential buildings, Große Kalugaer Straße (1940), Moscow, photographer unknown, 1940s repro from: *Deutsche Bauakademie zu Berlin, Dreißig Jahre sowjetische Architektur in der RSFSR* (Leipzig, 1951), illustration no. 50.

Fig. 2 _ Paul Artaria, Hans Schmidt, Schorenmatten Estate (1929/30), Basel-Eglisee, photographer unknown, 1929 © Wohngenossenschaft Lange Erlen, Basel

Fig. 3 _ "Industrial building in Germany during the 1920s", repro from: Hans Schmidt, *Beiträge zur Architektur* (Basel, 1965), p. 72.

Fig. 4 _ Hans Schmidt, *Studies on the problem of repetition in urban development*, Procurazie vecchie, St. Mark's Square, Venice (above), Rue de Rivoli, Paris (centre) and Bedford Square, London (below), repro from: Hans Schmidt, *Beiträge zur Architektur* (Basel, 1965), p. 187.

Fig. 5 _ Hans Schmidt, Karl Marx-Allee with the Haus des Lehrers as realized (a), and with standardized building along the edge of the street (b), repro from: Hans Schmidt, Rolf Linke, Gerd Wessel, *Gestaltung und Umgestaltung der Stadt. Beiträge zum sozialistischen Städtebau* (Berlin, Deutsche Demokratische Republik, 1970), p. 115.

Fig. 6 _ Auguste Perret, Reconstruction of Le Havre, Frankreich, 1945–64, axonometric view of the Place Gambetta with Bassin du Commerce, circa 1950, 86 x 140.4 cm, pencil on tracing paper on Japanese tissue paper © Fonds Perret. CNAM/SIAF/CAPA/Archives d'architecture du XXe siècle/Auguste Perret/UFSE/VG Bild-Kunst, Bonn 2015

Fig. 7 _ View from the Colonne de la Bastille to Boulevard Richard Lenoir, Paris, probably circa 1870, repro from: Sigfried Giedion, *Space, Time and Architecture. The Growth of a New Tradition* (Cambridge, Mass., edition 1967), p. 752.

Fig. 8 _ Edmund N. Bacon, *Stadtplanung von Athen bis Brasilia*, (Zurich, 1968) (*Design of Cities*, London, 1967).

Fig. 9 _ The so-called Triangle Area between Market Street West and Benjamin Franklin Parkway with the already partly realized Penn Center, Philadelphia, photographer unknown, aerial view circa 1960, Archive Stanislaus von Moos © holder of rights unknown

Fig. 10 _ Giacomo Barozzi da Vignola, Study on the perspective construction of space, 16th century, repro from: Edmund N. Bacon, *Stadtplanung von Athen bis Brasilia* (Zurich, 1968), p. 28.

Fig. 11 _ Fresco in the Vatican Library, "Sixtus V's Master Plan of Rome 1589", 16th century, repro from: Sigfried Giedion, *Space, Time and Architecture. The Growth of a New Tradition* (Cambridge, Mass., edition 1967), p. 83.

Fig. 12 _ "The architecture of motorways" taking Brasília as an example, repro from: Edmund N. Bacon, *Stadtplanung von Athen bis Brasilia* (Zurich, 1968), p. 225.

Fig. 13 _ City maps of Savannah, GA, USA, 1733, 1735, 1790, 1815, 1856, and after 1856, repros from: Edmund N. Bacon, *Stadtplanung von Athen bis Brasilia* (Zurich, 1968), pp. 206 and 207.

Fig. 14 _ "Conditions of seeing according to H. Maertens", repro from: Hans Schmidt, Rolf Linke, Gerd Wessel, *Gestaltung und Umgestaltung der Stadt. Beiträge zum sozialistischen Städtebau* (Berlin, 1970), p. 52.

Irma Leinauer

Modern Planning, Complex Construction: Industrialized Construction on Karl-Marx-Allee and Leninplatz

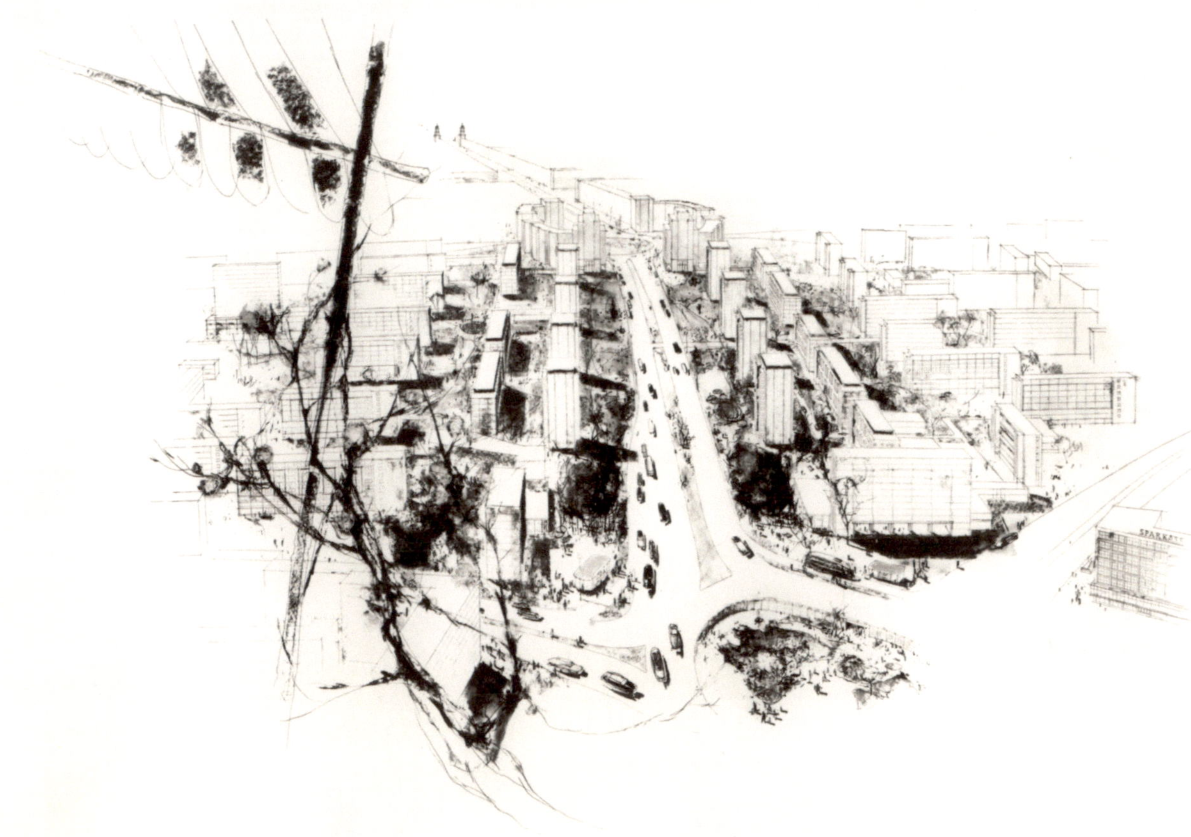

1 _ Collective Hermann Henselmann, Urban-developmental project suggestion for the continuation of building on Stalinallee with 8 tower blocks, June 1958

The second construction phase of Karl-Marx-Allee marks the beginning of a new period in the GDR in terms of construction, urban planning, and architecture. In 1959, construction began on a representative part of the so-called *Magistrale* (grand thoroughfare) that in addition to institutions of citywide importance also featured an entire residential area that met all the requirements of its residents. New building technologies grew beyond the experimental stage: *Plattenbauweise*, or prefabricated concrete slab construction, became the basis for all residential building. Urban planning turned away from closed block structures and was now based on the spatial principle of open plan building. Open spaces were no longer framed by buildings, but structured by them. Some ten years later, the neighboring Leninplatz was now built with prefab types. The location, symbolic content, and square character were clearly expressed by the architecture used, while, at the same time, serial residential architectural systems were employed with great flexibility.

Karl-Marx-Allee between Strausberger Platz and Alexanderplatz

On October 7, 1959, when the cornerstone was laid near Strausberger Platz on what was still called Stalinallee to mark the tenth anniversary of the founding of the GDR,[1] the large-scale project already had a complicated planning history behind it. As early as 1956, suggestions for the continuation to Alexanderplatz were submitted in the office of East Berlin's head architect Hermann Henselmann, now under new premises like looser construction and industrial construction types. In the end, however, these proposals were adamantly rejected by the top functionaries of the Bauakademie, the Building Ministry, and the Politbüro. Kurt Liebknecht, president of Deutsche Bauakademie, accused Henselmann's project of possessing an "anarchic character" like that of the Hansaviertel. "Western influence and a loss of unity" was the verdict of Kurt Magritz, the editor-in-chief of the journal *Deutsche Architektur*;[2] and Walter Ulbricht warned: "We should not try to imitate West Berlin ... The design leads to a break with the architecture of Stalinallee. It no longer corresponds to our idea of how to design the thoroughfare."[3] In a letter to Ulbricht, Henselmann rejected the accusations. "I am of the opinion that the street space needs to change, but not by dissolving completely, as in the models of the West – for example, at the Interbau [Hansa Viertel]."[4] All the same, the critique of the party leaders was primarily focused on a single structural characteristic, the functional type of the freestanding high-rise, which was equated with Western individualism. The leadership also failed entirely to realize what consequences modern architecture brought with it: the looser urban planning with freestanding buildings and new forms of construction, and the resulting design could no longer be combined with rules that were now out-dated (fig. 1).
At the same time as the ad acta plans of the head architect, new plans for the continuation of Stalinallee were ordered

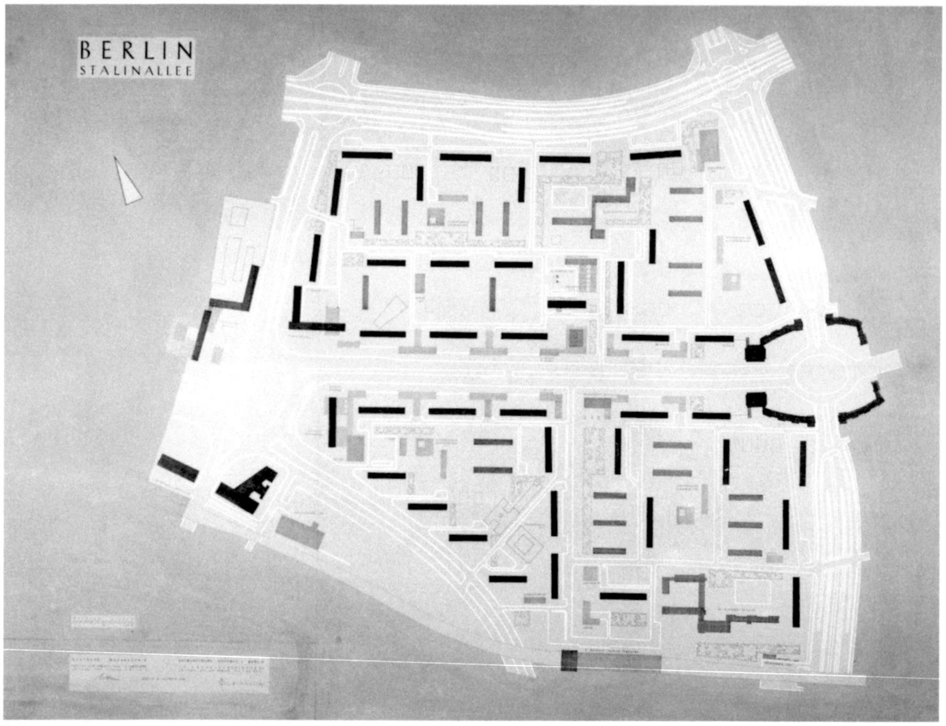

2 _ Internal competition result for the continuation of building on Stalinallee from September 1958 with a summary of the submissions by the collective Werner Dutschke and Edmund Collein

in September 1958 within just a few weeks, expressly rejecting all freestanding high-rises. This was followed by a very short, yet intense phase of planning involving seven groups of architects. Participants in this "internal" competition included the most important architects and urban planners in the GDR at the time: Richard Paulick, Hanns Hopp, Edmund Collein with Kurt W. Leucht and Hans Mertens from the Bauakademie, Otto Englberger from Weimar's Bauakademie, and Georg Funk from Dresden's Hochschule, and, once again Hermann Henselmann. Only Werner Dutschke from the Berliner Entwurfsbüro für Hochbau I (Berlin Studio for High-Rise Construction I) had not yet completed a project comparable in scale. In October 1958, the designs of Collein and Dutschke were selected, (fig. 2) and by February 1959 the building plan was finalized under Dutschke's direction. In terms of urban planning, a series of tasks had to be completed: despite looser, industrialized construction, reference had to be made to the part of Stalinallee that had already been built. Density and functions were supposed to correspond to the urban location. The task was not only to build an impressive thoroughfare, but also a complete residential area, sixty hectares in size for around 15,000 people in 4,600 apartments with all the institutions required. At the same time, it had to distinguish itself from Western residential construction. The emphasis placed on strictly right angles, creating clear forms and shapes, attested to this effort: all "free composition" with open, asymmetric flowing spaces was to be avoided.

Both the daily press and specialist journals in the GDR reported regularly on the planning and building for the continuation of Stalinallee, and in the West as well the press turned their attention to the project. As a journalist in the *Frankfurter Allgemeine Zeitung* commented, "Eight years after building began on the first section, built in a Stalinist imperial style, the 'first socialist street' is now getting a continuation with a more friendly feel, yet still colossal in scale. The new residential blocks – eight to ten stories high – are 'only' 84 meters long. The new stretch of the street is getting a worldly accent with the 13-story hotel Berlin Tourist, a cinema and the restaurant Moskau, which complements the already existing Stalinallee restaurants Warsaw, Budapest, and Prague, but is more friendly than these, with a glass pavilion surrounding a courtyard fountain. Lessons have apparently learned from West Berlin's Hansaviertel, albeit tentatively."[5]

Werner Dutschke and his collaborators,[6] most of them young graduates from the Technische Hochschule Dresden, created the urban scaffolding, and Josef Kaiser and his collective[7] were responsible for the architecture of important works of post-war modernism in Berlin – Kino International, Gaststätte Moskau, pavilions for specialized retail – and further developing residential construction types.

The boulevard was lined with residential high-rises and institutions important for the whole city – for trade, culture, and gastronomy. Despite the broad profile of the streets, the building was restrained, to allow for later urban enhancements.[8] The "optical architectural line" was formed by the flat pavilions together with Gaststätte Moskau and Kino International; they took up the lines of the old Stalinallee. Residential slabs along the street, that stood 125 meters apart, were set back from the road. Their height corresponded to the buildings of the older Stalinallee. With 500 residents per hectare of residential area, a relatively high residential density was sought, which was only permissible in direct proximity to the city center and which was in the upper range of what was planned across Germany in new residential areas (fig. 3).[9]

In its modernity, the representative ensemble on Karl-Marx-Allee marked a turn away from the "national tradition," taking up international formal language by using materials like steel, glass, and concrete, but also emphasizing the role of the capital city boulevard leading to the socio-political "cen-

3 _ Karl-Marx-Allee with the view towards Strausberger Platz in the direction of Alexanderplatz, July 1967

4 _ Housing area in the south with paddling pool and crèche, Singerstraße, circa 1968

tral square" on Spree Island. With his architectural collective, Josef Kaiser created significant buildings accentuating the central part of the Allee and structured the street fronts: the 13-story Hotel Berolina stood out with its contrasting blue color. It achieved importance across the GDR merely by its construction as the first prefab with "functional subdivisions." The ten floors with hotel rooms were built using industrial prefabrication, while the lower three floors of the "pedestal" were built using local concrete. The hotel was the first building torn down after 1990, forced to give way to a new office building.

Kino International, in contrast, has continued its success story as one of the last representatives of the classical film palace. Its central architectural element is the foyer on the upper floor, located behind a glazed façade. Cantilevered six meters above the sidewalk, it marks the cultural center of the "new" Karl-Marx-Allee, clearly visible and flooded with light. The three closed outer walls featured the concrete cast relief *Aus dem Leben der heutigen Menschen* (From the Life of Modern Man) using only two formed concrete elements.[10]

The ground floor of the building opposite the cinema, Gaststätte Moskau, is also set back from the street and more closed off than the upper floor. In contrast, the unadorned neon writing placed on the roof[11] underscores the effect of the top floor, entirely glazed and framed by filigreed window profiles. A characteristic element here is the entrance area with the forecourt featuring the mosaic *Aus dem Leben der Völker der Sowjetunion* (From the Lives of the Peoples of the Soviet Union),[12] and concrete latticework that significantly hovers over the forecourt, which according to Josef Kaiser lent "the modern Berlin building a touch of foreign folkloric."[13] With a restaurant, exhibition spaces, a concert café, a tea room and wine bar, a night bar, an interior courtyard and a rose garden, it offered an expansive, almost wastefully generous and transparent atmosphere. In recent years, the location has been renovated and is used for conferences.

The structures of the five store pavilions also exuded urbanity, both in terms of their architecture and their offerings: the ice cream parlor Mokka-Milch-Eisbar, the gallery Kunst im Heim, a shoe store Schuhhaus Zentrum, the fashion boutique Modesalon Madeleine, the florist Blumenhaus Interflor, and the salon Kosmetiksalon Babette. Taking up the lines of the old Stalinallee, they were arranged in rows, analogous to the residential units behind, rigorously symmetrical and utilizing the principle of repeating elements. On the street side, they were given large, framed windows with colorful glass listels that made the hall-like interior over two floors transparent to the outside world. Open stairwells led to the expanded sales floors on the upper gallery level. In the recessed, two floor elements, small window formats structured the façades, and their unified color with yellow bricks contrasted the white of the surrounding residential construction. In recent years, some of these pavilions have also been renovated as city landmarks.

In 1964, Haus des Lehrers and Kongresshalle were also completed, and their opening was celebrated on the 15th anniversary of the founding of the GDR. Here, Hermann Henselmann was chosen as architect, with an ensemble of buildings that marked the start of Karl Marx Allee, visible from afar, but above all oriented towards Alexanderplatz as a symbolic centerpiece. The vertical of Haus des Lehrers contrasted in geometrically rich arrangement with the somewhat receded, horizontal, and quadratic cube of the Congress Hall. The center of this flat structure, almost entirely in glass, was the large event hall cylindrically inserted into the structure, with its characteristic aluminum dome. The high-rise was equipped with a café, a restaurant, a library with reading room, club, seminar, and offices, and a cinema and lecture hall. The windowless third and fourth floors, featuring the frieze *Our Life* by Walter Womacka, seven meters high and running around the entire building, housed the holdings of the Pädagogische Zentralbibliothek. With concrete, steel, glass, and light metal, Henselmann sought to conform to the standards of classical modernism. The façade, the first in the GDR to hang in front of a steel concrete skeleton, had a nearly unified structure of glass and aluminum over all twelve floors, interrupted only by the decorative wall frieze.

Although ultimately built using on-site concrete, orientation for the building was taken from the prefab building block system, still in development, as can be seen from the bases

5 _ Ulf Eltze, Perspective drawing of the pavilions on Schillingstraße with cinema and hotel in line of sight, based on the development plan (1959) by the collective Werner Dutschke, 1959

of the windows and the width of the windows and panels. Screwed on aluminum pilaster strips emphasize the structure's verticality and the bright turquoise panels present a contrast to the surrounding residential high-rises built using large-scale prefab components.

Kongresshalle today continues to serve as an event location, after being modernized as an historical landmark. Haus des Lehrers was renovated to meet with new requirements, gutted and adapted to flexible office use. At first glance, nothing has changed about its appearance, but the structure has lost its role marking the entrance to Karl-Marx-Allee, due to the new construction on Alexanderplatz itself.

The urban ordering scheme of right angles was continued inside the residential area, where the buildings are arranged accordingly in relation to one another. Differentiation was achieved by varying the number of stories: ten, eight, or five floor residential buildings (fig. 4). Low buildings for kindergartens, schools, and laundries formed structured spaces together with the residential buildings and their green surfaces. The margins of the area were marked by slab buildings: diagonally placed along Alexanderstraße and stretched along the other main streets. A color concept for the entire ensemble underscored the architectural design. For the taller buildings, bright colors were chosen to keep their impact reduced despite their size, whereas the flat stores and infrastructural buildings were given more powerful color accents. A main structuring element was the "supply axis" for the residents that lead from the rail station Jannowitzbrücke in the south to the residential area in the north.

Along Schillingstraße, the "backbone" of the residential area, pavilion stores were lined up, with free placement emphasizing their character (fig. 5). Raised flowerbeds and a row of trees separated the generous pedestrian zone from the traffic. Along its visual axis, the ensemble with the hotel and the cinema marked a striking endpoint. In the course of the expansion of the living complex on the southern end of Schillingstraße at the end of the 1960s, isolated high-rises were arranged as dominants marking the entry to the residential area from a distance.

The complex on Karl-Marx-Allee marked the first step in the GDR on the way towards the industrialization of construction, and all realms were developed and used here: from apartment floor plans via the serial manufacture of large slabs with outer walls covered in ceramic, to rational montage (fig. 6). Already in planning the building, the requirements for the new manufacturing techniques were to be accounted for, including crane use and intermittent assembly lines (fig. 7). At the same time, for reasons of cost, the existing supply lines were to be kept accessible. For this reason, despite the de facto dissolution of the floor plan, none of the former streets were built over. A new factory was built for the serial production of bearing and non-bearing walls, ceilings, stairways, and ceramic-covered surfaces. The transportation of the finished elements using flatbed trucks and preparing cranes to move burdens of up to five tons was required. The eight to ten floor buildings using large-scale prefab components were a special challenge for the architects and construction engineers, since they had scarcely any experience with such high buildings. They decided to use a transverse wall system with supporting cross

7 _ Cyclic building site with crane rail and tower crane for the construction of the eight- and ten-storey residential buildings on Karl-Marx-Allee, 1961

6 _ Mounting and welding of a prefabricated external wall panel with French window on a five-storey QP-building in the residential area Karl-Marx-Allee, circa 1961

walls of heavy concrete and outer walls of light concrete (called *Querwandsystem,* the later QP-Serie). According to the principles of modern architecture, this mode of construction was legible on the outside of the building, so that prefabrication became the foundation for the architectural design (fig. 8).

The grid structure of the floor-high, 4.80 meter wide outside slabs, the size of a room, define the structure of the façade. The windows were placed in a horizontal format, lined up with the façade and emphasized in their arrangement over one another the vertical quality of the residential blocks. A covering with ceramic tiles in bright colors provided outer walls resistant to wind and weather that were also self-cleaning. Accents were marked by glass surfaces to floor level, with balconies or with window railings placed in front of them. In contrast, the design of the five-floor residential buildings was simpler, and the outer walls were simply plastered. Here too, there was an alternation of window forms: French windows together with the completely glazed stairway emphasized the functional structure of the sectional building. In terms of urban planning, the five-story residential buildings are striking not because of their individual design, but their arrangement. They were placed in lines in groups of two or three behind one another, and with shared green spaces formed the core of a residential group.

The residential area between Alexanderplatz and Strausberger Platz was the first residential complex in the GDR exclusively built using prefabricated slab construction, including type projection and serial production, and its buildings were "pioneers" of industrial assembly. They formed, although originally designed only for this location, the foundation for "repetitions" in Berlin and beyond as the QP series.

By the end of the 1990s, a large number of the apartment buildings had been renovated, but without any overarching design guidelines. The insulation systems installed on top of the characteristic ceramic façades were painted in inexplicable colors and patterns, concealing their original design intent. Only the buildings directly on the boulevard were listed as landmarks, and these were provided with ceramic façades with rear ventilation that in terms of color, material, and proportions were based on the historical surfaces.

Leninplatz

The planning and construction of Leninplatz was preceded by the development of residential building series beginning in the 1960s. Architectural policy sought to increase effectiveness by reducing construction area, rationalizing projection and production processes, and not least by creating apartment floor plans that were functional and simply structured. Here, the P2, whose prototype was erected by the Deutsche Bauakademie in 1962 in Berlin-Fennpfuhl, played a key role.[14] For the first time ceiling widths of six meters were achieved in prefabricated slab construction, and an additional innovation consisted in the floor plans that not

8 _ Façades of housing blocks, Karl-Marx-Allee, with ceramic cladding and front-mounted balconies, 1963

only placed the bathrooms and kitchens, but also the stairwells, elevators, and corridors in the building's interior.
At the same time, for central locations high-rises were planned as urban accents, a building type that was still vehemently rejected by the political elite in 1958, but just a few years later was accepted without any further discussion, at first with the "repeat project" of a 17-floor apartment house on Schillingstraße by Josef Kaiser and Johannes Gitschel using prefab slab construction elements of the QP series. In 1968, serial production began for the high-rise type WHH GT (Wohnhochhaus Großtafelbauweise, Residential High-Rise with Large Slabs)[15] with its prototypes on Fischerinsel. The weight of the elements was increased from the five tons of the QP series on Karl Marx Allee or the P2, to 6.3 tons. To stabilize the 18 or 21 floor buildings, they featured a construction that combined supporting cross walls and long walls.
In the general construction plan from 1968, the high-rises were usually planned for important locations, usually linked to traffic hubs and intended to form striking urban silhouettes: besides Fischerinsel along Leipziger Straße, at Jannowitzbrücke and at Leninplatz.[16] In 1967 a small competition was held for its construction, and designs were requested that included the now landscaped pile of rubble and the western part of Volkspark Friedrichshain. Among the six submitted works, the design of a collective under Hermann Henselmann from the Experimentalwerkstatt of the Bauakademie-Insitut für Städtebau and Architektur won first prize (fig. 9).[17] Notable here were the two new, yet related construction forms. On the northeast side of the semicircular square, Henselmann and his collaborators placed an up to 24 floor high-rise slab that in its stepped appearance represented an optical amplification of the mountain of rubble. Two rounded buildings placed diagonally across from one another followed the asymmetrical spatial situation. The collective from Experimentalwerkstatt developed the series P2 a step further, to create new, curved buildings using trapezoid intermediate elements.
The southern edge of the square was lined with the cubic, simple double residential high-rises from the QP series, part of the Karl Marx Allee residential area that also represented the marginal buildings for the new residential area to the south. For a Lenin Monument, Henselmann foresaw not a standard statue, but a library pavilion "in the form of spiral rolled, rising red flag, that took up the swing of the surrounding buildings and led to the vertical."[18]
After the competition, the local building authorities reworked the urban planning in several details, which then became the foundation for the final implementation of the project by a *Wohnungsbaukombinat* directed by Heinz Mehlan. Henselmann proposed for the main building of the ensemble a structure with eight steps, rising from 9 to 24 floors. This was changed and a triple-recessed residential high-rise with 17, 21, and 25 floors was built that was vertically structured by the offset components. In addition, a supermarket in the competition entry on the northern side with services was also replaced. Instead, a flat building placed in front of the high-rise housed a restaurant, café, and several small shops. The supermarket was relocated to the southern side of the ensemble. In designing the curved buildings, the series type P2, which until now was only 10 stories in height, was altered. It was given an additional floor, while the dimensions for the depth of the building were increased, enlarging the bedrooms. With the formation of trapezoid-shaped special axes, the distribution of apartments was altered to include more three and four room apartments so that in other locations in Berlin new urban planning could also be undertaken in prefab slab construction. The façade design gave the buildings a "modern feel," with loggias and balustrades in a colorful interaction with the ceramic cladding (fig. 10).
Henselmann's idea of a symbolic monument in Lenin's honor was abandoned. Instead, the Moscow sculptor and president of the Soviet Academy of Arts Nikolai Tomski was commissioned to create an immense statue. The artist created a monumental 19-meter high figure of Lenin with a stylized flag and designed it to match the surrounding buildings. The outlines of the flag held up high corresponded to the stepped high-rise, and the color of the red granite was echoed in the façades. The monument was surrounded by a star-like arrangement of light and dark granite plates, and the arrangement was lined with raised flowerbeds.

9 _ Collective Hermann Henselmann, prize-winning competition entry for the design of Leninplatz with library pavilion and banner sculpture, 1968

With Leninplatz, the policymakers created an ensemble in Berlin's center that served several times for symbolic festivities. The cornerstone was laid by Walter Ulbricht on an anniversary of the founding of the GDR, on October 7, 1968. Although at the end of the 1960s the city center still lacked a monument to Karl Marx and Friedrich Engels, at least with the ceremonial unveiling of the statue of Vladimir Ilyich Lenin a large-scale demonstration could be held to mark the one hundredth anniversary of Lenin's birth on April 19, 1970. In just one and one half years, with a massive concentration of efforts, the surrounding buildings had essentially already been completed. Leninplatz was renamed Platz der Vereinten Nationen (United Nations Square) in 1992, and that same year the 19-meter-high Lenin sculpture by Nikolai Tomski was torn down in a spectacular action, while the stepped high-rise and the round buildings have now been renovated as listed landmarks.[19]

10 _ Collective Heinz Mehlan, Model of the project selected for realization, Leninplatz with modified group of high-rise buildings and Lenin statue, 1969

NOTES

1 _ The stretch of the road leading from Alexanderplatz to Bahnhof Lichtenberg (Frankfurter Straße – Große Frankfurter Straße – Frankfurter Allee) was renamed Stalinallee in December 21, 1949 to mark Josef Stalin's 70th birthday. As part of de-Stalinization under Khrushchev, in November 1961 the name Stalin was deleted from public life in the Soviet Union and most of the socialist "brother states." In Berlin, the Stalin Monument was demolished on November 13, 1961, Stalinallee was renamed Karl-Marx-Allee from Alexanderplatz to Frankfurter Tor and the continuation was returned its original name, Frankurter Allee.

2 _ See Deutsche Bauakademie, *Protokoll über die Weiterführung der Präsidiumssitzung beim Stadtbauamt, Magistrat von Groß-Berlin am 1.9.1958*, Landesarchiv Berlin *(Bestand Bezirksparteiarchiv)*, IV-2/6/817.

3 _ In: *Niederschrift über Sitzung des Politbüros am 9.9.1958. Betr. Beratung über Vorlage ‚Berlin'*, Archivabteilung Baukunst der Akademie der Künste *(Nachlass Liebknecht)*, AcLbK-01-57.

4 _ A letter from Hermann Henselmann to Walter Ulbricht, Sept. 26, 1958, Landesarchiv Berlin *(Bestand Bezirksparteiarchiv)*, IV-2/6/817.

5 _ Sabina Lietzmann, "Ein Wolkenkratzer in Ost-Berlin: Baupläne für das Stadtzentrum. Die Stalinallee wird mondäner. Einflüsse des Hansaviertels," *Frankfurter Allgemeine Zeitung* (January 4, 1960).

6 _ Including Hans Eichner, Ulf Eltze, Eberhard Horn, Hermann Klauschke, Dieter Rogalla, Kurt Sadewasser, Reinhard Sonntag, and Günter Thielemann.

7 _ Including Günter Kunert, Heinz Aust, Gerhard Lehmann, Horst Bauer, Günther Wernitz, Klaus Deutschmann, and Arno Knuth.

8 _ See Werner Dutschke, "Zwischen Strausberger Platz und Alexanderplatz," *Deutsche Architektur* (1959) 10, p. 537.

9 _ In the Federal Republic as well, density was measured as "residential population density," i.e., the number of residents per hectare of residential area. For example, in the Hamburg construction plan of 1950, only in a few select areas of the core city were 500 residents/hectare allowed. See Baubehörde der Freien und Hansestadt Hamburg, ed., *Geschoßflächenzahlen. Grundlagen neuzeitlicher Stadtplanung* (Hamburg, 1960).

10 _ Artists: Waldemar Grzimek, Karl-Heinz Schamal, and Hubert Schiefelbein.

11 _ Klaus Wittkugel, a graphic designer and professor at Kunsthochschule Weißensee who became well-known for his posters, designed the advertising for all institutions along Karl-Marx-Allee, and chose the unadorned, thin futura font.

12 _ Artists: Bert Heller und Heinrich Jungebloedt.

13 _ Josef Kaiser, "Gaststätte 'Moskau' in Berlin," *Deutsche Architektur* (1964) 10, p. 211.

14 _ Developed by Wilfried Stallknecht, Achim Felz and Herbert Kuschy.

15 _ The basic project for the WHH GT was designed by Hans-Peter Schmiedel and Manfred Zumpe.

16 _ See Joachim Näther, "Der Generalbebauungsplan und das Stadtzentrum," *Deutsche Architektur* (1968) 6, p. 344.

17 _ With Hanspeter Kirsch, Karin Kirsch, Siegfried Klügel, Jörg Piesel, Werner Rösler, Wilfried Stallknecht, Erhard Stefke, and Gerd Wessel.

18 _ Christian Borngräber, "Hermann Henselmann," *Baumeister, Architekten, Stadtplaner: Biographien zur baulichen Entwicklung Berlins*, eds. Wolfgang Ribbe and Wolfgang Schäche (West Berlin, 1987), p. 573.

19 _ On the renovation, see Gerold Perler, "Die Tektonik des industriellen Bauens: Die Sanierung der Plattenbauten am Platz der Vereinten Nationen," *Die Karl-Marx-Allee zwischen Strausberger Platz und Alex. Berlin-Forschungen der Historischen Kommission zu Berlin*. Vol. VI, ed. Wolfgang Ribbe (Berlin, 2005), pp. 96–100.

PICTURE CREDITS

Fig. 1 _ Collective Hermann Henselmann, Urban-developmental project suggestion for the continuation of building on Stalinallee with 8 tower blocks, drawing: E. W. Schumacher, photographer unknown, June 1958, silver gelatin paper, Akademie der Künste, Berlin, Baukunstarchiv HHA 0120_001_878_14a © Akademie der Künste, Berlin

Fig. 2 _ Internal competition result for the continuation of building on Stalinallee from September 1958 with a summary of the submissions by the collective Werner Dutschke and Edmund Collein, photograph: Gisela Dutschmann, October 1958, Berlinische Galerie BG-AS 1436.002384 © Gisela Dutschmann/Berlinische Galerie

Fig. 3 _ Karl-Marx-Allee with the view towards Strausberger Platz in the direction of Alexanderplatz, photograph: Gisela Dutschmann, July 1967, repro from negative, Berlinische Galerie BG-AS 1436. 6902_B100139 © Gisela Dutschmann/Berlinische Galerie

Fig. 4 _ Housing area in the south with paddling pool and crèche, Singerstraße, photographer unknown, circa 1968, repro from: Krenz/Stiebitz/Weidner, eds., Städte und Stadtzentren in der DDR (Berlin, 1968), p. 32.

Fig. 5 _ Ulf Eltze, Perspective drawing of the pavilions on Schillingstraße with cinema and hotel in line of sight, based on the development plan (1959) by the collective Werner Dutschke, photograph: Gisela Dutschmann, 1959, silver gelatin paper, Berlinische Galerie BG-AS 1436.002390 © Gisela Dutschmann/Berlinische Galerie

Fig. 6 _ Mounting and welding of a prefabricated external wall panel with French window on a five-storey QP-building in the residential area Karl-Marx-Allee, photograph: J. Wolter/Deutsche Bauinformation, circa 1961, silver gelatin paper, Berlinische Galerie BG-AS 17/2013,275 © J. Wolter/Berlinische Galerie

Fig. 7 _ Cyclic building site with crane rail and tower crane for the construction of the eight- and ten-storey residential buildings on Karl-Marx-Allee, photograph: Gisela Dutschmann, 1961, repro from negative, Berlinische Galerie BG-AS 1436.006937_2 © Gisela Dutschmann/Berlinische Galerie

Fig. 8 _ Façades of housing blocks, Karl-Marx-Allee, with characteristic grid showing the joints of large, storey-high, room-wide panels, with ceramic cladding and front-mounted balconies, photograph: Herbert Fiebig, 1963, silver gelatin paper, Berlinische Galerie BG-AS 98/2012,17 © bpk/Herbert Fiebig

Fig. 9 _ Collective Hermann Henselmann, Institut für Städtebau und Architektur der Deutschen Bauakademie, prize-winning competition entry for the design of Leninplatz with library pavilion and banner sculpture, photographer unknown, 1968, silver gelatin paper, Akademie der Künste, Berlin HHA 120-846, F.1a © Akademie der Künste, Berlin

Fig. 10 _ Collective Heinz Mehlan, Wohnungsbaukombinat Berlin, Model of the project selected for realization, Leninplatz with modified group of high-rise buildings and Lenin statue, photograph: Gisela Dutschmann, 1969, Berlinische Galerie BG-AS 1436.002597_40 © Gisela Dutschmann/Berlinische Galerie

Large Housing Estates and Oppositions

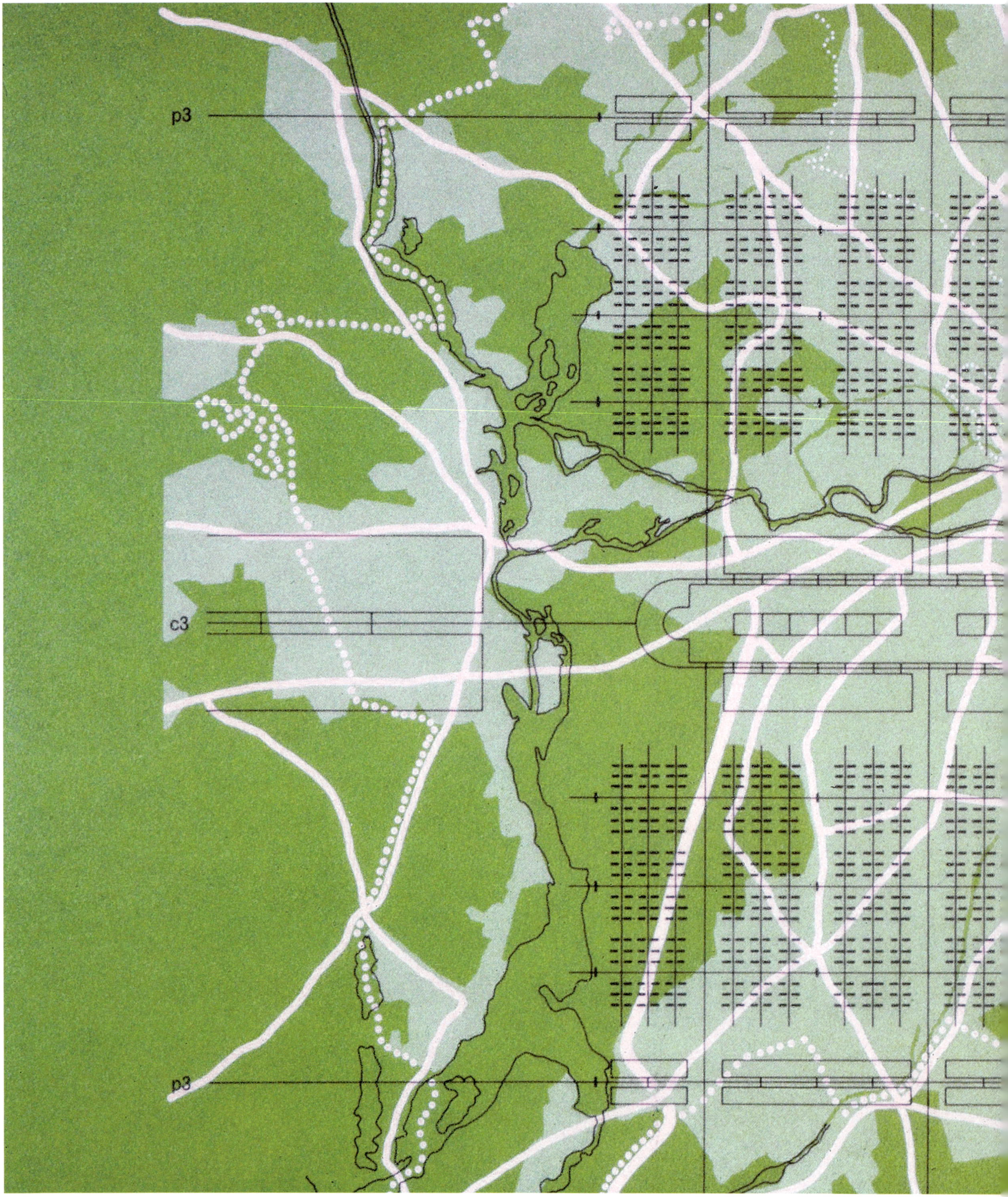

Fritz Haller, *totale stadt*, example design Berlin, 1968 (not built)

Werner Düttmann, Group of high-rise buildings in the Märkisches Viertel, Dannenwalder Weg, circa 1968

Hans Bandel, Shopping center in Wutzkyallee, housing estate Britz-Buckow-Rudow, 1967

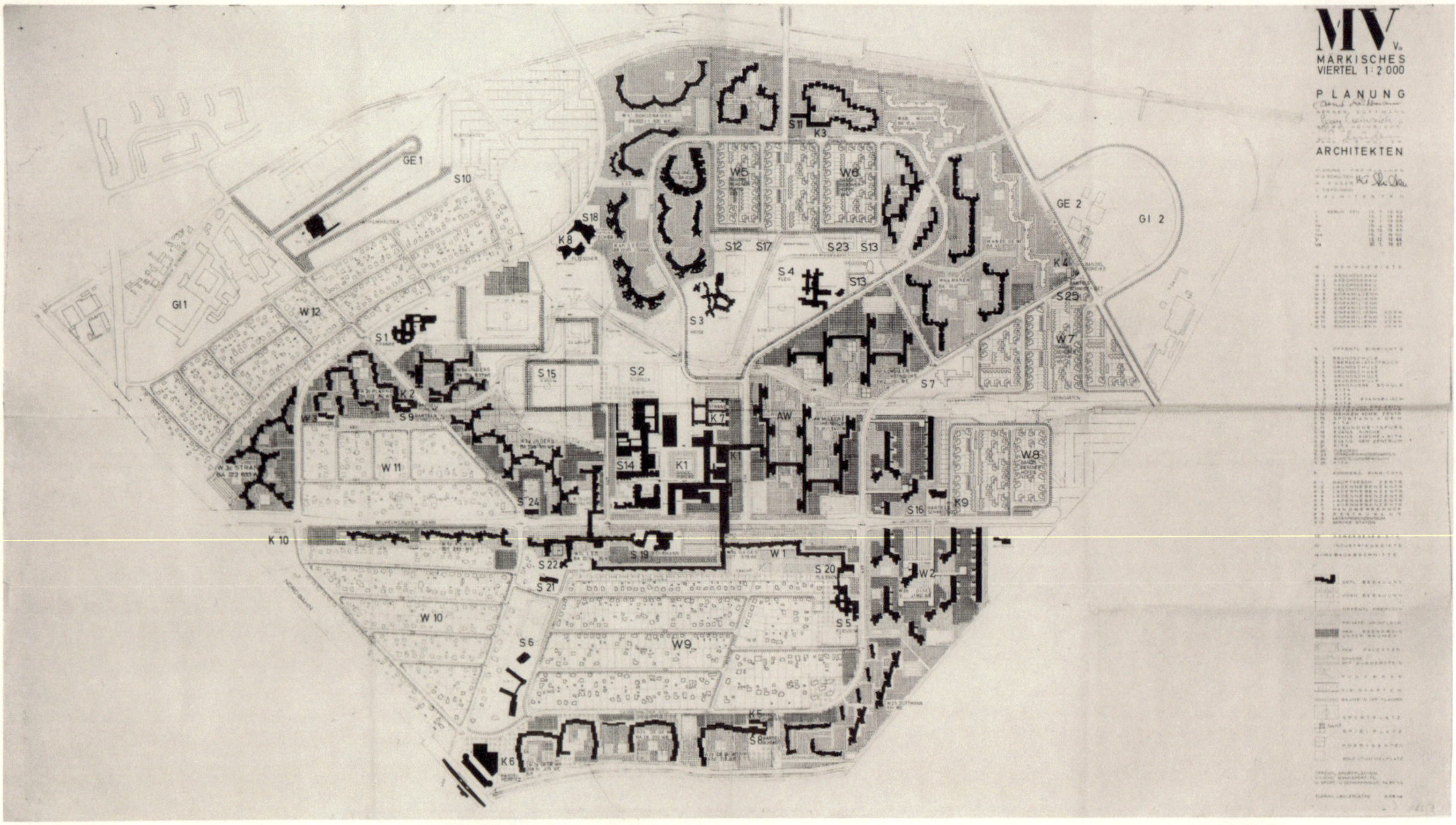

Werner Düttmann, Georg Heinrichs, Hans C. Müller, Märkisches Viertel, site plan 1:2000, 1967

Chen Kuen Lee, Residential buildings, Märkisches Viertel (1965-70), photograph: Heinrich Kuhn, circa

Heinrich Kuhn, Stationer's shop in an old building in West-Berlin, circa 1965

Heinrich Kuhn, Tobacconist's shop in the Märkisches Viertel, circa 1965

Heinrich Kuhn, Apartment houses from the *Gründerzeit* in West-Berlin, circa 1965

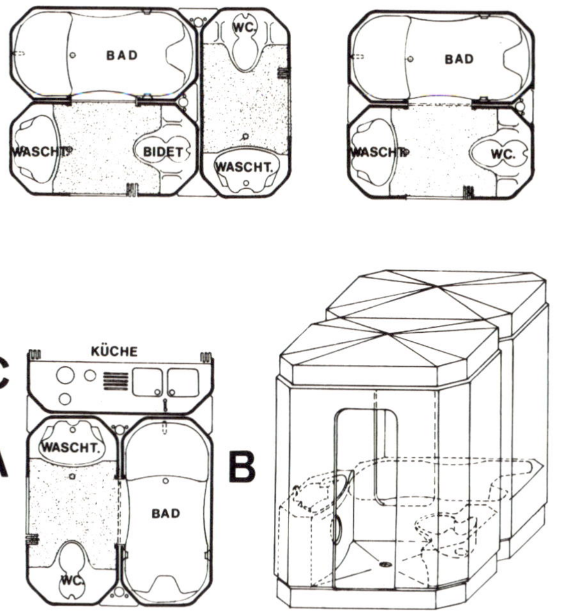

Georg Kohlmaier, Barna von Sartory, "Rucksack-WC," ground plans and isometry, 1969

Georg Kohlmaier, Barna von Sartory, "Rucksack-WC," façade simulation on old building, 1969 (not built)

Book cover of *Wohnste sozial haste die Qual. „jetzt reden wir". Betroffene des Märkischen Viertels* (Reinbek, 1975)

Book cover of *Die gemordete Stadt. Abgesang auf Putte und Straße, Platz und Baum* (Herbig, 1964)

Jürgen Holtfreter, Poster for the exhibition *Diagnose. Zum Bauen in West-Berlin*, 1968

Hartmut Frank

Crisis or Sea Change? Architecture Debates in West Berlin around 1967/68

During the international student unrest in 1968 many authors claimed that it also triggered tempestuous debates about architecture, its future direction and its current objectives. However closer scrutiny casts doubts on the notion of a direct correlation between political history and the discourses internal to a discipline. For one thing, after the Wall went up on August 13, 1961, the city's definitive partition was beyond any doubt an historical event of great political significance in West Berlin, but it did not trigger a noticeable shift in paradigm within the architectural community. For another, the issues covered by debates about architecture and urban planning in university milieus during the 1968 movements that gripped so many places from Mexico via Berkeley to West Berlin varied greatly. As far as I am aware, the UNAM students in Mexico did not suddenly discover an interest in urban renewal, as did the students at the Technical University in Berlin, and nor did the latter join their counterparts at the École des Beaux-Arts in Paris in calling for artistic imagination to seize power. What is beyond doubt is that in all these places political events shifted the discussion, including in architecture, much as they did in the humanities, unlike engineering and the natural sciences. In the case of architecture it was not so much new ideas and content that changed the course of discussion, but rather questions about its social relevance.

June 2, 1967

But the architecture debates in West Berlin came to a head a year before the legendary events of May 1968: on June 2, 1967 the student Benno Ohnesorg was shot by a civilian police officer outside the new opera house designed by Fritz Bornemann on Bismarckstraße in Charlottenburg during the breaking up of a demonstration against the visit of Shah Reza Pahlavi and his wife Farah Diba.[1] For several days, the people of West Berlin were deliberately misinformed about both events by the authorities and the media, especially by newspapers belonging to the dominant Springer group. The student bodies of the two biggest universities in West Berlin, the Freie Universität (FU) and the Technische Universität (TU), countered this disinformation in an unprecedented manner by delivering leaflets to every household in the city, informing them about what really had been happening. For the several days the campaign lasted, the TU students took over the north of West Berlin, and the FU students the south. At the TU, the hub of printing and distribution was located in the seminar rooms where Oswald Mathias Ungers taught at the Faculty of Architecture on Ernst-Reuter-Platz. This was no accident, as the campaign at the TU had been organized almost exclusively by architecture students, and Ungers' seminar boasted an efficient printer which was used for printing departmental publications.[2] Along with his wife and children, his assistants and many of his students Ungers himself had taken part in the demonstration which had been publicized in advance as a kind of happening. Kommune 1 had been distributing shopping bags with portraits of the shah and his wife which people could pull over their heads like masks. Nobody had foreseen the lethal escalation of the police operation against the protesters. The harmony between Ungers, then Dean of the Faculty of Architecture, and his politically committed students quickly broke down in the months that followed, and Ungers later stated on a number of occasions that the politicization of students was his main reason for leaving Berlin in 1969 and taking up a position as Dean of the School of Architecture at Cornell University in Ithaca, New York.

Ungers's grounds for moving to Cornell were probably more complex. They can perhaps be found in the construction culture in West Berlin after the Wall was built, a climate in which he rarely received commissions. His programmatic project for an elongated residential block across the River Havel at Rupenhorn for the housing association GSW, for example, had been halted at the last minute, even though it had been thoroughly detailed and was ready to build, and his social housing for the Märkisches Viertel in the north of the city bore little resemblance to the original design, as both bureaucrats and developers had imposed countless changes. And the resounding failure of the International Symposium on the Theory and Critique of Architecture, for which he had invited influential critics from the field to the TU in December 1967 had certainly hurt him (fig. 1).

Today, reading the proceedings of that conference produced on the very same printing press, it is hard to understand what went so badly wrong.[3] Ungers had succeeded in gathering 18 speakers from Western Europe and the United States for the four-day event, including such renowned figures as Sigfried Gideon, Friedrich Achleitner, Reyner Banham, Kenneth Frampton and Colin Rowe. The only striking thing about the list of speakers, which is almost a Who is Who? of architecture theory in the 1960s and 1970s – at a time when the discipline still did not have a chair of its own at any German university – is the absence of Italians, experts such as Ernesto Nathan Rogers, Manfredo Tafuri and Giancarlo De Carlo, especially as Ungers owed his own international reputation above all to the publication of his designs in Italian journals. Also missing were the representatives of Team X. Two years earlier he had invited them to a conference in Berlin, and he owed them a debt of gratitude for his contact with the protagonists of international debates at the time (fig. 2).[4] On the other hand, the week before, at his instigation, Peter and Alison Smithson had spent several days at the TU teaching a seminar on Mies van der Rohe's quest for timelessness.[5] In his introductory words to the symposium Ungers had explicitly mentioned the Smithson seminar and asked similar questions about whether architectural form could be independent of social, technical and historical developments and about the validity of the conventional approach to architecture as a discipline – a fundamental question that has lost none of its topicality today. At the time it flagged up the disconnect between the aims of the symposium and the discussion taking place between the participating architects and students, who became increasingly restless as they listened to contributions that were irrelevant in their eyes. The unease gradually gave way to aggressive heckling, finally culminating in the unfurling of a large banner which read: "Every building is good. Stop building." Sigfried Gideon left the venue in protest and went home early. As far as I am aware, the final colloquium announced in the programme, which was to be led by Jürgen Joedicke, never actually took place. Ungers felt his efforts to place the design process on a theoretical footing had been completely misunderstood, and when Colin Rowe then invited him to Cornell he did not hesitate – little suspecting what conflicts would await him there.

The mutual incomprehension that divided the organisers, speakers and audience could hardly have been greater. Some were concerned that the way architecture defined itself and the autonomy of formal aspects were obsolete, while others focussed explicitly on contemporary challenges for construction and the social role of the architect.

The Critical University

Many in the audience had recently begun discussing the social issues at meetings of the seminar known as Aktion 507. It took its name from the room in the Faculty of Architecture where the seminar was held, where students, research fellows and some younger architects working in the city would come together in several extremely mixed working groups to discuss fundamental questions facing the discipline. It was the only seminar at the TU that formed part of the anti-authoritarian *Critical University* set up at the Freie Universität on November 1, 1967 in response to the events in June. SDS, Students for a Democratic Society, played a key part in it, and it had been expressly prohibited by the FU Senate. As Rudi Dutschke put it, the *Critical University* set out to "restore the original substance of science as a process of human self-emancipation through enlightenment".[6] For the architecture seminar at the *Critical University*, this implied exploring – if not the revolutionary potential of architecture – at least its ability to change society.

In September 1968 Aktion 507 found an unexpected forum to present the status of its discussion and attract considerable public attention. Through the good offices of the BDA and the AIV – professional associations of architects with branches in West Berlin – the participants were tasked with mounting an exhibition at the annual *Bauwochen*. The previous year, a sizeable group of young, committed West Berlin architects who were involved in Aktion 507 had refused to display their work at an exhibition the Senat was planning for the 1967 *Bauwochen* in protest at the construction policies of the Berlin state government (Senat) and the all-pow-

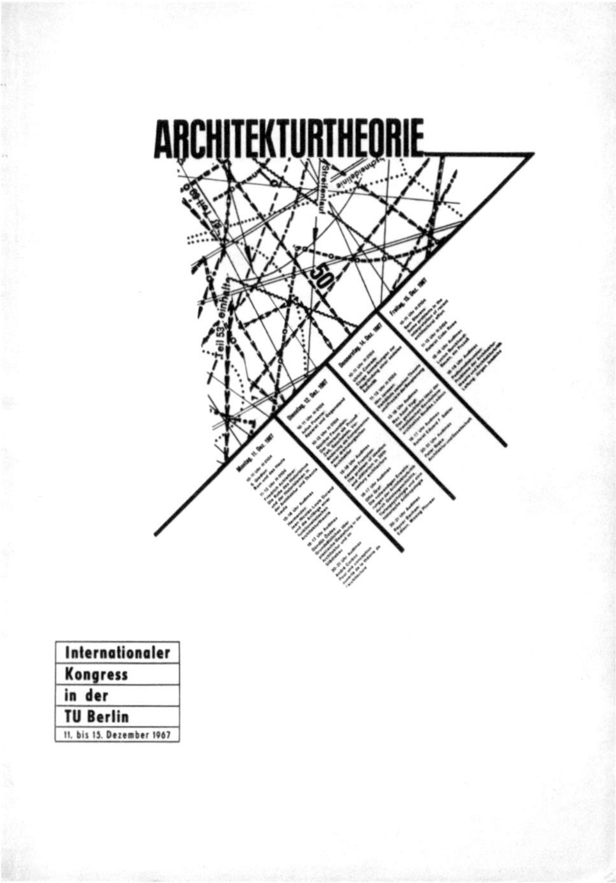

1 _ Volume of papers, Architectural Theory. International Congress in the TU West-Berlin 11th to 15th December 1967, *Veröffentlichungen zur Architektur*, ed. O. M. Ungers (June 1968) 14

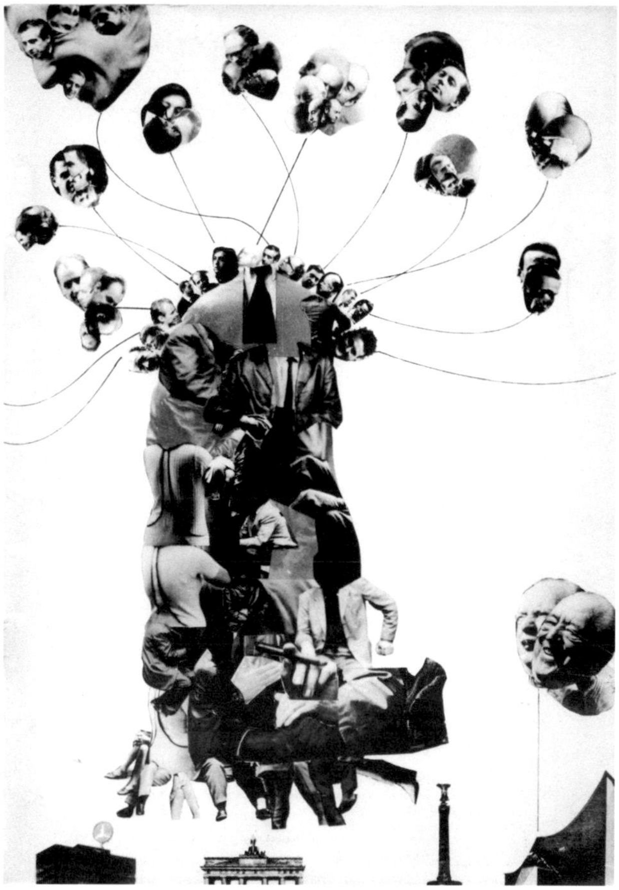

2 _ Stefan Wewerka, Collage for the title page of *Veröffentlichungen zur Architektur*, ed. O. M. Ungers (June 1966) 3

erful public-interest housing corporations. This time they used the skeleton of the Architecture Library on Ernst-Reuter-Platz designed by Hans Scharoun to stage an exhibition of their own entitled *Diagnosis of Building* in West Berlin. The discussion enabled them to air much of their criticism.

The catalogue to that event is a document of the era (fig. 3).[7] It does not conceal the heterogeneity of the various threads of debate in Aktion 507, and its improvised nature vividly illustrates the ferment in the architecture community in West Berlin. Technical questions and approaches internal to the discipline dominate, whereas Dutschke's idea of self-emancipation through enlightenment barely makes an impact. A number of contributions take issue with the revolving door between politics and the housing corporations in West Berlin. There are embryonic and fairly general efforts towards a critique of land speculation and the subsidy-based capitalism specific to West Berlin, and some sardonic comments are made about the ideological utterances of architects and architectural critics. No alternatives are formulated and no concrete demands are made. The manifesto at the front of the catalogue was signed by 69 members of Aktion 507. It unabashedly poses generalized demands about fostering critical, enlightened public discourse, involving stakeholders in the planning process, placing land under social ownership and developing new interdisciplinary methods. And it reiterated the long-standing professional insistence that the planning departments in council construction departments and housing corporations should be closed down.

The one concrete issue related to a major Mies van der Rohe exhibition at the Academy of Arts and the ceremonial inauguration of the Neue Nationalgalerie on September 15, 1968. It was the demand to rebuild the memorial to Rosa Luxemburg and Karl Liebknecht originally designed by Ludwig Mies van der Rohe and destroyed by the Nazis near the Landwehr Canal, close to Mies's gallery in West Berlin, and not next to Friedrichshain Park in East Berlin, where it had originally stood. There is a report of a ground-breaking ceremony for the statue on the date of the opening, and of a collection to fund it, which could only be interpreted as a provocation in rigidly anti-communist West Berlin so soon after the building of the Wall. The report had sparked contemptuous comment in the local press and the West German weekly *Spiegel*.[8]

The second edition of the catalogue came with an insert, the *Planer-Flugschrift*, a "pamphlet for planners" produced by an ad-hoc group within Aktion 507 that focussed on teaching methods in higher education (fig. 3).[9] It called for the founding of a planning faculty to replace the Faculty of

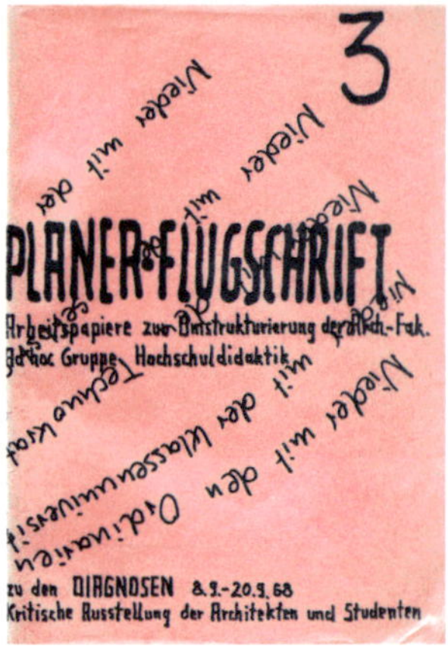

3 _ Left: Discussion materials for the exhibition *Diagnose zum Bauen* in West-Berlin on the occasion of the Building Weeks from the 8th to the 20th September, 1968. Center: Signatories to the manifesto for the exhibition. Right: Ad hoc group university didactics, *Planer-Flugschrift 3. Arbeitspapiere zur Umstrukturierung der Arch.-Fak.* (Working papers for the restructuring of the Faculty of Architecture)

Architecture at the TU, which had originated as Schinkel's Building Academy, arguing that unlike the artistic architect, who was now socially irrelevant, planners with a scientific training had the genuine potential to change society. The appeal fell on fertile soil, and it had consequences. Soon afterwards the TU founded a Department of Planning and Social Theory and renamed the rump of the architecture faculty Department of Construction Planning and Implementation, sending a message that in future its work would be less artistic and more scientific in nature. The new focal themes were industrial prefabrication, process management and stakeholder participation.

It is enough to read the list of signatories to the manifesto at the Diagnosis exhibition to appreciate the broad spectrum of positions reflected in Aktion 507. The manifesto hints at the internal contradictions (fig. 3). There are not many student signatures. Far more signatories are research fellows at the Faculty of Architecture and professionals who already had a reputation of their own, such as Josef Paul Kleihues, Egbert Kossak and Heiner Moldenschardt. Ungers and other TU professors will not be found on the list. Hardly any of the signatories were later harmed by their involvement with Aktion 507, and many became influential architects in the West Berlin of the 1970s and 1980s.

Young Berlin Architects

How little their creative aspirations as architects were actually influenced by the debates in Aktion 507 is clear from the presentation *Junge Berliner Architekten* (Young Berlin Architects) that Josef Paul Kleihues published in an issue of the *Deutsche Bauzeitung* (*db*) in August 1968, just before the Diagnosis exhibition, together with a commentary by guest editor Julius Posener (fig. 4).[10] Kleihues' "young architects" were born in the 1920s and 1930s.[11] Most of them had, indeed, refused to take part in the exhibition the Senat had planned to hold in September 1967. Others he included were Werner Düttmann, who had headed the Construction Department at the Senat for many years, his successor Hans Müller, Georg Heinrichs and Oswald Mathias Ungers. Hans Bandel was also featured, although he was born in 1918 and a little older. Since 1961 Bandel had been the liaison architect for Walter Gropius on the project to build Gropius-Stadt in the Britz-Buckow-Rudow area.

Most of these choices were quite evidently based on Kleihues's personal creative preferences. Almost all the architects he presented were either fostering updated forms of 1920s modernism or committed to the kind of contemporary trends represented by, for example, James Stirling, the Smithsons, Cedric Price, Shadrach Woods and other members of Team X. The only exceptions to this canon are Heinz

4 _ Guest editor Josef Paul Kleihues, *Junge Berliner Architekten*, *db* (1968) 8

Schudnagies, who was influenced by Hans Scharoun, and Johannes Uhl, with his extremely artistic personal style. Had Ulrich Conrads been asked to contribute a similar article for *Bauwelt*, his choice would presumably have been diametrically opposed to the one put together by Kleihues.

All architects were invited to submit their views by responding to questions compiled for a survey by the *Deutsche Bauzeitung* in 1934.[12] Their answers also highlight how far most of those presented had moved away from the positions of Aktion 507, assuming they had ever shared them. Julius Posener rightly remarked in his commentary that the answers differed greatly and painted a less consistent picture than the buildings – whether built or designed – that were being described. He did acknowledge, however, that in both their words and their works an entire generation of architects had been engaged in a serious conflict with "the primacy of meaning or form". In the light of this observation, the question Ungers had asked nine months earlier about the autonomy of form in the design process seems a lot less far-fetched and irrelevant to the time than the critics of his symposiums had sought to argue. With his incomparable irony, Posener concludes that "as an architect the revolutionary ... suffers from a crippling awareness that ideals are in any case unachievable in a society that has not yet been changed".[13]

Kleihues's choice of built and unbuilt projects was by no means without an ulterior motive. Its clear target was the dominant trend in West Berlin's post-war architecture, with its emphatically anti-monumental and unpretentious functionalism – aside from a sporadic sprinkling of work by Hans Scharoun and his school. This architecture, with its homogenized and standardized lack of character, culminating in the big residential estates of the 1960s which were increasingly seen as failures, was nevertheless still bent on becoming the norm for the large-scale rehabilitation schemes in Wedding, Kreuzberg and Charlottenburg, fuelled by a great deal of West German money. He contrasted this with examples of a new design awareness that the originators had usually acquired during periods of studying and working with teams in Britain and France. In his preamble, he explicitly mentions the recent failed competitions for the

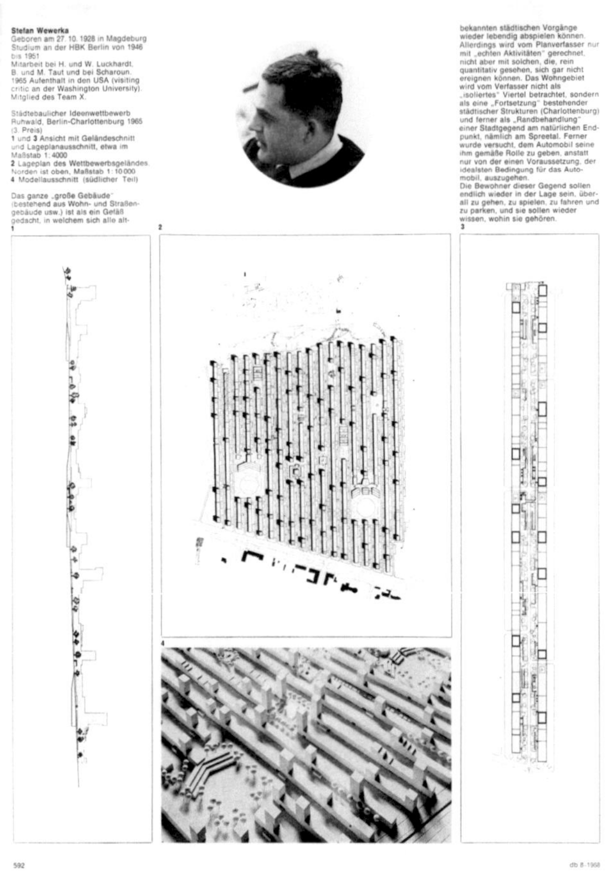

5 _ Stefan Wewerka, 3rd prize in the urban-developmental competition for ideas, Ruhwald, 1965, *db* (1968) 8, p. 592.

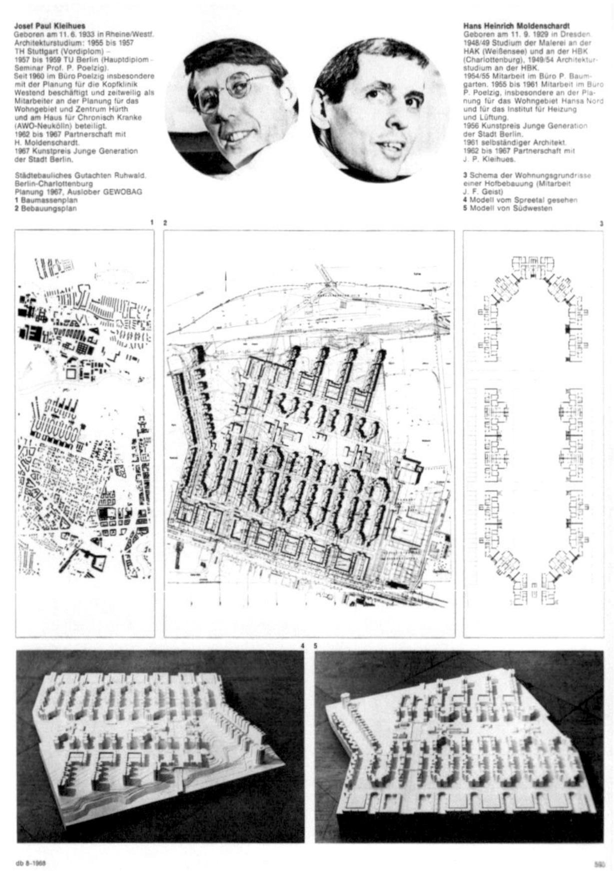

6 _ Josef Paul Kleihues and Hans Heinrich Moldenschardt, Urban-developmental report, Ruhwald, for GEWOBAG, 1967, *db* (1968) 8, p. 593.

French Lycée and for the Ruhwald site in Charlottenburg's Westend. After the Märkisches Viertel project, which for all its declared ambitions had been rather disappointing, the Ruhwald competition in 1965 in particular had aroused great hopes. Ever since the turn of the last century, the Ruhwald district had attracted one new proposal after another from well-known names in the discipline. Kleihues presented both the first prize by René Gagès and Volker Theissen and the entry from Stefan Wewerka, who – along with Ludwig Leo – was without a doubt one of the secret heroes of the younger generation. Parallel to this he showed an expert report on the same site submitted after the competition by himself and Heiner Moldenschardt (figs. 5 and 6). He did not, however, include Ungers's Ruhwald design, featuring instead the same architect's programmatic project – also never implemented – for an extensive development at Rupenhorn. Ungers had already publicized his Ruhwald project himself in one of the journals produced by his Chair.[14]

The three projects for a big estate on the Ruhwald site that were selected as examples by Kleihues indicate how far the discussion during the 1960s in West Berlin had departed from the conceptual typologies applied only a few years earlier to Gropius-Stadt and the Märkisches Viertel. Instead of loosely scattering low apartment blocks and free-standing buildings within a broad green space, ideas were now being mooted for new approaches to urban construction where roads, open spaces and residential buildings were to be merged with their infrastructure to create a new whole, not dissimilar to traditional urban geometries of road, square and block – a trend that was to reach full fruition a decade later at the IBA in Berlin under the leadership of Kleihues and Hardt-Waltherr Hämer.

When reading the answers to the questions put to the young Berlin architects by the *db* editors, it is not so much the spectrum of issues that is surprising, but rather the positive assessment of the new inner-city motorway most of the interview partners have. Several of them refer to the *Kollektivplan* of 1946 as the intellectual root of the biggest public construction project in West Berlin for many years, and believe it will inject urgently required modernization into the island city. By contrast, the architects surveyed seem barely aware of the major subsidy scheme launched after the Wall was built to boost the West Berlin economy, which had been suffering from a lack of investment: the planning process initiated in 1962 for radically restructuring the city by means of large-scale demolition of inner-city quarters that had been left largely undamaged by war-time air raids.[15] Although the results of a competition for ideas had been presented by some important urban designers from the Federal

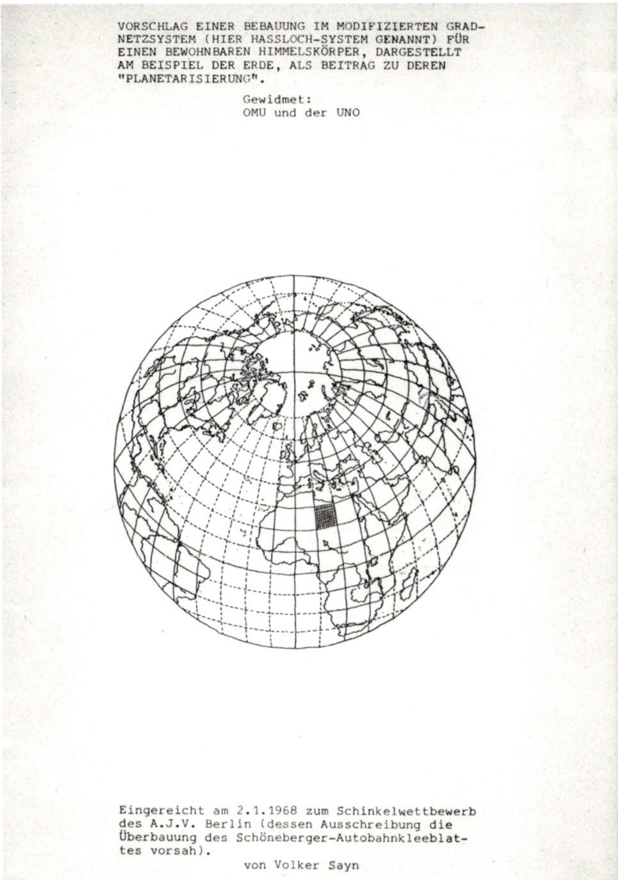

VORSCHLAG EINER BEBAUUNG IM MODIFIZIERTEN GRAD-NETZSYSTEM (HIER HASSLOCH-SYSTEM GENANNT) FÜR EINEN BEWOHNBAREN HIMMELSKÖRPER, DARGESTELLT AM BEISPIEL DER ERDE, ALS BEITRAG ZU DEREN "PLANETARISIERUNG".

Gewidmet:
OMU und der UNO

Eingereicht am 2.1.1968 zum Schinkelwettbewerb des A.J.V. Berlin (dessen Ausschreibung die Überbauung des Schöneberger-Autobahnkleeblattes vorsah).

von Volker Sayn

7 _ Volker Sayn, Entry for the "Planetarisation" of the Earth, submission to the Schinkel Competition of the AIV Berlin, 1968, *Veröffentlichungen zur Architektur*, ed. O. M. Ung (May 1968) 13

Republic during the *Bauwochen* in 1964, the architecture community had taken little notice of them. The implications of this did not crystallize into issues for architecture until hefty criticism of monotonous, ghetto-like estates on the urban periphery began to erupt around 1968. At first, these issues were only raised in seminars at the newly constituted departments of the TU, but gradually – as the rehabilitation plans became urban reality in the wake of extensive clearance and demolition – they were lodged in the consciousness of practising architects as tasks to be addressed.[16] Over the subsequent two decades, these practising architects took a greater interest in aspects of rehabilitation, engaging in intense debates about closing off block perimeters and the public or semi-public use of urban spaces. For the time being, however, the discussion in architecture before and after 1968, until the real estate crisis in the 1970s, continued to focus on questions of form and colour, and the relationship of building design to the new transport infrastructures, and at best incidentally the challenges posed by industrialization and prefabrication in construction, only occasionally interrupted by polemical architectural utopias, such as Volker Sayn's proposal for the Schinkel competition in 1968 to "planetise the Earth" by building endless ribbon cities along the meridians (fig. 7).[17]

NOTES

1 _ Uwe Soukup, *Wie starb Benno Ohnesorg? Der 2. Juni 1967* (Berlin, 2007).

2 _ TU Berlin, Lehrstuhl für Entwerfen VI or Prof. Dipl.-Ing. O.M.Ungers, ed., *Veröffentlichungen zur Architektur* (Berlin, 1965–1969).

3 _ *Architekturtheorie. Internationaler Kongress in der TU Berlin 11. bis 15. Dezember 1967, Veröffentlichungen zur Architektur* 14, ed. Jörg Pampe (Berlin, June 1968).

4 _ *Team X Treffen, Veröffentlichungen zur Architektur* 3, ed. Ulrich Fleming and Hartmut Schmetzer (Berlin, June 1966).

5 _ *A.+ P. Smithson, Mies van der Rohe, Veröffentlichungen zur Architektur* 20, ed. Jörg Pampe (Berlin, November 1968).

6 _ Rudi Dutschke in an interview in: *Der Stern* on November 26, 1967. See also: Rudi Dutschke, *Mein langer Marsch* (Reinbek, 1981), p. 64.
On the *Critical University* see also: Tilmann Fichter, *Kleine Geschichte des SDS* (Berlin, 1977).

7 _ *Materialien zur Diskussion. Diagnose zum Bauen in West-Berlin*, printed by Gerhard Rump (Berlin, 1968).
(The quotations below are taken from the expanded second edition, probably published in late September 1968.)

8 _ See article: "Stumpfer Stern," *Der Spiegel* (1968) 39.

9 _ Ad-hoc Gruppe Hochschuldidaktik, *Planer-Flugschrift 3. Arbeitspapiere zur Umstrukturierung der Arch.-Fak. Zu den Diagnosen 8.9.-20.9.1968. Kritische Ausstellung der Architekten und Studenten* (Berlin, 1968).

10 _ Guest editor Josef Paul Kleihues, *Junge Berliner Architekten, db* (1968) 8 (*Deutsche Bauzeitung* with *baukunst* and *werkform*).

11 _ Ibid., p. 570.

12 _ Ibid., pp. 608–610.

13 _ Julius Posener, "Reflexionen," *Deutsche Bauzeitung* (1968) 8, pp. 574/575.

14 _ O.M. Ungers, "Gutachten Ruhwald," *Veröffentlichungen zur Architektur* 9, ed. Guido Ast (Berlin, August 1967).

15 _ Rolf Schwedler, „Bericht des Senators für Bau- und Wohnungswesen," *Stadterneuerung in Berlin*, published for the Berliner *Bauwochen* 1964, pp. 2–7.

16 _ Cf. e.g.: Hartmut Frank, Olaf Gibbins, Ulf Kadritzke, Berd Künkel, Joachim Schlandt, "Gründerzeitmuseum und Bildungsfelder – Alternativen zur Stadtsanierung in Berlin-Kreuzberg?", *Bauwelt* (1969) 47.

17 _ Volker Sayn, *Vorschlag einer Bebauung im modifizierten Grad-Netz-system für einen bewohnbaren Himmelskörper, dargestellt am Beispiel der Erde, als Beitrag zu deren „Planetarisierung", Veröffentlichungen zur Architektur* (Berlin, May 1968) 13. (Dedicated to OMU and the UN, submitted on January 2, 1968 to the Schinkel competition held by A.I.V. Berlin, for which the brief sought a superstructure for the motorway interchange at Schöneberg).

PICTURE CREDITS

Fig. 1 _ Volume of papers, *Architectural Theory. International Congress in the TU West-Berlin 11th to 15th December 1967*, ed. Jörg Pampe, repro from: TU Berlin, Lehrstuhl für Entwerfen VI o. Prof. Dipl.-Ing. O. M. Ungers, ed., *Veröffentlichungen zur Architektur* (Berlin, June 1968) 14.

Fig. 2 _ Stefan Wewerka, Collage for the title page, publication of the meeting of Team X in Berlin-West, 1965, repro from: TU Berlin, Lehrstuhl für Entwerfen VI o, Prof. Dipl.-Ing. O. M. Ungers, ed., *Veröffentlichungen zur Architektur* 3, ed. Ulrich Fleming and Hartmut Schmetzer (Berlin, June 1966).

Fig. 3 _ Left: Discussion materials for the exhibition *Diagnose zum Bauen* in West-Berlin on the occasion of the Building Weeks from the 8th to the 20th September, 1968. Center: Signatories to the manifesto for the exhibition. Right: Ad hoc group university didactics, *Planer-Flugschrift 3. Arbeitspapiere zur Umstrukturierung der Arch.-Fak. Zu den Diagnosen 8.9.-20.9.1968. Kritische Ausstellung der Architekten und Studenten* (Berlin, 1968).

Fig. 4 _ Guest editor Josef Paul Kleihues, *Junge Berliner Architekten, db* (1968) 8 (*Deutsche Bauzeitung* united with *baukunst* and *werkform*)

Fig. 5 _ Stefan Wewerka, 3rd prize in the urban-developmental competition for ideas, Ruhwald, 1965, repros from: *db* (1968) 8, p. 592.

Fig. 6 _ Josef Paul Kleihues and Hans Heinrich Moldenschardt, Urban-developmental report, Ruhwald, for GEWOBAG, 1967, repros from: *db* (1968) 8, pp. 592–593.

Fig. 7 _ Volker Sayn, Entry for the "Planetarisation" of the Earth, submission to the Schinkel Competition of the AIV Berlin, 1968, repro from: TU Berlin, Lehrstuhl für Entwerfen VI o. Prof. Dipl.-Ing. O. M. Ungers, ed., *Veröffentlichungen zur Architektur* (Berlin, May 1968) 13.

Architecture and Art

Hans Scharoun with landscape planner Hermann Mattern, Berliner Philharmonie (1960–63), circa 1963

Hans Scharoun, Concert hall of Berliner Philharmonie, photograph: Mila Hacke, 2012

Hermann Fehling, Daniel Gogel, Max Planck Institute for Educational Research (1972–74, planning since 1964), entrance area, circa 1974

Hermann Fehling, Daniel Gogel, Max Planck Institute for Educational Research, entrance area, photograph from inside, circa 1974

Ludwig Mies van der Rohe, Neue Nationalgalerie (1965–68), circa 1968

Ludwig Mies van der Rohe, Design for the Neue Nationalgalerie Berlin, interior, 1962–65

Hermann Henselmann, Haus des Lehrers with mosaic in natural stone by Walter Womacka (1961–64), 1965

Hermann Henselmann, Congress Hall and Haus des Lehrers, postcard, circa 1967

Hermann Henselmann, Congress Hall, entrance area with stairs, circa 1964

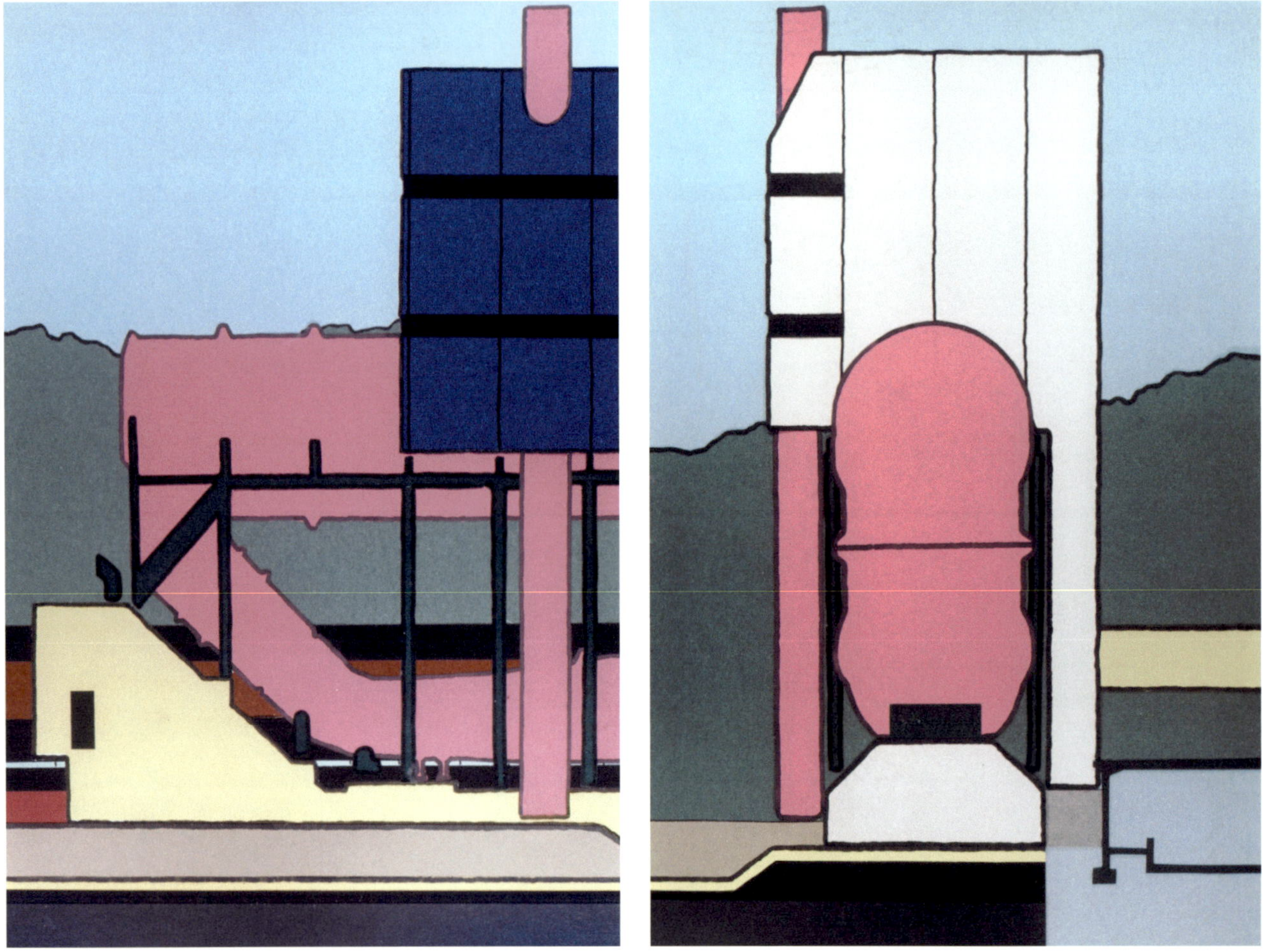

Ludwig Leo, Color study for the Circulation Tank 2 of the Institute of Hydraulic Engineering and Shipbuilding (UT 2), circa 1967

Ludwig Leo and Christian Boës, Circulation Tank 2 of the Institute of Hydraulic Engineering and Shipbuilding (1967–74), photograph: Thomas Bruns, 2011

Epilogue

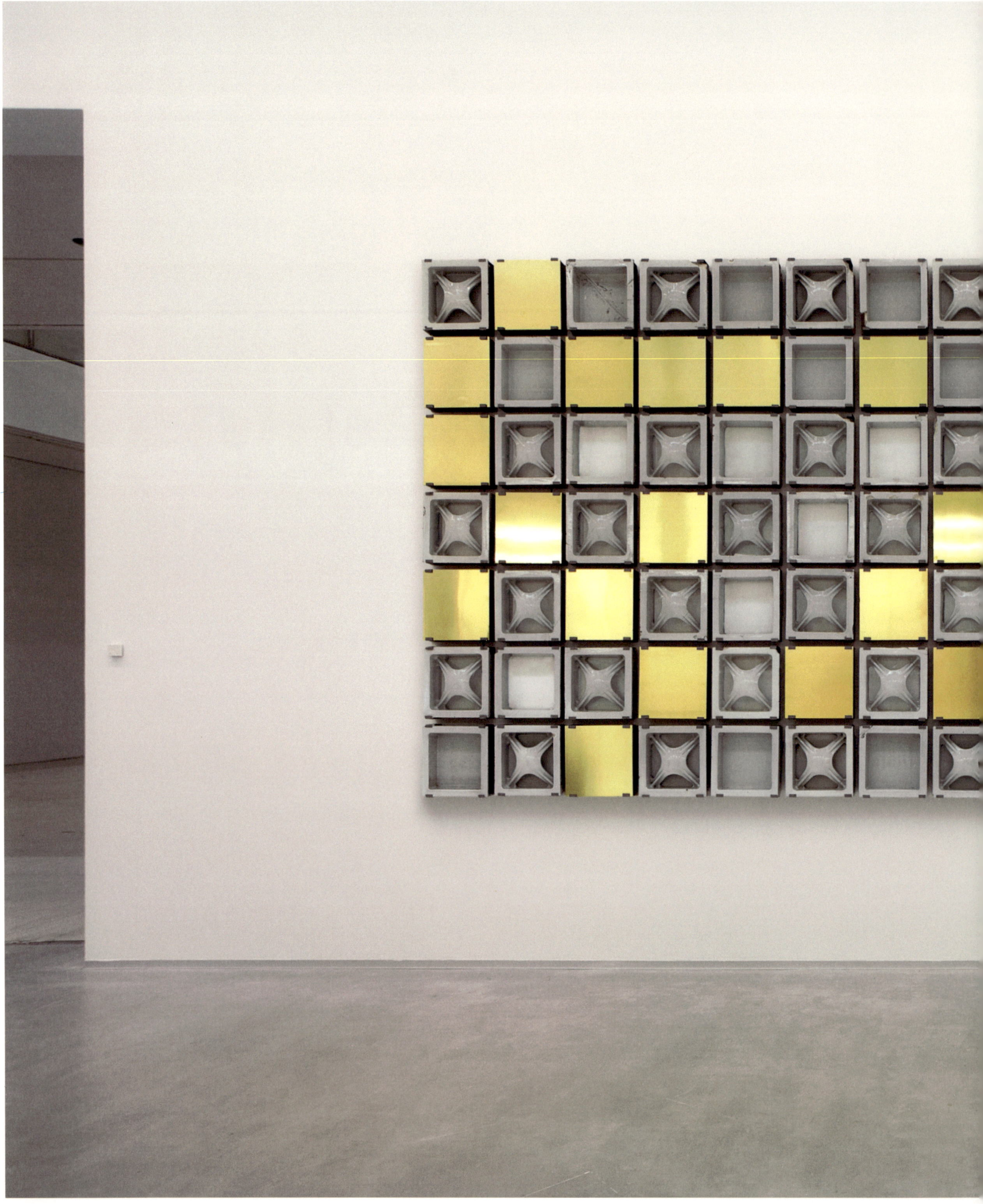

ES IST SOWEIT NORMAL, ICH KENNE
DAS ANDERE LEBEN HALT NUR VON ERZÄHLUNGEN

MAN WÄCHST AUF, INTERESSEN ÄNDERN SICH,
ABER ALLE SIND GENAUSO GEBLIEBEN, WIE SIE WAREN

DIE SCHRANKWAND SIEHT AUCH FAST AUS WIE EIN TOWER
DAS GEHT ALLES SO IN DIESE RICHTUNG

ICH WILL ES NICHT ALS IRGENDWELCHE MATTSCHEIBE SEHEN. ICH KANN JA DAS FENSTER AUFMACHEN, DANN KANN ICH ALLES SPÜREN

Bernd Trasberger, *Hertie*, 2009
Beate Gütschow, *S#11*, 2005
Stephen Willats, *Eine postmoderne Lebensform*, 1992/93
Stephen Willats, *Eine postmoderne Lebensform*, 1992/93
Karsten Konrad, *Lost Island*, 2004

Catalogue of Exhibited Works

Prologue

Icons of International Post-War Modernism

Ludwig Mies van der Rohe, Representation pavillion of the German Empire, Barcelona, 1929, exterior views, photographs: unknown author, circa 1929, each circa 11.3 x 22.2 cm, BG-AS 3.9.2-4

Ludwig Mies van der Rohe, Representation pavillion of the German Empire, Barcelona, 1929, interior views, photographs: unknown author, circa 1929, each circa 11.4 x 22.5 cm, BG-AS 3.9.5,7,11

Le Corbusier, Unité d'habitation (1945), Marseille, photograph: Paul Koslowski, 1997, p. 2

Ludwig Mies van der Rohe, Commonwealth Promenade apartment buildings, construction period 1953-56, Chicago, photograph: Hedrich-Blessing Photographers, 1957-58, Chicago History Museum HB-20816-A, p. 3 (not in the exhibition)

Yona Friedman, Ville Spatiale, project, perspective, 1958-59, 34.3 x 49.5 cm, felt-tip pen on transparent paper, Museum of Modern Art (MoMA), New York, Gift of The Howard Gilman Foundation Acc.n.: 1192.2000, p. 4 (not in the exhibition)

René Burri, Office building by Oscar Niemeyer (1957-60), National Congress, Brasília, 1960, p. 5

Berlin – A City Destroyed

Photographer unknown, Aerial photograph of Leipziger Platz with adjacent urban area to the east, 29.5 x 29 cm, silver gelatin paper, reproduction from „Berlin. Planungsgrundlagen für den städtebaulichen Ideenwettbewerb, Hauptstadt Berlin'". Memorandum, 1957, p. 42, fig. 4, repro 2015, Berlinische Galerie BG-AS 108/2014, p. 16

Photographer unknown, Aerial photograph of Mehringplatz with southern part of Friedrichstadt, circa 1955, 29.5 x 41.5 cm, silver gelatin paper, reproduction from „Berlin. Planungsgrundlagen für den städtebaulichen Ideenwettbewerb ‚Hauptstadt Berlin'". Memorandum, p. 40, fig. 2, repro 2015, Berlinische Galerie BG-AS 108/2014

Greater-Berlin center, mapping of war damage, situation in 1945, from: „Berlin. Planungsgrundlagen für den städtebaulichen Ideenwettbewerb ‚Hauptstadt Berlin'". Memorandum, 1957, repro 2015, 17.9 x 25.6 cm, Berlinische Galerie BG-AS 123/2012,1

Berlin – Divided City

Will McBride, 2 young men in Bernauer Straße, the newly constructed Wall in the background, 1961, 37.3 x 54.7 cm, silver gelatin paper, Berlinische Galerie BG-FS 028/95,13, p. 19

Herbert Tobias, Shortly after the building of the Wall, Bernauer Straße, 1961, 34.4 x 34.6 cm, silver gelatin paper, Berlinische Galerie BG-FS 008/96,3

Herbert Tobias, Untitled (wreaths laid in front of a walled-up house), 1961, 34.4 x 34.5 cm, silver gelatin paper, Berlinische Galerie BG-FS 008/96,6

Photographer unknown, Untitled (Wedding. Wall and screen Schwedter Straße/corner of Gleimstraße – Gleimtunnel), January 18, 1962, 18.1 x 24 cm, silver gelatin paper, Berlinische Galerie BG-FS 041/86,62

Photographer unknown, Untitled (Wedding. Barbed wire barrier at the sector border), August 16, 1961, 15.1 x 21.5 cm, silver gelatin paper, Berlinische Galerie BG-FS 041/86,62

Berlin – New City

Hans Scharoun, Entry to the international urban-developmental competition "Capital City Berlin", 1957, 2nd prize, isometry, 25 x 42 cm, silver gelatin paper, reproduction from „Berlin. Planungsgrundlagen für den städtebaulichen Ideenwettbewerb ‚Hauptstadt Berlin'", 1957. Memorandum, repro 2015, Berlinische Galerie, p. 6

Alexander Naumov, Sketch for the urban-developmental "Competition for ideas for a socialist re-design of the center of the capital of the GDR – Berlin", photograph: Gisela Dutschmann, 1959, repro from negative, 2015, Berlinische Galerie BG-AS 1436.001634, p. 7

Alison and Peter Smithson, Capital City Berlin 1957/58, Governmental department buildings, perspective of the main transport axis, 33 x 44.4 cm, ink on transparent paper, Frances Loeb Library, Harvard University Graduate School of Design, Deutsches Architekturmuseum, Frankfurt am Main, p. 85

Lindemann & Lüdicke Berlin, Reconstruction and new building of Berlin (West), scale 1:50000, German Planning Atlas – Atlas of Berlin, 1959, 43 x 60 cm, color print, Berlinische Galerie BG-AS 16.35

Risen from Ruins

The new Kaiser Wilhelm Memorial Church

Auguste-Viktoria-Platz, circa 1910, model circa 1987, 20 x 180 x 115 cm, wood, metal, parish of Kaiser Wilhelm Memorial Church

Breitscheidplatz after 1965, model circa 1987, 20 x 180 x 100 cm, wood, metal, parish of Kaiser Wilhelm Memorial Church

Egon Eiermann, Model of Kaiser Wilhelm Memorial Church, photograph: Carl Albiker, 1957, 8.5 x 11.7 cm, silver gelatin paper, Berlinische Galerie BG-AS 117.2.2, repro 2015

Egon Eiermann, Model of Kaiser Wilhelm Memorial Church, interior, photograph: Carl Albiker, 1957, silver gelatin paper, 12.2 x 17.1 cm, Berlinische Galerie BG-AS 117.2.1, repro 2015

Egon Eiermann, Kaiser Wilhelm Memorial Church, montage of the glass-concrete honeycomb, photographer unknown, silver gelatin paper, 17.2 x 23.2 cm, private archive

Egon Eiermann, New Kaiser Wilhelm Memorial Church, photograph: Otto Borutta, 1963, repro from 9 x 12 cm negative, Berlinische Galerie BG-AS 1/2015,3, p. 22

Egon Eiermann, New Kaiser Wilhelm Memorial Church, interior: photographer unknown, 1963, 17.2 x 23.2 cm, silver gelatin paper, Berlinische Galerie BG-AS 17/2013,1011, p. 23

Conversion of the Reichstag Building

Max Krajewsky, Reichstag, south lobby before reconstruction, 24.07.1959, 23.4 x 17.4 cm, silver gelatin paper, Akademie der Künste, Berlin, Baukunstarchiv PBA WV 103, F. 174, repro 2015

Max Krajewsky, Reichstag, entrance hall before reconstruction, 24.07.1959, 23.4 x 17.5 cm, silver gelatin paper, Akademie der Künste, Berlin, Baukunstarchiv WV 103, F. 171

Max Krajewsky, Reichstag, hall beneath the dome before reconstruction, 24.07.1959, 17.3 x 23.3 cm, silver gelatin paper, Akademie der Künste, Berlin, Baukunstarchiv WV 103, F. 173

Max Krajewsky, Reichstag, hall beneath the dome before reconstruction, 24.07.1959, 17.4 x 23.4 cm, silver gelatin paper, Akademie der Künste, Berlin, Baukunstarchiv WV 103, F. 172

Hans Döllgast, competition for the redevelopment of the Reichstag building in Berlin, 1960, 43.8 x 39.6 cm, pencil, watercolour, Kunstbibliothek, Berlin HdZ 970

Paul Baumgarten, Redevelopment of the Reichstag building, sketch for the new dome, handwritten note: "Dome must be rebuilt, although in a different form. It now has 'content' and the large open staircase fulfils a purpose", 1964, 31 x 52 cm, blueprint, Akademie der Künste, Berlin, Baukunstarchiv WV 103, Plan 30, p. 24

Paul Baumgarten, Redevelopment of the Reichstag building, reception hall with view to the west door, 1961-69, 50 x 57 cm, ink and pencil on transparent paper, Akademie der Künste, Berlin, Baukunstarchiv WV 103, Plan 42

Paul Baumgarten, Redevelopment of the Reichstag building, interior of the reception hall with view to the plenary chamber, 1961, 50.8 x 70.2 cm, pencil on transparent paper, Akademie der Künste, Berlin, Baukunstarchiv WV 103, Plan 43

Paul Baumgarten, Redevelopment of the Reichstag building, cross-section west-east, 1961, 30 x 52.5 cm, pencil on transparent paper, Akademie der Künste, Berlin, Baukunstarchiv WV 103, Plan 27

Paul Baumgarten, Redevelopment of the Reichstag building, west view, 1961-69, 31 x 52 cm, pencil on blueprint, Akademie der Künste, Berlin, Baukunstarchiv WV 103, Plan 28

Photographer unknown, Reichstag, view from the west, 1961-69, 11.5 x 24 cm, silver gelatin paper, Akademie der Künste, Berlin, Baukunstarchiv PBA WV 103, F. 120

Paul Baumgarten, Redevelopment of the Reichstag building, assembly hall, photograph: Wallace Driver, circa 1969, 20.9 x 30 cm, silver gelatin paper, Akademie der Künste, Berlin, Baukunstarchiv WV 103, F. 115, p. 25

Paul Baumgarten, Redevelopment of the Reichstag building, foyer to the plenary chamber with the sculpture *Cosmos* by Bernhard Heiliger, photograph: Karl E. Jacobs, circa 1969, 12.9 x 17.6 cm, silver gelatin paper, Akademie der Künste, Berlin, Baukunstarchiv WV 103, F. 123, p. 25

Klaus Mehner, Redevelopment of the Reichstag building, interior of the plenary chamber, 1961-69, 24.3 x 30 cm, silver gelatin paper, Akademie der Künste, Berlin, Baukunstarchiv WV 103, F. 133b

Paul Baumgarten, Redevelopment of the Reichstag building, south entrance with the window of the Council of Elders with balustrade by Chrukin, photograph: Wolfgang Lücking, 1961-69, 23.3 x 17.3 cm, silver gelatin paper, Akademie der Künste, Berlin, Baukunstarchiv WV 103, F. 74

Paul Baumgarten, Reichstag, Federal President's reception hall with view of the Brandenburg Gate, photograph: Liselotte Orgel-Köhne, circa 1969, repro from negative, Akademie der Künste, Berlin, Baukunstarchiv WV 103. Neg. 94

Paul Baumgarten, Reichstag, lobby with seating group and artwork, photographer unknown, circa 1969, 18 x 23.7 cm, silver gelatin paper, Akademie der Künste, Berlin, Baukunstarchiv WV 103, F. 183

Privy Council Building

Roland Korn, Hans-Erich Bogatzky and Klaus Pätzmann, Privy Council Building, façade front and rear, circa 1961, pencil on transparent paper, European School of Management and Technology

Roland Korn, Hans-Erich Bogatzky and Klaus Pätzmann, Privy Council Building, view of façade from Schloßplatz, circa 1961, pencil on transparent paper, European School of Management and Technology

Roland Korn, Hans-Erich Bogatzky and Klaus Pätzmann, Privy Council Building, façade, rear view, circa 1961, pencil on transparent paper, European School of Management and Technology

Roland Korn, Hans-Erich Bogatzky and Klaus Pätzmann, Privy Council Building, view of façade from Breite Straße with side wing, circa 1961, pencil on transparent paper, European School of Management and Technology

Roland Korn, Hans-Erich Bogatzky and Klaus Pätzmann, Privy Council Building, site plan showing front building and side wing with layout of atrium, circa 1961, pencil on transparent paper, European School of Management and Technology

Roland Korn, Hans-Erich Bogatzky and Klaus Pätzmann, Privy Council Building, photograph: Gisela Dutschmann, 1965, repro from 6 x 6 cm negative, Berlinische Galerie BG-AS 1436.007254, p. 26

Roland Korn, Hans-Erich Bogatzky and Klaus Pätzmann, Privy Council Building, insertion of the projection above the doorway IV from the palace, photographer unknown, 1963, 16.2 x 23.8 cm, silver gelatin paper, Berlinische Galerie BG-AS 95/2012,33, p. 26

Doug Hall, Privy Council Building, main entrance hall, ground floor, from the series Remnants of the GDR, August 1992, 129.5 x 101 cm, C-Print, Berlinische Galerie BG-FS 033/93, p. 27

Urban Spaces/ Urban Dreams

Breitscheidplatz

Otto Borutta, Breitscheidplatz and the new Kaiser Wilhelm Memorial Church, circa 1965, repro from 9 x 12 cm negative, Berlinische Galerie, p. 46

Helmut Hentrich, Hubert Petschnigg, Europa-Center, postcard, circa 1968, p. 48

Engelbert Kremser, Europa-Center, photomontage, 1969, 41.3 x 49 cm, silver gelatin paper on cardboard, Berlinische Galerie BG-AS 86/2014,3, p. 49

Engelbert Kremser, Design for the Europa-Center, view from the Zoo high-rise building, photomontage, 1969, 41.5 x 48.3 cm, silver gelatin paper on cardboard, Berlinische Galerie BG-AS 86/2014,1

Mehringplatz

Hans Scharoun, Development plan Mehringplatz, urban-developmental report, competition first prize, model, 1962, 120 x 116 x 19 cm, wood, plastic, Akademie der Künste, Berlin, Baukunstarchiv WV 223, model 32,

Werner Düttmann, New building on Mehringplatz, model, 1967-70, 31.5 x 100 x 98 cm, wood, plastic, Berlinische Galerie BG-AS 94/2014,1

Werner Düttmann, Housing construction on Mehringplatz, isometry of the urban-developmental situation, circa 1966, 39.9 x 60 cm, blueprint, Akademie der Künste, Berlin, Baukunstarchiv Düttmann WV 34, Plan 1

Mehringplatz, Report of the invited architects, model, photographs of the models: unknown authors, 1966-65, 17.7 x 13.1 cm and 24 x 17.4 cm, silver gelatin paper, Akademie der Künste, Berlin, Baukunstarchiv Düttmann-34, 34/7-12

Kulturforum

Hans Scharoun, "Kulturforum" with Senate guesthouse, photograph of the model: Reinhard Friedrich, 1964, 18.2 x 24 cm, silver gelatin paper, Berlinische Galerie, p. 79

Otto Borutta, Philharmonic Hall in the urban context, circa 1963, repro from 6 x 7 cm negative, Berlinische Galerie, p. 78

Model Kulturforum, 1992, 32 x 187 x 152 cm, wood, plastic, Berliner Philharmonie

Planning for the Center of East-Berlin

Gerhard Kosel with Hanns Hopp and Hans Mertens, Marx-Engels-Forum with central building, urban-developmental study, out of competition, for the "Competition for ideas for a socialist re-design of the center of the capital of the GDR – Berlin" as further development of a design dated early 1958, 1959, photograph: Gisela Dutschmann, repro from 13 x 18 cm negative, Berlinische Galerie BG-AS 1436.001758_B19725, p. 72

Hermann Henselmann, Design for a "German Pantheon", June 24, 1958, counter design to the idea of the governmental high-rise building by the collective Kosel, buildings on the central square/Spreeinsel, bird's-eye-view from the west, 24.08.1958, 58.8 x 75.5 cm, ink and crayon on transparent paper, Akademie der Künste, Berlin, Baukunstarchiv HHA 120-148, Plan 1, p. 73

Hermann Henselmann, Design for a "German Pantheon", June 24, 1958, counter design to the idea of the governmental high-rise building by the collective Kosel, bird's-eye-view to the north-east with buildings around the central square on the Spreeinsel, 24.08.1958, 60 x 75.8 cm, ink and crayon on transparent paper, Akademie der Künste, Berlin, Baukunstarchiv HHA 120-148, Plan 2

Hermann Henselmann, Sketched ideas with views of the "Tower of Signals", design out of competition for the "Competition for ideas for a socialist re-design of the center of the capital of the GDR – Berlin", 1959, 85 x 120 cm, pencil and crayon on transparent paper, Akademie der Künste, Berlin, Baukunstarchiv HHA 120-147, Plan 1, p. 74

Hermann Henselmann, View from the Spree to the central building, photograph of the drawing: unknown author, 1962, 32.5 x 37.5 cm, silver gelatin paper, Akademie der Künste, Berlin, Baukunstarchiv HHA 120-848, F. 10a

Hermann Henselmann, Interior of the central building, photograph of the drawing: unknown author, 1962, 32.5 x 37.3 cm, silver gelatin paper, Akademie der Künste, Berlin, Baukunstarchiv HHA 120-848, F. 11a

Collective Municipal Building Offices: Peter Schweizer, Dorothea Tscheschner, Hubert Martinez, Central area with television tower in its final position and cubistic low building as central building, photograph of the model, view from the south-west, December 1964, photographer unknown, 23.5 x 17.7 cm, silver gelatin paper, repro 2015, Berlinische Galerie Bestand G.F. Kühne

Gisela Dutschmann, Realised television tower in the urban context (1964-69), photograph taken from the high-rise building on the Fischerinsel, 1970, repro from 6 x 6 cm negative, Berlinische Galerie BG-AS 1436.007716, p. 75

Josef Kaiser, Ministry of Foreign Affairs of the GDR, collaged view: Dieter Urbach, circa 1967, 60.3 x 59.8 cm, opaque white and ink on silver gelatin paper, Berlinische Galerie BG-AS 2033.1.1

Josef Kaiser, Ministry of Foreign Affairs of the GDR, contact print of the negative by Gisela Dutschmann on archive index card, silver gelatin paper on paper, 18.7 x 24.9 cm, April 1967, Berlinische Galerie BG-AS 1436.007228, p. 76

The Marx-Engels-Brücke seen from the Altes Museum. In the background is the newly built Ministry of Foreign Affairs of the GDR, circa 1968, photograph: Wohlrabe, Landesdenkmalamt Berlin II_B 1048, negative interpretation: Arwed Messmer, 2009, p. 77

Dieter Andree, Large pub-restaurant *Ahornblatt* with housing on Leipziger Straße, circa 1986, 17.7 x 17.7 cm, silver gelatin paper, Berlinische Galerie BG-AS 17/2013,556, p. 53

Alexanderplatz

Gisela Dutschmann, Alexanderplatz with Haus des Lehrers, 1966, repro from 6 x 6 cm negative, Berlinische Galerie BG-AS 1436.005840, p. 47

Heinz Lieber, Panorama Alexanderplatz, 1972, 22.8 x 92.8 cm, silver gelatin paper, Berlinische Galerie BG-AS 77/2014, p. 50-51

Gisela Dutschmann, View along Karl-Marx-Allee from the corner of Grunerstraße, 1964, repro from 6 x 6 cm negative, Berlinische Galerie BG-AS 1436.005839, p. 51

Rem Koolhaas, View along the Wall towards the Axel Springer high-rise, 1971, Office for Metropolitan Architecture, p. 52

Leninplatz

Hermann Henselmann, Leninplatz (since 1992 Platz der Vereinten Nationen), competition entry, 10-storey ribbon development, views and ground plans, 1967-71, repro from negative, 28 x 27.3 cm, 2015, Akademie der Künste, Berlin, Baukunstarchiv HHA 120-890, 2

Hermann Henselmann, Competition Leninplatz with Lenin monument, ground plans, cross-section, views, 1967-71, repro from negative, 28 x 28 cm, 2015, Akademie der Künste, Berlin, Baukunstarchiv HHA 120-890, 3

Hermann Henselmann, Winning competition entry by the collective Hermann Henselmann for the design of Leninplatz with library pavilion and banner sculpture, 1968, 32.5 x 37.3 cm, silver gelatin paper, Akademie der Künste, Berlin, Baukunstarchiv HHA 120-846, F. 1a

Collective Manfred Jäkel, Lothar Kwasnitza, Dieter Urbach, Competition entry housing construction Leninplatz, collaged perspective: Dieter Urbach, 1967, repro from 13 x 18 cm negative, Berlinische Galerie BG-AS 44/2013,260, p. 80

Collective Hermann Henselmann, Heinz Mehlan, Realisation of housing construction Leninplatz with Lenin monument by Nikolai W. Tomski, 1968-70, photograph: Gisela Dutschmann, 1971, repro from 6 x 6 cm negative, Berlinische Galerie BG-AS 1436.004602, p. 81

Techno-Geometries

Traffic Planning

Werner Düttmann, Highway bridge Mecklenburgische/Rudolfstädter Straße, 1958, 91 x 146 cm, charcoal and graphite on transparent paper, Akademie der Künste, Berlin, Baukunstarchiv Düttmann WV 10, Plan 1

Josef Kaiser, Elevated road at Alexanderplatz, junction Liebknechtstraße, with roadside development, perspective drawing, photograph: Gisela Dutschmann, 1960, repro from 13 x 18 cm negative, 2015, Berlinische Galerie BG-AS 1436.003349, p. 100

Photographer unknown, Autobahn, Schöneberger Interchange/west ring road, planning drawing, 1965, 15.7 x 22.9 cm, silver gelatin paper, Berlinische Galerie BG-FS 041/86,30

Photographer unknown, System of highways, planning drawing, 1965, 13.4 x 22.8 cm, silver gelatin paper, Berlinische Galerie BG-FS 041/86,32

Junction Halensee with Rathenauplatz, 03.06.1960, postcard, Archive Frank Seehausen, p. 107

Gisela Dutschmann, Tunnel Grunerstraße and Haus des Lehrers, photograph from 1969, repro from 6 x 6 cm negative, Berlinische Galerie BG-AS 1436.006725, p. 107

Georg Kohlmaier, Barna von Sartory, Autobahn planning Oranienplatz, photomontage, 1969, 90 x 90 x 1 cm, silver gelatin paper on press board, Berlinische Galerie BG-AS 83/2014,5, p. 101

Georg Kohlmaier, Barna von Sartory, Moving pavements on the Kurfürstendamm, reproduction based on collage, 1969, 104.5 x 127.5 cm, Berlinische Galerie BG-AS 79/2014,1, p. 113

Georg Kohlmaier, Barna von Sartory, Routes of the moving pavements in West-Berlin, 1969, 52 x 85.9 cm, felt-tip pen and ink on transparent paper, Berlinische Galerie BG-AS 79/2014,22

Georg Kohlmaier, Barna von Sartory, Moving pavements, model 1969, 8.5 x 23.2 cm, silver gelatin paper, Berlinische Galerie BG-AS 79/2014,5

Georg Kohlmaier, Barna von Sartory, photomontage Moving pavements, 1969, 29.6 x 21.1 cm, silver gelatin paper, Berlinische Galerie BG-AS 79/2014,4

Georg Kohlmaier, Barna von Sartory, photomontage Moving pavements on the Kurfürstendamm, 1969, 104.5 x 127.5 cm, silver gelatin paper, Berlinische Galerie BG-AS 79/2014,1

Tower of Signals

Hermann Henselmann, Model for the "Competition for ideas for a socialist re-design of the center of the capital of the GDR - Berlin", photograph: K. Hoffmeister, 1958-59, 14 x 11.7 cm, silver gelatin paper, repro 2015, Akademie der Künste, Berlin, Baukunstarchiv HHA 120-892, F. 06b

Hermann Henselmann, Photo-collage Tower of Signals, entry for the "Competition for ideas for a socialist re-design of the center of the capital of the GDR - Berlin", photographer unknown, 1958-59, C-Print, 30 x 20.3 cm, Akademie der Künste, Berlin, Baukunstarchiv HHA 120-847, F. 31c

Hermann Henselmann, Tower of Signals, Forum of the Nation, entry for the "Competition for ideas for a socialist re-design of the center of the capital of the GDR - Berlin", model, photographer unknown, 1958-59, 32.5 x 37.3 cm, silver gelatin paper, repro 2015, Akademie der Künste, Berlin, Baukunstarchiv HHA 120-847, F. 22

Hermann Henselmann, Tower of Signals with Marienkirche (Church of Our Lady), entry for the "Competition for ideas for a socialist re-design of the center of the capital of the GDR - Berlin", model, photographer unknown, 1958-59, 32.5 x 37.3 cm, silver gelatin paper, repro 2015, Akademie der Künste, Berlin, Baukunstarchiv HHA 120-847, F. 24a

Fernsehturm

Hermann Henselmann, Sketch of the sphere of the TV tower, 1958/59, 33.5 x 36.6 cm, pencil and crayon on transparent paper, Akademie der Künste, Berlin, Baukunstarchiv HHA 120-147, Pl.3

Karl-Heinz Kraemer, TV tower under construction, circa 1967, 30 x 20.5 cm, silver gelatin paper, Berlinische Galerie BG-AS 1/2014,16, p. 102

Karl-Heinz Kraemer, TV tower under construction, montage of façade segments, 1968, 30 x 20.2 cm, silver gelatin paper, Berlinische Galerie BG-AS 3015.1.10, p. 102

Josef Kaiser, Design for the entrance building of the TV tower, 1964, collage of images: Dieter Urbach, 1964, repro from 13 x 18 cm negative, Berlinische Galerie BG-AS 44/2013,237, p. 103

Dieter Urbach, Collaged interior perspective of the entrance building of the TV tower according to a design by Josef Kaiser, 1964, repro from 18 x 13 cm negative, Berlinische Galerie BG-AS 44/2013,240a, p. 103

Tower Restaurant Steglitz

Ralf Schüler, Ursulina Schüler-Witte, Design of the Tower Restaurant Steglitz, photo-collage, 1972, 22.5 x 29.7 cm, silver gelatin paper, Berlinische Galerie BG-AS 1904.70.006a

Ralf Schüler, Ursulina Schüler-Witte, Design of the Tower Restaurant Steglitz, photo-collage, 1972, 22.5 x 29.7 cm, silver gelatin paper, Berlinische Galerie BG-AS 1904.70.006b, p. 104

Ralf Schüler, Ursulina Schüler-Witte, Tower Restaurant Steglitz with underground station Schloßstraße, 1972, 45 x 29.7 cm, C-Print, Berlinische Galerie BG-AS 1904.70.011, p. 105

Tegel Airport

Meinhard von Gerkan, Volkwin Marg, Tegel Airport, seating goup, circa 1972, Archiv gmp Architekten von Gerkan, Marg und Partner

Meinhard von Gerkan, Volkwin Marg, Tegel Airport, seating groups, circa 1972, C-Print, repro 2015, Archiv gmp Architekten von Gerkan, Marg und Partner

Meinhard von Gerkan, Volkwin Marg, Tegel Airport, exterior view with approch road, circa 1972, C-Print, repro 2015, Archiv gmp Architekten von Gerkan, Marg und Partner

Meinhard von Gerkan, Volkwin Marg, Tegel Airport, interior, circa 1972, C-Print, repro 2015, Archiv gmp Architekten von Gerkan, Marg und Partner

Meinhard von Gerkan, Volkwin Marg, Tegel Airport, competition model, 1965, 6 x 120,5 x 84 cm, wood, paper, cardboard, press board, Archiv gmp Architekten von Gerkan, Marg und Partner

Meinhard von Gerkan, Volkwin Marg, Tegel Airport, aerial view: unknown author, circa 1975, C-print, repro 2015, Berlin State Archive, p. 106

Large-Scale Structures

Ulrich Müther with Gerhard Lehmann, Rüdiger Plaethe, Helmut Stingl, Large pub-restaurant *Ahornblatt*, Gertraudenstraße (demolition: 2000), photograph: Gisela Dutschmann, 1977, repro from 6 x 6 cm negative, Berlinische Galerie BG-AS 1436.006422, p. 107

Josef Kaiser, Großhügelhaus ("large hill house"), collaged perspective: Dieter Urbach, 1971, repro from 15 x 12 cm negative, Berlinische Galerie BG-AS 1/2015,16

Josef Kaiser, Großhügelhaus ("large hill house", collaged perspective with residents: Dieter Urbach, 1971, repro from 15 x 12 cm negative, Berlinische Galerie BG-AS 44/2013,100b, p. 108

Ralf Schüler, Ursulina Schüler-Witte, Ribbon development Grunewald, cross-section, 1973, repro from negative 2015, Berlinische Galerie, p. 110-111

Bernhard Boës, Ribbon development Grunewald, perspective drawing based on a design by Schüler/Schüler-Witte, 1973, 24 x 54.8 cm, ink on transparent paper, Berlinische Galerie BG-AS 1904.55.1, p. 111

Georges Candilis, Alexis Josic, Shadrach Woods with Manfred Schiedhelm, Presentation plan for the competition "Development of the fruit-growing site of the Freie Universität Berlin", 1963, 122 x 121 x 1 cm, print, paper, acrylic glas, Berlinische Galerie BG-AS 27/2012,1, p. 112

Georges Candilis, Alexis Josic, Shadrach Woods with Manfred Schiedhelm, Competition model "Development of the fruit-growing site of the Freie Universität Berlin", 1963, 4 x 110 x 100 cm, wood, paper, cardboard, Berlinische Galerie BG-AS 27/2012,5

Serial Diversity

The layout of pages 126 and 127 was inspired by the design of a selection of Heinz Mosch buildings completed in Berlin, in: *Die Bauunternehmung Heinz Mosch* (Berlin/Bonn et al., 1971), no pag. Design concept: J. Meier BDW (Bauunternehmung Heinz Mosch); Tausch und Rüsse Werbeagentur Berlin.

All photographs are in the collection of Berlinische Galerie.

Column 1
Klaus Müller-Rehm, 22-storey housing blocks of the large-scale housing estate BBR (after 1972: Gropiusstadt), Sollmannweg 2, Berlin-Neukölln, construction period 1970-73, photograph: Schubmann+Ploch, 1977, 30 x 30 cm (detail), color print

Joachim Härter, Office building, Storkower Straße, Berlin-Prenzlauer Berg, photograph: Karl-Heinz Kraemer, 1967, 17 x 23.1 cm (detail), silver gelatin paper

Column 2
Josef Kaiser, Johannes Gitschel, High-rise tower block, Schillingstraße 30, Berlin-Mitte, 1964-1966, photograph: Gisela Dutschmann, 1966, scan from a slide (detail)

Siegfried Fehr, 15-storey housing block, Kandeler Weg 1, Berlin-Spandau, photograph: Walter Köster, 1963, 23 x 17.5 cm, silver gelatin print

Gehag, View of 14-storey tower block in the housing estate BBR (after 1972: Gropiusstadt), Berlin-Neukölln, Fritz-Erler-Allee 16, planning department of the Gehag, construction period 1964-65, photograph: Waldemar Titzenthaler, circa 1965, 23.4 x 17.5 cm, silver gelatin paper

Column 3
Astra Zarina Haner, V.S. Stefano d. Cacco, Erwin Eickhoff, Siegfried Hoffie, Residential building in the Märkisches Viertel, Treuenbrietzener Straße 17-27, construction period 1970-71, photograph: Ulrich, 1971, 13 x 18 cm, silver gelatin paper

Wilfried Stallknecht, Achim Felz, Herbert Kuschy, Residential building type P2, Erich-Kuttner-Straße 9-15, Berlin-Lichtenberg, photograph: Wolter, Deutsche Bauinformation, 1962, 12.6 x 17.5 cm, (detail), silver gelatin paper

Wolfgang Ortmann, 25-storey housing block, Leipziger Straße 45, photographer unknown, 1977, scan from a slide (detail)

Hans C. Müller, Georg Heinrichs, Residential and commercial building ensemble, so-called Opernviertel (Opera Quarter), Bismarckstraße 23-31, Berlin-Charlottenburg, photograph: Rolf Koehler, 1969, 17.9 x 23.4 cm (detail), color print

Column 4
Residential building, Grüntaler Straße 23, Berlin-Wedding, photograph: Rolf Koehler, 1967, silver gelatin paper

Wils Ebert, View of 14-storey high-rise building, Otto-Suhr estate, Alte Jakobstraße 144, Berlin-Kreuzberg, photographer unknown, circa 1962, 20.9 x 29.3 cm, silver gelatin paper

Hermann Klauschke, Office building, Storkower Straße, Berlin-Prenzlauer Berg, photograph: Karl-Heinz Kraemer, 1967, 16.6 x 22.4 cm (detail), silver gelatin paper

Otto Hagemann, 15-storey residential building in the Otto-Suhr estate, Berlin Kreuzberg, Alexandrinenstraße 100, photograph: Max Rudolph, 1964, 22.6 x 17.3 cm, silver gelatin paper

Wils Ebert, View of 14-storey high rise building in the "Spring Project", Berlin-Kreuzberg, Alte Jakobstraße 144, Nauenburger Straße (1959-62), photographer unknown, circa 1962, 21.2 x 29.4 cm, silver gelatin paper

Column 5
Hans Peter Schmiedel, Manfred Zumpe, 21-storey high-rise residential building Fischerinsel (1967-73), photographer unknown, 1970, scan from a slide (detail)

Wils Ebert, 18-storey high-rise residential building in BBR (after 1972: Gropiusstadt), Imbuschweg 30, Berlin-Neukölln, photographer unknown, 1967, 10 x 14.4 cm, silver gelatin paper

Heinz Graffunder, Housing area, Rathausstraße, photograph: Zentralbild/Ritter, 1969, 21.2 x 13.7 cm (detail), silver gelatin paper

Embassy of the Democratic People's Republic of North Korea, Glinkastraße 5-7, photographer unknown, 1974, scan from a slide (detail)

Column 6
Gehag, 15-storey residential high-rise building, Ritterstraße 95, Berlin-Kreuzberg, photograph: Waldemar Titzenthaler, 1968, 23.6 x 17.6 cm (detail), silver gelatin paper

Josef Kaiser, Johannes Gitschel, Tower block, Schillingstraße 30, Berlin-Mitte, 1964-1966, photograph: Gisela Dutschmann, 1966, Scan from negative (detail)

Wils Ebert, Fritz Gaulke, Werner Weber, 8-storey house type in the Paul-Hertz estate, Berlin-Charlottenburg, Klausingring 26, photograph: Wolfgang Lücking, 1962, 21.1 x 29.5 cm (detail), silver gelatin paper

High-rise apartment block, photograph: Eberhard Piltz, 18.2 x 23.8 cm, silver gelatin paper

Column 7
Gehag planning department, 14-storey tower block in the housing estate BBR (after 1972: Gropiusstadt), Berlin-Neukölln, Fritz-Erler-Allee 16, photograph: Waldemar Titzenthaler, 1968, 17.4 x 23.3 cm (detail), silver gelatin print

Hans C. Müller, Georg Heinrichs, Ensemble of residential and commercial buildings, so-called "Opernviertel", Bismarckstraße 23-31, photograph: Rolf Koehler, 1969, 17.9 x 23.4 cm (detail), color print

Hans C. Müller, Georg Heinrichs, Residential building in the Märkisches Viertel (1967-70), Wilhelmsruher Damm 122, photograph: Ulrich, 1970, 13 x 18 cm (detail), silver gelatin paper

Hans Bandel, 9-storey residential building in BBR, the so-called "Gropiusstadt", Theodor-Loos-Weg 6-12, photographer unknown, 1967, 21.2 x 30.2 cm (detail), silver gelatin paper

René Gages, Volker Theißen, Werner Weber, 18-storey residential building in the Märkisches Viertel (1966-69), Wilhelmsruher Damm 83-145, photographer unknown, 12.5 x 17.2 cm (detail), silver gelatin paper

Heinz Scharlipp, Günter Boy, Helmut Riechert, Wolfgang Vieroth, Motel, Unter den Linden, corner of Friedrichstraße, photographer unknown, 1967, scan from a slide (detail)

Column 8
Joachim Härter, Office building, Storkower Straße, Berlin-Prenzlauer Berg, photograph: Karl-Heinz Kraemer, 1967, 17 x 23.1 cm (detail), silver gelatin paper

Wilhelm Vormeier, 15-storey high-rise building, Krowelstraße 6, Berlin-Spandau, photograph: Willi Huschke, 1969, 23.9 x 18.2 cm (detail), silver gelatin print

Collective Peter Senf, Office building Wiratex, Unter den Linden 62-68, Berlin-Mitte, photograph: Karl-Heinz Kraemer, 1965, 17.9 x 16.8 cm (detail), silver gelatin paper

Gehag planning department, 14-storey tower block in the housing estate BBR (after 1972: Gropiusstadt), Berlin-Neukölln, Fritz-Erler-Allee 16, photograph: Waldemar Titzenthaler, 1968, 23.4 x 17.5 cm (detail), silver gelatin print

Column 9
Klaus Müller-Rehm, 22-storey high-rise blocks in the large-scale estate Heerstraße Nord, Berlin-Spandau, Maulbeerallee, from 1971, planning 1968-71, photograph: Schubmann +Ploch, 1977, 29 x 20 cm (detail), color print

Josef Kaiser, Johannes Gitschel, Tower block, Schillingstraße 30, Berlin-Mitte, 1964-1966, photograph: Gisela Dutschmann, 1966, Scan from negative (detail)

Collective Peter Senf, Office building Wiratex, Unter den Linden 62-68, photographer unknown, 1965, 17 x 23.4 cm (detail), silver gelatin paper

Klaus Müller-Rehm, 22-storey high-rise buildings in the large-scale estate Heerstraße Nord, Berlin-Spandau, Maulbeerallee, from 1971, planning 1968-71, photograph: Schubmann+Ploch, 1977, 20.5 x 28.8 cm (detail), color print

Hans Bandel, 9-storey residential building in BBR (after 1972: Gropiusstadt), Neuköllner Straße 267, photographer unknown, 1967, 21.2 x 30.2 cm (detail), silver gelatin paper

Column 10
Hans Bandel, 9-storey residential building in BBR (after 1972: Gropiusstadt), Neuköllner Straße 267, photographer unknown, 1967, 21.4 x 30.4 cm, (detail), silver gelatin paper

Guest house of the central committee, Wallstraße 57, Berlin-Mitte, photographer unknown, 1969, demolition 1998, scan from a slide (detail)

Gehag planning department, 14-storey tower block, large-scale housing estate BBR (after 1972: Gropiusstadt), Johannisthaler Chaussee 360, photograph: Waldemar Titzenthaler, 1968, 23.3 x 17.5 cm (detail), silver gelatin paper

Collective Werner Strassenmeier, Restaurant Lindencorso, Unter den Linden, corner of Friedrichstraße, Berlin-Mitte photographer unknown, 1966, demolition 1993, scan from a slide (detail)

Hans Stephan (general planning), Richard Kappey, Residential buildings on Falkenhagener Feld, photograph: Willi Huschke, 1966, 12.7 x 17.9 cm (detail), silver gelatin paper

Residential high-rise building, photograph: Eberhard Piltz, 18 x 23.9 cm (detail), silver gelatin paper

Page 128ff
Poster for the exhibition *Typenbauten für Stadt und Industrie* (Building types for city and industry), an exhibition in the context of an international conference on typified design projects, 1957, 41.7 x 29.7 cm, offset print, Berlinische Galerie BG-AS 72/2014

The Slab-Type Block
Franz Heinrich Sobotka, Gustav Müller, Pepper-House, photographer unknown, circa 1964, 22.9 x 17.6 cm, silver gelatin paper, Berlinische Galerie BG-AS 2030.2.1, p. 128

Franz Heinrich Sobotka, Gustav Müller, Pepper-House with exhibition pavilion *Bauzentrum Berlin*, photographer unknown, circa 1964, 16.8 x 21.5 cm, Berlinische Galerie BG-AS 2030.2.2

Collective Peter Senf, Office building of the GDR's foreign trade company Wiratex, photograph: Gisela Dutschmann, 1964, repro from 6 x 6 cm negative, Berlinische Galerie BG-AS 1436.008238, p. 128

Josef Kaiser, Ministry for Foreign Affairs, View of the model, photographer unknown, circa 1964, 24 x 30 cm, silver gelatin paper, Nachlass Josef Kaiser, p. 128

Emil Leibold with Herbert Boos, Hanno Walther, Berlin Ministry for Foreign and inner German Trade, before 1965, 44 x 88 cm, ink, pencil and gilt bronze on transparent paper, Berlinische Galerie BG-AS 5.107

Slab-Type Block with Low Building
Helmut Hentrich, Hubert Petschnigg, Europa-Center during construction, aerial view: Otto Borutta, circa 1964, 17.2 x 22.5 cm, silver gelatin paper, Berlinische Galerie, p. 129

Roland Korn, Heinz Scharlipp, Hans-Erich Bogatzky, Interhotel Stadt Berlin, 1971, photograph: Gisela Dutschmann, 1971, repro from 6 x 6 cm negative, Berlinische Galerie BG-AS 1436.005918, p. 129

Hermann Henselmann, Exterior view of the Haus des Lehrers with Congress Hall, photograph: Vera und Dieter Breitenborn, circa 1964, 18.1 x 20.5 cm, silver gelatin paper, Akademie der Künste, Berlin, Baukunstarchiv 120-919, F. 12

Hermann Henselmann, Exterior view of the Haus des Lehrers with Congress Hall, photographer unknown, circa 1964, 32.5 x 37.3 cm, silver gelatin paper pasted on album sheet, Akademie der Künste, Berlin, Baukunstarchiv HHA 120-875, F. 16

Hermann Henselmann, Exterior view of the Haus des Lehrers with Congress Hall, photograph: Konrad Hoffmeister, circa 1964, 22 x 29.6 cm, silver gelatin paper, Akademie der Künste, Berlin, Baukunstarchiv 120-919, F. 15

The High-Rise Building
Hans Wolff-Grohmann, High-rise building Handjeryplatz, model, 1962, 30 x 80 x 65 cm (incl. cap), wood, cardboard, metal, Kunstbibliothek Berlin, p. 130

Klaus Müller-Rehm, Spindel-House, Sollmannweg, large-scale housing estate Britz-Buckow-Rudow (BBR) (from 1972, Gropiusstadt), model, circa 1970, 35 x 40 x 36 cm, cardboard, paper, wood, plastic sheet, Berlinische Galerie BG-AS 10/2014, p. 130

Walter Gropius, Alexander Svianovic, Residential high-rise building "Ideal", large-scale housing estate Britz-Buckow-Rudow (BBR), photograph of the model: Robert D. Harvey, circa 1966, 23.4 x 17.2 cm, silver gelatin paper, Berlinische Galerie, p. 131

Georg Heinrichs, Residential and commercial building in the Opernviertel, model, circa 1965, 36.5 x 148 x 61 cm, wood, cardboard, plastic, Berlinische Galerie BG-AS 94/2014,2

Paul Schwebes, Commerical and office building Philips-House, An der Urania, model, 1969-70, 43 x 123 x 68.5 cm, wood, plastic, cardboard, Berlinische Galerie BG-AS 94/2014,3

Bernhard Binder, Office building at Ernst-Reuter-Platz, model, 1969-74, 30 x 39.5 x 83 cm, wood, cardboard, paper, plastic, Berlinische Galerie BG-AS 42/2014

Klaus Müller-Rehm, „Sternhaus", Residential area Heerstraße Nord, 1966, 30 x 58 cm, pencil on transparent paper, Berlinische Galerie BG-AS 2.7.7.2.1, p. 132

Klaus Müller-Rehm, „Sternhaus", Residential area Heerstraße Nord, ground plan of upper floor, 1966, 47 x 42 cm, pencil auf transparent paper, Berlinische Galerie BG-AS 2.7.7.1.2, p. 132

Klaus Müller Rehm, Residential buildings Heerstraße Nord, normal floor type C, 1968, 50 x 80.5 cm, felt-tip pen on transparent paper, Berlinische Galerie BG-AS 2.7.6.3.3, p. 132

Manfred Zumpe, 30-storey residential tower block using large panel construction method 6.3 MP, drawing of elevation, 1971, 22.1 x 22.1 cm, silver gelatin paper, Berlinische Galerie BG-AS 17/2013,342a, p. 133

Manfred Zumpe, Ground plan of 30-storey residential tower block using large panel construction method 6.3 MP, 1971, 20 x 20 cm, silver gelatin paper, Berlinische Galerie BG-AS 17/2013,342c, p. 133

Hans-Peter Schmiedel, Design for a residential and commercial complex, Leipziger Straße, 42 x 48 cm, collage, ink and gouache on paper, Berlinische Galerie BG-AS 5.101.1, p. 10

Manfred Zumpe, Design for residential tower block type, 1962, 66 x 98 cm, ink on transparent paper, Berlinische Galerie BG-AS 19/2013,20

Manfred Zumpe, Hans-Peter Schmiedel, Design for residential tower block type, 1962, 27 x 40 cm ink on transparent paper, Berlinische Galerie BG-AS 19/2013,19, p. 135

Hans-Peter Schmiedel, Design for residential tower block type, perspective drawing, 1960s, 45 x 34,5 cm, ink on parchment paper, Berlinische Galerie BG-AS 93/2014,1

Klaus Müller-Rehm, Residential area Heerstraße Nord, façade and ground plan forms, 1970, 60 x 90 cm, ink on transparent paper, Berlinische Galerie BG-AS 2-7-41-1, p. 136-137

Josef Kaiser, Design for a monolithic industrial building, residential high-rise blocks using sliding panel and tunnel sheeting methods, circa 1969, 90 x 106 cm, print on plastic sheet, estate of Josef Kaiser, p. 134

Large Housing Estates and Oppositions

Large-Scale Housing Estate
Fritz Haller, *totale stadt*, example design Berlin, 1968, repro from negative, gta-Archiv/ETH Zürich, estate of Fritz Haller no. 189-FX-2-7-8-35, p. 160-161

Fritz Haller, *totale stadt*, example design Berlin, 1968, repro from negative, gta-Archiv/ETH Zürich, estate of Fritz Haller no. 189-FX-2-7-8-32

Fritz Haller, *totale stadt*, example design Berlin, 1968, repro from negative, gta-Archiv/ETH Zürich, estate of Fritz Haller no. 189-FX-2-7-8-33

Fritz Haller, *totale stadt*, example design Berlin, 1968, repro from negative, gta-Archiv/ETH Zürich, estate of Fritz Haller no. 189-FX-2-7-8-34

Werner Düttmann, Group of high-rise buildings in the Märkisches Viertel, Dannenwalder Weg, photograph: Uwe Rau, circa 1968, 21.1 x 29.6 cm, silver gelatin paper, Akademie der Künste, Berlin, Baukunstarchiv Düttmann-35, F. 35/49, p. 162

Werner Düttmann, Märkisches Viertel, Dannenwalder Weg, photograph: Willi Huschke, circa 1968, 17.7 x 24 cm, silver gelatin paper, Akademie der Künste, Berlin, Baukunstarchiv Düttmann-35, F. 35/80

Werner Düttmann, Märkisches Viertel, Dannenwalder Weg, photographer unknown, 16.5 x 23.5 cm, silver gelatin paper, Akademie der Künste, Berlin, Baukunstarchiv Düttmann-35, F. 35/77

Werner Düttmann, Märkisches Viertel, Dannenwalder Weg, model, photograph: Uwe Rau, 1960s, 17 x 22.6 cm, silver gelatin paper, Akademie der Künste, Berlin, Baukunstarchiv Düttmann-35, F. 35/24

Hans Bandel, Shopping center in Wutzkyallee, housing estate Britz-Buckow-Rudow, (after 1972 Gropiusstadt), in the background the 27-storey residential high-rise building by Manfred Hinrichs, photograph 1967, 28.1 x 20.7 cm, silver gelatin paper, Berlinische Galerie BG-AS 2026.6.59

Werner Düttmann, Georg Heinrichs, Hans C. Müller, Märkisches Viertel, site plan 1:2000, 1967, 100 x 182 cm, diazo print on paper, Berlinische Galerie BG-AS 2.63.1, p. 164

Werner Düttmann, Georg Heinrichs, Hans Christian Müller, Märkisches Viertel, model, 1972, 6 x 180 x 99 cm, wood, Berlinische Galerie

Chen Kuen Lee, Residential buildings, Märkisches Viertel, photograph: Heinrich Kuhn, circa 1970, repro from negative 2015, estate of Heinrich Kuhn, p. 164

Manfred Joachim Hinrichs, 27-storey high-rise building in Britz-Buckow-Rudow (BBR), model, 1968, 18.5 x 65.3 x 25.3 cm, wood, plastic, metal, Berlinische Galerie BG-AS 3/2015,1

Heinrich Kuhn, Tobacconist's shop in the Märkisches Viertel, circa 1970, repro from negative 2015, estate of Heinrich Kuhn, p. 165

West-Berlin's Old Buildings

Heinrich Kuhn, Stationer's shop in an old building in West-Berlin, circa 1970, repro from negative 2015, estate of Heinrich Kuhn, p. 165

Heinrich Kuhn, Apartment house from the Gründerzeit in West-Berlin, circa 1970, repro from negative 2015, estate of Heinrich Kuhn, p. 166

Heinrich Kuhn, Old building in West-Berlin, rear courtyard, circa 1970, repro from negative 2015, estate of Heinrich Kuhn, p. 166

Heinrich Kuhn, Old building in West-Berlin, breakfast kitchen, circa 1965, estate of Heinrich Kuhn, p. 166

Heinrich Kuhn, Demolition of an old building in West-Berlin, circa 1970, repro from negative 2015, estate of Heinrich Kuhn, p. 166

Oppositions

Georg Kohlmaier, Barna von Sartory, „Rucksack-WC", ground plans and isometry, 1969, repro from negative, Berlinische Galerie BG-AS 80/2014,4 a-b, p. 167

Georg Kohlmaier, Barna von Sartory, „Rucksack-WC", façade simulation on old building, photo-collage, 1969, 30 x 22 cm, silver gelatin paper, p. 167

Aktion 507, *Diagnose zum Bauen in West-Berlin. - Kommt! Seht! Diskutiert!* Discussion materials for the exhibition in the TU Berlin on the occasion of the Building Weeks conference 8th–20th September 1968, Berlinische Galerie BG-AS 76/2014

Johannes Beck, Heiner Boehncke, and Gerhard Vinnai, eds., *Wohnste sozial haste die Qual. „jetzt reden wir". Betroffene des Märkischen Viertels. Mühsamer Weg zur Solidarisierung* (Reinbek, 1975) book cover: 19 x 11.5 cm, photograph: Helga Reidemeister (Heike Lange, Horst Lange, Jürgen Holtfreter, Andreas Reidemeister), p. 168

Jürgen Holtfreter, Poster for the exhibition *Diagnose. Zum Bauen in West-Berlin*, 1968, 83.8 x 58.8 cm, Akademie der Künste, Berlin, Kunstsammlung KS Plakat 10685, p. 169

Alexander Mitscherlich, *Die Unwirtlichkeit unserer Städte. Anstiftung zum Unfrieden* (Frankfurt/Main, 1965)

Volume of papers, Architectural Theory, International Congress in the TU West-Berlin, 11th–15th December 1967, ed. Jörg Pampe, *Veröffentlichungen zur Architektur* 14, ed. TU Berlin Lehrstuhl für Entwerfen VI o. Prof. Dipl.-Ing. O. M. Ungers (Berlin, June 1968), private archive

Wolf Jobst Siedler, Elisabeth Niggemeyer, and Gina Angreß, *Die gemordete Stadt. Abgesang auf Putte und Straße, Platz und Baum.* Herbig Verlag, 1964, Berlinische Galerie

Stefan Wewerka, title page for the publication *Treffen des Team X in Berlin-West*, 1965, private archive

Architecture and Art

Berliner Philharmonie

Hans Scharoun, Berliner Philharmonie, photograph: Otto Borutta, circa 1963, repro from 6 x 8 cm Dia, Berlinische Galerie, p. 180

Mila Hacke, concert hall of Berliner Philharmonie, 2012, p. 181

Hans Scharoun, Façade of the Berlin Philharmonic Hall, photograph: Reinhard Friedrich, 18 x 24 cm, silver gelatin paper, Akademie der Künste, Berlin, Baukunstarchiv WV 222, F.14

Max Planck Institute for Educational Research

Hermann Fehling, Daniel Gogel, Max Planck Institute for Educational Research, entrance area, photograph from outside, photograph: Rudolf Keßler, circa 1974, Archive of the Swiss Architecture Museum, Basel, p. 182

Hermann Fehling, Daniel Gogel, Max Planck Institute for Educational Research, entrance area, photograph from inside, photograph: Rudolf Keßler, circa 1974, Archive of the Swiss Architecture Museum, Basel, p. 183

Neue Nationalgalerie

Ludwig Mies van der Rohe, Neue Nationalgalerie, photograph: Karl-Heinz Schubert, circa 1968, 12.2 x 23 cm, silver gelatin paper, Berlin State Archiv, F Rep. 290 no. 0141075, p. 184

Ludwig Mies van der Rohe, Design for the Neue Nationalgalerie Berlin, interior, collage, 1962-65, 75.5 x 101.5 cm, paper, bpk / Nationalgalerie NG 4/71d

Ludwig Mies van der Rohe, Design for the Neue Nationalgalerie Berlin, interior, collage, 1962-65, 75.5 x 101.5 cm, paper, bpk / Nationalgalerie NG 4/71e, p. 185

Ludwig Mies van der Rohe, Design for the Neue Nationalgalerie Berlin, interior, collage, 1962-65, 75.5 x 101.5 cm, paper, bpk / Nationalgalerie NG 4/71f

Ludwig Mies van der Rohe, Neue Nationalgalerie, 1962-65, 75.5 x 101.5 cm, ink on paper, NG 4/71b

Ludwig Mies van der Rohe, Neue Nationalgalerie, 1962-65, 75.5 x 101.5 cm, ink on paper, NG 4/71c

Ludwig Mies van der Rohe, Presentation folder for the construction of the Neue Nationalgalerie, 1963, HdZ 12388,05

Ludwig Mies van der Rohe, Neue Nationalgalerie, rear view, photograph: Otto Borutta, 1968, color print, Berlinische Galerie BG-AS 1/2015,15

Ludwig Mies van der Rohe, Neue Nationalgalerie, model, 1965-68, 34.5 x 213.9 x 166.8 cm, wood, cardboard, Kunstbibliothek, Berlin

Haus des Lehrers

Hermann Henselmann, Haus des Lehrers with mosaic in natural stone by Walter Womacka, photograph: Gisela Dutschmann, 1965, repro from 6 x 6 cm negative, Berlinische Galerie BG-AS 1436.005831, p. 186

Hermann Henselmann, Congress Hall and Haus des Lehrers, postcard, circa 1967, private archive, p. 187

Hermann Henselmann, Congress Hall, entrance area with stairs, photograph: Rudolf Hartmetz, circa 1964, 17.4 x 17.5 cm, silver gelatin paper, Akademie der Künste, Berlin, Baukunstarchiv HHA 120-919, F. 18, p. 187

Hermann Henselmann, Haus des Lehrers and Congress Hall, photographer unknown, 32.5 x 37.3 cm, silver gelatin paper pasted on album sheet, Akademie der Künste, Berlin, Baukunstarchiv HHA 120-875, F. 7

Hermann Henselmann, Interior view of the Haus des Lehrers, photographer unknown, 32.5 x 37.3 cm, silver gelatin paper pasted on album sheet, Akademie der Künste, Berlin, Baukunstarchiv HHA 120-875, F. 62

Haus der Verlage (Publishers' House) and Press Café

Willi Neubert, Press Café Berlin, circa 1969, 57.7 x 100 cm, paper on hard fibre, oil and acrylic, collage, estate of Willi Neubert

Willi Neubert, Press Café Berlin, circa 1969, 74.3 x 88 cm, watercolour on hard fibre, estate of Willi Neubert

Willi Neubert, Haus der Verlage and Press Café Berlin, view from south, photographer unknown, circa 1970, 10,4 x 14,6 cm, silver gelatin paper, estate of Willi Neubert

Willi Neubert, Press Café Berlin, interior view with ceiling design, photographer unknown, circa 1970, 10,4 x 14,6 cm, silver gelatin paper, estate of Willi Neubert

Willi Neubert, Press Café Berlin under construction, exterior view, photographer unknown, circa 1970, 10,4 x 14,6 cm, silver gelatin paper, estate of Willi Neubert

Willi Neubert, Press Café Berlin, exterior view by night, photographer unknown, circa 1970, 10,4 x 14,6 cm, silver gelatin paper, estate of Willi Neubert

Willi Neubert, Press Café Berlin under construction, mural (detail), photographer unknown, circa 1970, 10,4 x 14,6 cm, silver gelatin paper, estate of Willi Neubert

Circulation Tank 2

Ludwig Leo, Color study for the Circulation Tank 2 of the Institute of Hydraulic Engineering and Shipbuilding (UT 2), circa 1967, 36 x 24 cm, Akademie der Künste, Berlin, Baukunstarchiv LLA-176, F. 46, p. 188

Ludwig Leo, Color study for the Circulation Tank 2 of the Institute of Hydraulic Engineering and Shipbuilding (UT 2), circa 1967, 36 x 24 cm, Akademie der Künste, Berlin, Baukunstarchiv LLA-176, F. 50, p. 188

Ludwig Leo, Christian Boës, Circulation Tank 2 of the Institute of Hydraulic Engineering and Shipbuilding (UT 2), site plan with existent buildings in the surrounding area, 1972, 60 x 153 cm, ink on transparent paper, Akademie der Künste, Berlin, Baukunstarchiv LLA 16, Plan 1

Ludwig Leo, Christian Boës, Circulation Tank of the Institute of Hydraulic Engineering and Shipbuilding, east views, 1967-68, 59.7 x 21 cm, ink on transparent paper, Akademie der Künste, Berlin, Baukunstarchiv LLA-13, Plan 1

Ludwig Leo, Christian Boës, Circulation Tank of the Institute of Hydraulic Engineering and Shipbuilding, views from the west, 1967-68, 60.5 x 22 cm, ink on transparent paper, Akademie der Künste, Berlin, Baukunstarchiv LLA-13, Plan 2

Ludwig Leo, Christian Boës, Circulation Tank of the Institute of Hydraulic Engineering and Shipbuilding, elevation drawing, 1967-68, 60 x 94.6 cm, ink on transparent paper, Akademie der Künste, Berlin, Baukunstarchiv LLA-13, Plan 9

Thomas Bruns, Circulation Tank 2 of the Institute of Hydraulic Engineering and Shipbuilding, (UT2) by Ludwig Leo and Christian Boës, 2011, 153 x 182.5 cm, archival pigment print on Hahnemühle baryt-paper, Staatliche Museen zu Berlin, Nationalgalerie, p. 189

Werner Düttmann, House Annemarie Vogel, Weinmeisterhornweg 31, photograph: Ingeborg Lommatzsch, circa 1966, 30.2 x 34.4 cm, silver gelatin paper, Akademie der Künste, Berlin, Baukunstarchiv Düttmann GF 29, F. 1

Werner Düttmann, House Dr. Menne, Zingerleweg 29/31, photograph: Ingeborg Lommatzsch, 1964-66, 29.7 x 39.9 cm, silver gelatin paper, Akademie der Künste, Berlin, Baukunstarchiv Düttmann GF 29, F. 2

Werner Düttmann, House Dr. Menne, Zingerleweg 29/31, photograph: Ingeborg Lommatzsch, circa 1966, 29.7 x 39.9 cm, Akademie der Künste, Berlin, Baukunstarchiv Düttmann GF 29, F. 3

Werner Düttmann, House Dr. Menne, Zingerleweg 29/31, photograph: Ingeborg Lommatzsch, circa 1966, 29.7 x 39.9 cm, Akademie der Künste, Berlin, Baukunstarchiv Düttmann GF 29, F.4

Epilogue

Evol, *(there's a) Hole in the Morning*, 2014, 297 x 201 cm, spray paint on cardboard

Beate Gütschow, *S#11*, 2005, 180 x 232 cm, LightJet Print, p. 194-195

Karsten Konrad, *Lost Island*, 2004, 50 x 120 x 120 cm, plaster, acrylic glass, polystyrene, painted chipboard, p. 198-199

Karsten Konrad, *DDR [aussen]*, 2005, 120 x 105 x 40 cm, medium density fibreboard, found objects

Friederike von Rauch, *Philharmonie 1*, 2010, 110 x 110 cm, edition 1/5 (+2 AP), Archival Pigment Print on aluminium

Friederike von Rauch, *Philharmonie 2*, 2010, 110 x 110 cm, edition 1/5 (+2 AP), Archival Pigment Print on aluminium

Friederike von Rauch, *Philharmonie 3*, 2010, 110 x 110 cm, edition 1/5 (+2 AP), Archival Pigment Print on aluminium

Friederike von Rauch, *Philharmonie 4*, 2010, 110 x 110 cm, edition 1/5 (+2 AP), Archival Pigment Print on aluminium

Bernd Trasberger, *Hertie*, 2009, 374 x 860 x 15 cm, ceramic tile, brass, wood, p. 192-193

Stephen Willats, *Eine postmoderne Lebensform*, 1992/93, 126 x 76.5 cm, different materials, Berlinische Galerie BG-G 12549/14 1/2, p. 196

Stephen Willats, *Eine postmoderne Lebensform*, 1992/93, 126 x 76.5 cm, different materials, Berlinische Galerie BG-G 12549/14 2/2, p. 197

Exhibition Media Room

GDR-magazine program 1968/41 (excerpts)

Direction: Nina Hartung, Günter Weschke
Production DEFA-Studio
02.39 min
On loan from: Progress Film-Verleih GmbH

Collaged city and interior perspectives of the planned development of Berlin, capital city of the GDR,
by Dieter Urbach, 1964-1970
Projected photographs
Acquired with budget funds of the Berlinische Galerie, 2013

"Vorhang auf! F:7" – A Berlin feature dated 12.12.1960
Excerpt: Werner Düttmann in conversation with Thilo Koch
Author: Friedrich Luft
Editor: Dagmar Fambach
07.35 min
Copyright: Sender Freies Berlin

Bauen in Berlin (Building in Berlin), 1969/70
A film made by the advertising agencies Zühlke + Scholz KG, by Michael Raven
Commissioned by the construction company Heinz Mosch
11 min
Donation by Family Heinz Mosch

Die gemordete Stadt (The Murdered City), 1964/65
Answer print
Editor: Ulrich Conrads, based on a book by Wolf Jobst Siedler and Elisabeth Niggemeyer
Direction: Manfred Durniok
40.52 min
Copyright: rbb Rundfunk Berlin-Brandenburg
On loan from: UCA, BTU Cottbus

Acknow-ledgements

The exhibition has received backing from the following artists and photographers:

Thomas Bruns

Evol

Beate Gütschow

Mila Hacke

Karsten Konrads

Hendrik Krawen

Arwed Messmer

Friederike von Rauch

Bernd Trasberger

Many important objects have been donated to the museum in the context of preparations for this exhibition. We would like to express our immense gratitude to the following institutions, families and individuals for the confidence they have shown in the Berlinische Galerie:

Andrea Aust

Hermes Hausverwaltung AG: Florian Geistler

Family Hopf

Sabine Krüger

Family Heinz Mosch

Family Oberste-Wilms

Werner Herzog

Manfred Hinrichs

Georg Kohlmaier

Christine Nestler

Elisabeth von Sartory

Ursula Schneider

Ingeburg Schwarz

Gerd Wessel

Manfred Zumpe

The following institutions and individuals have assisted us with our research or kindly provided individual loans:

Berlin Academy of the Arts, architectural archive: Eva-Maria Barkhofen, Petra Albrecht, Jürgen Kaulfuß, Juliane Kreißl, Tanja Morgenstern

Berlin Academy of the Arts, art collection: Anna Schultz

The German Museum of Architecture, Frankfurt am Main: Wolfgang Welker, Inge Wolf

ESMT European School of Management and Technology: Vera Dorsch, Antje Niebuhr

ETH-Zurich, gta archive: Filine Wagner

gmp Architekten, von Gerkan, Marg und Partner: Michael Kuhn, Hanne Banduch, Heidi Knaut

IKMZ/University library of the BTU Cottbus-Senftenberg: Simone Kossack

Institute of Regional Development and Structural Planning, Erkner: Alexander Obeth, Kai Drewes, Anja Pienkny

Michael Kaiser

The parish of the Kaiser Wilhelm Memorial Church: Reverend Martin Germer

Art Library, State Museums of Berlin – Prussian Cultural Heritage: Elke Blauert, Moritz Wullen

State Archive Berlin: Andreas Matschenz, Aileen Tomzek

State Office for Historical Monuments, Berlin: Jörg Haspel, Norbert Heuler

Museum Neukölln: Julia Dilger

Nationalgalerie im Hamburger Bahnhof - Museum für Gegenwart – Berlin, State Museums of Berlin – Prussian Cultural Heritage: Johanna Lemke

Neue Nationalgalerie, State Museums of Berlin – Prussian Cultural Heritage: Ute Smeteck, Dieter Scholz

Company archive Axel Springer SE: Rainer Laabs

Mario Schwennicke

The text authors and exhibition curator would like to thank the following people, whose cordial support, research, inspiration and criticism has proved essential for the development of such insights into the epoch of Berlin building during the 1960s:

Hinrich Baller

Dieter Bankert

Maria Bortfeldt

Boris von Brauchitsch

Ulrich Domröse

Ull Eisel

Alfred Englert

Teresa Fankhänel

Helmut Geisert

Karla Gogel

Alexander Hoff

Christine Hoh-Slodczyk

Lucia Kaiser

Annelie Lütgens

Isabelle McKinnon

Hans Räde

Mathias Sauerbruch und Louisa Hutton

Wolfgang Schöddert

Matthias Seidel

Donata Valentien

Lutz Vetter

Karin Wilhelm

Imprint

This catalogue is published on the occasion of the exhibition Radically Modern. Planning and Construction in 1960s Berlin 29.05. to 26.10.2015

Berlinische Galerie
Landesmuseum für Moderne Kunst, Fotografie und Architektur
Stiftung öffentlichen Rechts
Alte Jakobstraße 124-128
10969 Berlin

Tel +49 (0)30-78 902-600
Fax +49 (0)30-78 902-700
bg@berlinischegalerie.de
www.berlinischegalerie.de

CATALOGUE
Editor: Thomas Köhler and Ursula Müller for Berlinische Galerie, Landesmuseum für Moderne Kunst, Fotografie und Architektur
Concept: Ursula Müller
Academic Assistance: Anna Maria Heckmann, Gunnar Klack, Dirk Weilemann
Support Image Research: Ulrike Kohl
Managing Editor: Diana Artus, Geoffrey Steinherz
English Translation: Brian Currid, Lucinda Rennison, Katherine Vanovitch
Design: Uta Grundmann, Dagmar Puzberg
Typeface: corporate
Paper: Olin Rough, high white, 130 g/m², Cover: 400 g/m²
Production: MEDIALIS, Berlin
Catalogue production was supported by Wüstenrot Stiftung.

Cover reproduction:
Collective Manfred Jäkel, Lothar Kwasnitza, Dieter Urbach, Competition entry housing construction Leninplatz, collaged perspective: Dieter Urbach, 1967

Photo credits
Akademie der Künste, Baukunstarchiv/Berlinische Galerie: p. 6
Andree, Dieter: p. 53
Berlinische Galerie: pp. 22, 46, 78, 112, 129 bottom, 130 bottom, 131, 132, 136/137, 164 top, 180
Bruns, Thomas: p. 189
dr. julius | ap für Karla Gogel: pp. 182, 183
Dutschmann, Gisela/Berlinische Galerie: pp. 7, 26 top, 47, 51 top, 75, 76, 81, 107 top, 109, 126 (column 2, fig. 1), 127 (column 6, fig. 2/column 9, fig. 2), 128 middle, 129 top, 186
FLC/VG Bild-Kunst, Bonn 2015: p. 2
Friedman, Yona/VG Bild-Kunst, Bonn 2015: p. 4
gta Archiv/ETH Zürich: pp. 160/161
Gütschow, Beate: pp. 194/195
Hacke, Mila: p. 181
Hall, Doug: p. 27
Hedrich Blessing Photographers: p. 3
Henselmann, Andreas/Akademie der Künste, Berlin: pp. 73, 74
Holtfreter, Jürgen/Akademie der Künste, Berlin: p. 169
Jacobs, Rolf/Akademie der Künste, Berlin: p. 25 bottom
Kaiser, Michael: pp. 100, 128 bottom, 134
Koehler, Rolf: pp. 126 (column 3, fig. 4/column 4, fig. 1), 127 (column 7, fig. 2)
Kohlmaier, Georg/von Sartory, Elisabeth/Berlinische Galerie: pp. 101, 113, 167
Konrad, Karsten: pp. 198/199
Kraemer, Karl-Heinz/Berlinische Galerie: pp. 102, 126 (column 1, fig. 2/column 4, fig. 3), 127 (column 8, fig. 1 and 3)
Kremser, Engelbert/Berlinische Galerie: p. 49
Krüger, Sabine: pp. 164 bottom, 165, 166
Krüger-Verlag: p. 48
Leo, Morag/Akademie der Künste, Berlin: p. 188
Magnum Photos/Agentur Focus: p. 5
Office for Metropolitan Architecture: p. [illegible]
Legal successor Baumgarten, Paul/Akademie der Künste, Berlin: p. 24
Legal successor Driver, Wallace/Akademie der Künste, Berlin: p. 25 top
Legal successor Friedrich, Reinhard / Berlinische Galerie: p. 79
Legal successor Hartmetz, Rudolf / Akademie der Künste, Berlin: p. 187 bottom
Legal successor Huschke, Willi: p. 127 (column 8, fig. 2/column 10, fig. 5)
Legal successor Köster, Walter: p. 126 (column 2, fig. 2)
Legal successor Kosel, Gerhard; Hopp, Hanns; Mertens, Hans/Berlinische Galerie: p. 72
Legal successor Lieber, Heinz: pp. 50, 51
Legal successor Luftbildtechnik GmbH, Berlin Charlottenburg: p. 16
Legal successor Piltz, Eberhard: p. 127 (column 6, fig. 4/column 10, fig. 6)
Legal successor Rau, Uwe /Akademie der Künste, Berlin: p. 162
Legal successor Schubert, Karl-Heinz/Landesarchiv Berlin: p. 184
Legal successor Titzenthaler, Herloff: pp. 126 (column 2, fig. 3), 127 (column 6, fig. 1/column 7, fig. 1/column 8, fig. 4/column 10, fig. 3 and 4)
Legal successor Wolff-Grohmann, Hans/Kunstbibliothek Berlin: p. 130 top

Reidemeister, Helga: p. 168
Rudolph, Max: p. 126 (column 4, fig. 4)
Schlegel, Thomas/VEB Bild und Heimat Reichenbach: p. 187 top
Schubmann+Ploch: pp. 126 (column 1, fig. 1), 127 (column 9, fig. 1 and 4)
Schüler-Witte, Ursulina/Berlinische Galerie: pp. 104, 105, 110, 111,
Trasberger, Bernd: pp. 192–193
Ulrich: pp. 126 (column 3, fig. 1), 127 (column 7, fig. 3)
Unbekannter Rechteinhaber: p. 107 bottom
Unknown holder of rights/Berlinische Galerie: pp. 23, 26 bottom, 126 (column 3, fig. 3/column 4, fig. 2 and 5/column 5, fig. 1, 2 and 4), 127 (column 6, fig. 3/column 7, fig. 4, 5 and 6/column 9, fig. 3 and 5/column 10, fig. 1 and 2), 128 top, 163
Unknown holder of rights /Landesarchiv Berlin: p. 106
Urbach, Dieter/Berlinische Galerie: pp. 80, 103, 108
VG-Bild-Kunst, Bonn: pp. 18, 185
Willats, Stephen: pp. 196/197
Wohlrabe/Landesdenkmalamt Berlin/Arwed Messmer: p. 77
Wolter/Deutsche Bauinformation: p. 126 (column 3, fig. 2)
Zentralbild/Ritter: p. 126 (column 5, fig. 3)
Zumpe, Manfred/Berlinische Galerie: pp. 133, 135

© for the reproductions
Anders, Jörg P.: p. 185
Arndt & Partner Berlin/Zürich: pp. 198, 199
Dutschmann, Gisela: p. 72, 100
Hawlik, Markus: pp. 6, 7, 16, 22, 23, 24, 25, 26, 46, 47, 48, 49, 50, 51, 53, 72, 73, 74, 75, 76, 78, 79, 80, 81, 101, 102, 103, 104, 105, 107, 108, 109, 110, 111, 112, 113, 128, 129, 130 bottom, 131, 132, 133, 134, 135, 136, 137, 162, 163, 164, 167, 180, 186, 187
Katz, Dietmar: p. 130 top
Kohl, Uli; Moser, Henning, 2015: pp. 192, 193

We have made every effort to identify copyright holders. However, if we have failed to inform someone, we ask to contact the publisher.

Published by
Ernst Wasmuth Verlag
Tübingen · Berlin
www.wasmuth-verlag.de

ISBN: 978-3-940208-32-3 (Exhibition)
ISBN: 978-3-8030-0793-3 (Book Trade)

EXHIBITION
Curator: Ursula Müller
Project idea: Ursula Müller, Thomas Steigenberger
Academic assistance:
Anna Maria Heckmann, Gunnar Klack, Dirk Weilemann
Academic advisory council:
Dr. Andreas Butter, Institut für Regionalentwicklung und Strukturplanung, Erkner,
Dr.-Ing. Dr. sc. phil. Bruno Flierl, Architekt, Publizist,
Prof. Dipl. Ing. Hartmut Frank, HafenCity Universität Hamburg,
Prof. Dr. Stanislaus von Moos, Universität Zürich,
Prof. Dr. Kerstin Wittmann-Englert, Technische Universität Berlin
Support: Frank Schütz, Ulrike Kohl
Film programme: Ursula Müller, Anne Bitterwolf
Supervision film digitalization: Maria Bortfeldt
Compilation of Berliner Wochenschau sequences: Dirk Schaefer
Exhibition architecture: David Saik
Registrar: Frank Schütz
Conservation: Andreas Piel, Maria Bortfeldt
Mounting: Sabina Fernandez
Head of installation: Wolfgang Heigl, Roland Pohl
Installation: RT Ausstellungstechnik
Public Relations: Bureau N
The exhibition was enabled by Kulturstiftung des Bundes.

Staff of the Berlinische Galerie – Landesmuseum für Moderne Kunst, Fotografie und Architektur

Director: Dr. Thomas Köhler
Director of administration: Birgitta Müller-Brandeck

Management office: Wiebke Heß
Assistant to the director: Anne Bitterwolf
Assistant to the director of administration: Daniela Siegel
Projectmanagement Joint Venture: Barbara Heinrich

Collections
Fine Art: Dr. Stefanie Heckmann (HoD), Guido Faßbender, Annemarie Seyda, Christian Tagger, Anja Elisabeth Witte, Christiane Necker
Photography: Ulrich Domröse (HoD), Kerstin Diether, Tanja Keppler
Graphic Art: Dr. Annelie Lütgens (HoD), Katharina Hoffmann
Architecture: Ursula Müller (HoD), Frank Schütz
Artists' Archives: Dr. Ralf Burmeister (HoD), Philip Gorki, Wolfgang Schöddert, Julia Moldenhawer
Library: Sabine Schardt (HoD), Marion Molnos, Christina Strauch
Conservation: Andreas Piel (HoD), Maria Bortfeldt, Sabina Fernandez, Corinna Nisse
Trainee Curators: Anna Maria Heckmann, Gunnar Klack, Dirk Weilemann, Barbara Susanne Werr, Anne Wriedt

Marketing & Communication:
Ulrike Andres (HoD), Diana Brinkmeyer, Fiona Finke, Michaela Englert (Trainee), Carolin Wagner (Trainee), Clemens Wildt (FSJ Kultur)
Friends of the museum:
Stephanie Krumbholz, Sophie Bertone, Elena Schoubye

Administration
Organisation and IT:
Christiane Friedrich (HoD), Martin von Piechowski, Jan Salzberger
Finance and controlling:
Susanne Teuber (HoD), Laila Ayyache, Kerstin Böhme, Karin Rasper
Human Resources: Christian Monschke (HoD), Cornelia Remky
Visitors' service: Carola Semm (HoD), Helmut Andersen, Christiane Boese, Friederike von Born-Fallois, Brigitte Heilmann, Nihal Isigan, Gerhard Jende, Frank Lambertz, Daniela Lamprecht, Matthias Linde, Katarina Roters, Olaf Schümann, Nasrin Sheikh Zadeh, Reza Soltani
Museumshop: Carsten Fedderke, Dr. Eva-Maria Kaufmann, Reinhard Kuh, Merwe Reckenfelderbäumer, Dirk Schäfer
Technical department: Roland Pohl (HoD), Wolfgang Fleischer, Robert Frank, Ralf Geelhaar, Wolfgang Heigl, Andreas Kamprath, Frank Rohrbeck

Media partners

BauNetz
dérive
domus DEUTSCHE AUSGABE
kulturradio rbb 92,4
uncube digital magazine for architecture and beyond
WELTKUNST
ARCH+
3pigs